OFF THE BEATEN PATH™ SERIES

Iowa

FOURTH EDITION

by Lori Erickson

Revised and Edited by
Tracy Stuhr

The Globe Pequot Press

Old Saybrook, Connecticut

The prices and rates listed in this guidebook were confirmed at press time. We recommend, however, that you call establishments before traveling to obtain the most current information.

Cover and text design: Laura Augustine
Cover photo: Images © PhotoDisc, Inc.
Maps created by Equator Graphics © The Globe Pequot Press
Illustrations by Carol Drong
Drawing on page 70 based on a photograph, © Mike Whye.

Library of Congress Cataloging-in-Publication Data

Erickson, Lori.
     Iowa : off the beaten path / Lori Erickson. —4th ed. / revised and edited by Tracy Stuhr.
     p. cm. —(Off the beaten path series)
  Includes index.
  ISBN 0-7627-0266-4
  1. Iowa—Guidebooks. I. Stuhr, Tracy. II. Title. III. Series.
    F619.3.E75   1999
  917.7704´33—dc21   98-36365
                                         CIP

Manufactured in the United States of America
Fourth Edition/First Printing

Help Us Keep This Guide Up to Date

Every effort has been made by the author and editors to make this guide as accurate and useful as possible. However, many things can change after a guide is published—establishments close, phone numbers change, hiking trails are rerouted, facilities come under new management, etc.

We would love to hear from you concerning your experiences with this guide and how you feel it could be made better and be kept up to date. While we may not be able to respond to all comments and suggestions, we'll take them to heart and we'll also make certain to share them with the author. Please send your comments and suggestions to the following address:

The Globe Pequot Press
Reader Response/Editorial Department
P.O. Box 833
Old Saybrook, CT 06475

Or you may e-mail us at:
editorial@globe-pequot.com

Thanks for your input, and happy travels!

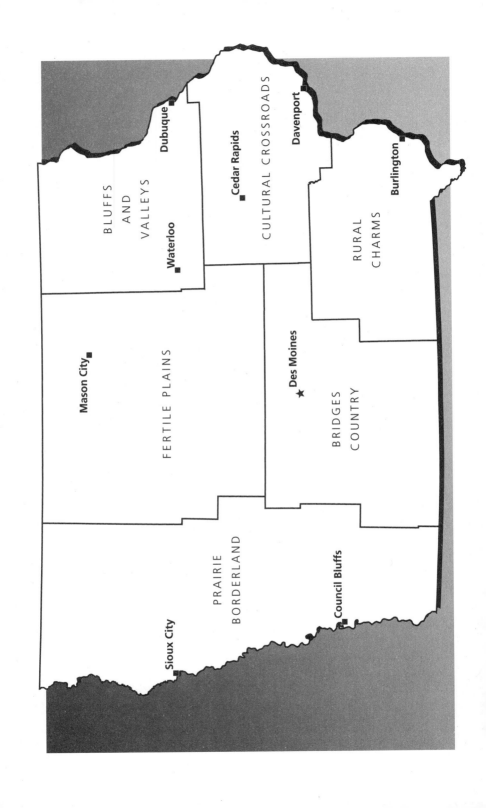

BLUFFS AND VALLEYS

Dubuque

CULTURAL CROSSROADS

Davenport

Cedar Rapids

Waterloo

RURAL CHARMS

Burlington

FERTILE PLAINS

Mason City

Des Moines

BRIDGES COUNTRY

PRAIRIE BORDERLAND

Sioux City

Council Bluffs

Contents

Introduction vi

Bluffs and Valleys 1

Cultural Crossroads 29

Rural Charms 61

Bridges Country 85

Fertile Plains 113

Prairie Borderland 143

Indexes 173

    General 173

    Restaurants 180

    Lodgings 180

    About the Author 182

Introduction

The summer I was eight, my parents decided to take me, my two sisters, and my brother on an Iowa vacation. We children, dumbfounded, didn't understand what they could possibly mean by an Iowa vacation—after all, we *lived* here. How *boring!* What sort of a vacation is that? Why couldn't we go to a dude ranch or to a cabin by a lake in Minnesota? *Why, why* couldn't we go to Disneyland? None of our friends took Iowa vacations. Quite naturally we thought we were being punished. We blamed each other: "Why did you go to the park without permission? Why did you break that window? Why, oh why, didn't we mind the baby-sitter?" And we would ask each other darkly, "Why do Mom and Dad persist in putting the words *fun* and *educational* together, as if they don't know that they cancel each other out?

Perhaps they thought it would be cheaper or just more manageable. With four children ranging in age from ten to two, I can imagine this had some appeal. It probably helped as well that my father and mother had grown up in Storm Lake and Postville, respectively, and so there were places we could stay, home bases from which to extend our travels. Perhaps it really was meant to be a cultural experience, a way to learn about our own backyard. If this was so, it was probably a secondary consideration. Nonetheless, I do remember visiting Bily Clock in Spillville, the Grotto in West Bend, the "World's Smallest Church" in Festina, and the Little Brown Church in Nashua. And for the culmination of the trip there was a visit to Arnolds Park, a place we already knew and loved.

It seems funny in retrospect that so homely a trip should have remained so firmly etched in my memory, that I learned at such an early age how much my home state had to offer. Unlike our earlier and some of our subsequent family vacations, this Iowa trip is one that we still vividly remember, one in which we did (miraculously) learn and have fun. It may be that at that age we were still content, as children, to get along with one another, that we still (mostly) obeyed our parents, that there was little strife and a lot of fun. My mother, an indefatigable seeker of harmony, kept us occupied in the car singing songs, from the spirited "Waltzing Matilda" to the more personal and seriously probing "Do Your Ears Hang Low?" My father, blessed with a rather formidable curiosity and a fertile imagination, made us look, really look, and ask questions to seek out stories. It could be too that Iowa just has a lot to offer that is child-size— nothing too big or too overwhelming, just the right size for burrowing in, just the right shape for the imagination to find a jumping-off place.

Since that first childhood experience, I have continued my explorations of Iowa and have found, throughout the years, old things to cherish, passing things to mourn, new discoveries to delight in. I have been astounded on my most recent trips at the enormous number of heritage museums, preservations, and restorations; no county and hardly a single town is without some remnant of the past that has been saved, in one shape or another, for the wandering traveler to explore. Prairie is being preserved, houses have been restored, historic buildings are being dedicated to new uses, bicycle paths are being created from abandoned railroad tracks. Everywhere the land, its people, and their landmarks are bending and changing to find new shapes, new ways to survive and prosper.

Long before I was asked to revise this edition, I bought my first copy of *Iowa: Off the Beaten Path,* thrilled to see that there was such a guide. With it I have discovered places I hadn't heard of before and would have ignorantly passed by. Obviously, if you are reading this book, you are looking for the same kind of adventures. I hope you will be pleased to learn that more than one hundred new entries have been added to this edition; there are also new lists of interesting regional events, as well as lists of places to stay and places to eat. This book does not, by any means, provide a complete list of unique attractions in the state of Iowa, though I think it is representative of the many things Iowa has to offer to the wandering or weekend traveler. Much of the text has remained the same, updated to reflect current hours and prices. I have also added new sidebars to include some personal perspectives and reminiscences, as well as to highlight some of each area's attractions, events, and stories.

A few pointers on using this guidebook: Keep a state map in your glove compartment as you travel because most of these attractions are off the interstates, and you may find yourself lost without one. I'd also recommend that you call ahead to verify hours and prices. Though all were correct at press time, they change frequently. The prices for restaurants are divided into three categories:

Inexpensive—less than $6.00

Moderate—$6.00 to $13.00

Expensive—more than $13.00

I would like to add that this edition could not have been developed without Lori Erickson's unflagging encouragement and support. Equally, I would like to thank the many people who have given me so many suggestions and recommendations: family, friends, and strangers. In particular I'd like to acknowledge the help I've received from convention bureaus, visitor centers, and chambers of commerce across the state. Nor can I forget the many volunteers and employees and helpful citizens who, in countless ways, continue to give so generously of their time.

In closing, I'd like to suggest that we can all give back to this rich and beautiful state. It's important to patronize our small and independent businesses; they stand as fresh symbols of where we have come from and where we are going. We need to keep everything as beautiful as we find it and to make donations where and when we are able. Remember to talk to the folks you meet along the way—everything, everyone, has a story. In other words, please be generous with your ears and your time. Listen to the many voices of Iowa, to the farmers, the meat packers, the teachers, the factory workers, the businesspeople, the artists, the children, and the retired. Listen to the farms, to the steely roar and prowl of farm machinery, to the eloquence of a faded barn, to the snort and snuffle of pigs. Listen to the voices of the cities and towns, to the sounds of demolition, construction, and renewal. Listen to the voices of the parades, the festivals, the celebrations; to the museums, the cemeteries, and the long-quiet mounds. Listen to the low-throated rumble of advancing thunder and to the lush stillness of snow; to the reedy tune of crickets on a summer night; to meadowlarks, robins, and the quarrel of jays. Listen, deeply, to the whispering silence of corn.

No, Iowa is not boring, but it does demand a fresh and almost childlike imagination to really appreciate it, an imagination that is attentive and searching. I would have to say that curiosity and imagination are really the most important things for you to pack on this trip.

From the limestone bluffs bordering the Mississippi to the loess hills flanking the Missouri River, from the natural lakes in the north and across the central plains to the southern border, Iowa is, above all, a place to savor, to enjoy, to visit and revisit. Welcome—and happy exploring!

—Tracy Stuhr, Editor

Fun Facts About Iowa

- Leads the country in pork production
- Has the highest literacy rate in the nation
- Ranks thirtieth in population density nationally
- One of only seven states to shrink in population during the 1980s
- Has more than 90 percent of its land under cultivation
- Its highest point, in northern Osceola County, at 1,670 feet, was constructed by mound builders
- Stretches 332 miles from east to west and 214 miles from north to south
- Leads the country in corn and soybean production in most years
- Has 100,000 farms
- Temperatures range from below zero in the winter (with wind chills dipping into double digits) to over 100 in summer. Temperatures can fluctuate by as much as fifty degrees during a single day.

For More Information

For further information on the state of Iowa, contact the following:

Division of Tourism

Iowa Department of Economic Development
200 East Grand Avenue
Des Moines, IA 50309
(515) 242–4705
(800) 545–IOWA
http://www.state.iowa.us

Eastern Iowa Tourism Association
PO Box 485
Vinton, IA 52549
(319) 472–5135
(800) 891–EITA
http://www.easterniowatourism.org
E-mail: eita@easterniowatourism.org

Central Iowa Tourism Region
PO Box 454
Webster City, IA 50595
(515) 832–4808
(800) 295–5842
E-mail: citr@netins.net

Western Iowa Tourism Region
502 East Coolbaugh Street
Red Oak, IA 51566
(712) 623–4232
(888) 623–4232
E-mail: witr@netins.net

Iowa Department of Natural Resources
Wallace State Office Building
Des Moines, IA 50319-0034
(515) 281–5145

Iowa Department of Transportation
800 Lincoln Way
Ames, IA 50010
(515) 239–1101

Iowa Department of Cultural Affairs
State Historical Building
600 East Locust Street
Des Moines, IA 50319
(515) 281–6258

Iowa Lodging Association
Iowa Bed and Breakfast Innkeepers Association
9001 Hickman Road #2B
Des Moines, IA 50322
(515) 278–8700
(800) 888–INNS

Bluffs and Valleys

Northeast Iowa is a land of thickly wooded hills, steep bluffs, secluded valleys, and scenic vistas—countryside that in many places seems more like that of New England than the Midwest. From river towns rich in history to immigrant enclaves where old-world traditions remain strong, northeast Iowa offers a host of unique treasures.

River Region

Begin your tour of northeast Iowa in Dubuque, one of my favorite destinations in the entire state. Much of what makes the city so appealing relates to its long and colorful history as a Mississippi River town. The city is named after Julien Dubuque, a French-Canadian fur trader who received permission in 1788 from the Fox Indians to work the lead mines in the area. The territory was opened to white settlement in 1833, and soon hundreds of new residents—many of them immigrants—were pouring into the new town. The next hundred years saw the decline in mining and the growth of the lumbering, boatbuilding, shipping, and meatpacking industries. As the city grew rich, its citizens filled its streets with magnificent homes and buildings, structures that stand today as eloquent reminders of the city's past.

One good place to learn more about that history is at *The Mississippi River Museum,* a complex of sites describing the rich heritage of America's most famous waterway. Inside are exhibits on the Indians, explorers, gamblers, adventurers, and steamboat pilots who lived and worked on the Mississippi. Among the museum's highlights are the historic side-wheeler *William M. Black,* a 277-foot vessel permanently docked near the museum, and the *National Rivers Hall of Fame,* an exhibit honoring such river heroes as Mark Twain, explorers Lewis and Clark, and inventor Robert Fulton. The complex forms one of the largest river museums in the country and provides a vicarious thrill for anyone who's ever dreamed of following Huck Finn's journey down the Mississippi.

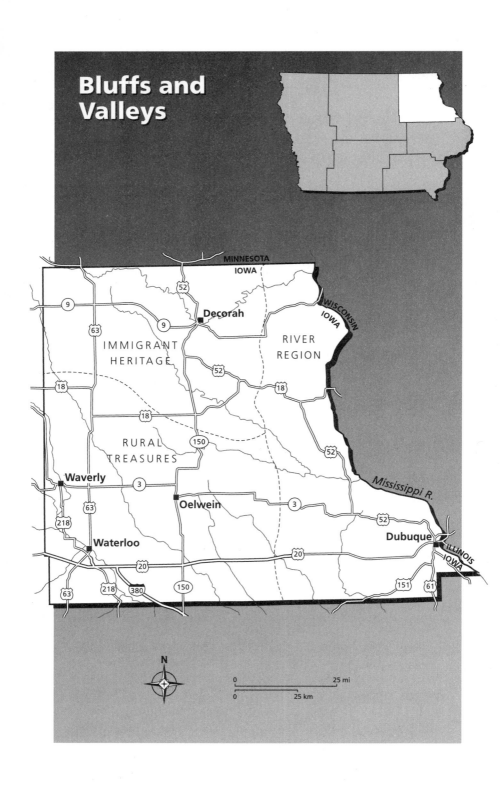

Bluffs and Valleys

MINNESOTA
IOWA

WISCONSIN
IOWA

52

Decorah

9

63

9

IMMIGRANT
HERITAGE

52

RIVER
REGION

18

18

18

150

RURAL
TREASURES

52

Waverly

3

63

Oelwein

3

218

52

Waterloo

Dubuque
ILLINOIS
IOWA

20

20

63

218

380

150

151

61

Mississippi R.

N

0   25 mi
0   25 km

BLUFFS AND VALLEYS

The Mississippi River Museum is located next to the Mississippi in the Ice Harbor area in downtown Dubuque. It's open from 10:00 A.M. to 5:00 P.M. daily. Admission is $6.00 for adults and $3.00 for children (under 7 free). Call (319) 557–9545 for information.

Another good way to sample the history of the city—and some delicious food as well—is on a **Victorian House Tour and Progressive Dinner** held at four of Dubuque's loveliest old mansions. At each stop you'll receive a tour of the house and introduction to its history, plus an elegantly served dinner course. The meal begins with an appetizer at the Mathias Ham House, a home built in the Italian villa style by a man who grew rich off the area's lead mines. Next it's on to the Redstone Inn for soup and French bread. The main course is served at the Ryan House, a restaurant that once was the home of "Hog" Ryan, a Civil War general. Your last stop will be for dessert and coffee at the Mandolin Inn, which gets its name from a window overlooking its grand staircase that features Saint Cecelia (the patron of musicians) holding a mandolin.

The Victorian House Tour and Progressive Dinner is available to group tours throughout the year and to individual diners on the second and fourth Friday evenings of June through October, as well as during the Christmas season. Reservations are required, and the price is $40 per person. For information call the Mississippi River Museum at (319) 557–9545.

Once you've had a peek at the **Redstone Inn,** you may want to return to stay the night. The Redstone was built in 1894 as a wedding present for the daughter of a wealthy industrialist and is now owned by the Dubuque Historic Improvement Company, a group of local citizens who wanted to save and preserve one of the city's best-loved landmarks. The wine-colored mansion is built in a gloriously Victorian style, complete with towers, turrets, and cupids frolicking across the ceiling in the front parlor. Fifteen rooms are open to guests, and rates range from $60 to $175 per night. You'll find the Redstone Inn at 504 Bluff Street; call (319) 582–1894 for reservations.

Another of my favorite places to stay in Dubuque is the **Hancock House,** a magnificent Queen Anne mansion with a spectacular view of the city. The house is owned by Chuck and Susan Huntley, who also

Hancock House

operate a gift shop and dried-flower-arranging business in their home. They provide complimentary homemade baked goods and beverages to their guests as well as a hearty, full breakfast each morning. Nine rooms are available to guests, all of which have private baths. The Hancock House (319 –557–8989) is located at 1105 Grove Terrace, and rates range from $75 to $150.

A pleasant place to stop while you're in Dubuque—at any time of the year—is the **Dubuque Arboretum and Botanical Gardens.** The gardens showcase many different plant and tree collections, including a formal herb garden, woodland wildflowers, lily ponds, and one of the largest public hosta gardens in the United States with over 13,000 hosta plants of more than 700 varieties. You will be accompanied by the sound of trickling waterfalls and on Sundays by musical concerts. All of this was developed by volunteers from the community and the admission is free. The gardens are open from Arbor Day through October 8 from 8:00 A.M. to sunset. The rest of the year they are open during the week from 9:00 A.M. to 5:00 P.M., on Saturdays from 9:00 A.M. to 1:00 P.M., and closed on Sundays. Get to the arboretum by taking Highway 52 (Central Avenue) to West Thirty-second Street to Arboretum Drive in Marshall Park. Call (319) 556–2100 for more information.

For evening entertainment in Dubuque, two performance centers in the downtown area offer a variety of shows in elegant settings. The **Five Flags Theater** was built in 1910 and was modeled after the great music halls of Paris. Today it has undergone a plush restoration that will make you think you've gone back a century in time. A few blocks away is the **Grand Opera House,** a hundred-year-old stage where Ethel Barrymore, George M. Cohan, and Sarah Bernhardt once performed. After years of service as a movie house, it is once again home to live community theater.

And according to its resident acting company, the venerable old building is haunted—literally—by the spirits of actors who once performed here. "Where else would old actors go once they died?" asks one performer who's heard the ghostly voices. "It seems logical they'd go back to the place they'd loved best."

Regardless of whether ghosts make an appearance during a performance, you're likely to enjoy a show at either one of the stately old theaters. Five Flags Theater is located at Fourth and Main Streets and can be reached at (319) 589–4254. The Grand Opera House is at 135 Eighth Street; call (319) 588–4356 for more information.

There are a number of other attractions in the Dubuque area that are well worth a visit, including many fine bed-and-breakfasts, the Old Jail Gallery and Art Center, County Courthouse, riverboat gambling on the *Diamond Jo Riverboat Casino,* trolley tours, and several

"Going Up?"

*N*ot far from the Hancock House is one of the city's most unusual attractions, the **Fenelon Place Elevator.** Described as the "world's steepest, shortest railway," the elevator connects downtown Dubuque with the residential neighborhoods on top of a steep bluff. It was built in 1882 by J. K. Graves, a businessman who worked downtown but liked to return home each day for lunch and a nap. The problem was that it took him a good hour to drive his horse and buggy there and back again. To solve the problem, he commissioned a small cable car modeled after those he had seen on trips to Europe and had it installed on the bluff near his home. Now he could easily fit in both lunch and a nap, and he returned to work each day a happy man.

Then Graves's neighbors started asking permission to use the elevator, and

soon it had become a fixture of the city. In the intervening years, the cars and support structure have been rebuilt several times, so even if it seems like you're going to tumble to the ground as you're riding it, rest assured, the cars are safe. The elevator is even listed on the National Register of Historic Places—quite an honor for a machine designed to give a businessman time enough for a nap.

The Fenelon Place Elevator is located at 512 Fenelon Place and is open from April 1 through November 30, from 8:00 A.M. to 10:00 P.M. Round-trip rates are $1.50 for adults and 50 cents for children. (And while you're in the area, browse through the Cable Car Square shopping district at the foot of the elevator, an area of renovated homes and buildings that now house gift shops, antiques stores, and boutiques.)

beautiful parks and nature areas. For more information on what to see and do in the city, call the Dubuque Convention and Visitors Bureau at (319) 557–9200 or (800) 798–8844.

Five miles south of Dubuque on Highway 52 is the *Crystal Lake Cave,* which is open from May 1 to November 1. The cave was discovered accidentally in 1868 when some miners, drilling for lead, happened upon this incredible natural cave. In 1932 one of these miners christened it and opened it to the public. Tours through the cave wind along a three-quarter-mile track, and the temperature hovers around fifty degrees so you will want to dress accordingly. You will see anthrodites—otherwise known as cave flowers—a rare form of aragonite crystals, as well as large formations of brown onyx, which only take about a million years or so to form. There are delicate hollow "soda straw" stalactites through which water flows, and a crystal "chandelier" formed of still-growing, active stalactites. The cave is open from 9:00 A.M. to 5:00 P.M. daily from Memorial Day to Labor Day; the rest of the season the hours vary. Call (319) 556–6451 or (319) 872–4111 for more information.

Ten miles northwest of Dubuque on County Road C9Y is an Iowa dining landmark that you shouldn't miss: *Breitbach's Country Dining* in the small town of Balltown. Breitbach's likes to boast that it's the only restaurant in the world to be visited by both the outlaw Jesse James and the actress Brooke Shields, but that's not the restaurant's only claim to fame: Breitbach's has been refreshing the palates of weary travelers since 1852, making this the oldest bar and restaurant in continuous operation in Iowa history.

The Breitbach family has owned this former stagecoach stop for more than a century, and visitors today are likely to be greeted with a hearty welcome by fifth-generation owner Mike Breitbach. The key to the restaurant's longevity is simple: homemade, delicious food, reasonable prices, and a welcoming and cozy atmosphere. Breitbach's is open for breakfast, lunch, and dinner from 7:00 A.M. to 9:00 P.M. daily, until 10:00 P.M. on weekends. For information call (319) 552–2220.

Before heading north along the Mississippi, you may want to take a short detour east to the small town of Dyersville. One of its attractions is the *National Farm Toy Museum,* a facility housing thousands of rare and antique farm toys as well as newer items, all designed to reflect the agricultural heritage of the nation. There's also a multimedia show describing the lives of farm families from the post–Civil War era to the present.

The National Farm Toy Museum (319–875–2727) is located near the junction of Highways 136 and 20. Hours are 8:00 A.M. to 7:00 P.M. every day. Admission is $4.00 for adults and $1.00 for children (under 6 free).

Dyersville has become known as the "Farm Toy Capital of the World" not only because of the museum but also because of the fact that three of the world's major farm toy manufacturers are located here: The Ertl Company, Scale Models, and Spec-Cast. Each November the town hosts the National Farm Toy Show, an event that attracts thousands of toy collectors and exhibitors. If you can't make it to the show, you can still visit the *Ertl Toy Factory* at Highways 136 and 20 throughout the year. Free guided tours are given Monday through Friday; call (319) 875–5699 for reservations. There are also several outlet stores here that sell factory seconds and overruns.

Another attraction in Dyersville is the *Basilica of St. Francis Xavier,* one of the finest examples of Gothic architecture in the Midwest. The church has a main altar of Italian marble and Mexican onyx, a pulpit of butternut, and twin towers that rise to a height of 212 feet. It was given the title of basilica in 1956 in recognition of its outstanding architecture and spiritual significance and is one of only thirty-five basilicas in the United States.

Visitors are welcome to visit the church at 104 Third Street SW, and information packets are available at the main entrance for self-guided tours. The basilica is open daily from sunrise to sunset.

Three miles northeast of Dyersville is the *Field of Dreams Baseball Diamond,* a former movie set that has taken on a life of its own. The movie *Field of Dreams,* filmed here in 1988, tells the story of an Iowa farmer who plows up his field to build a diamond so that a ghostly baseball team can return to play. Since then thousands of fans from as far away as Japan have visited the diamond, which still remains among the cornfields. Visitors can sit and dream on the bleachers, walk the bases, and toss a few baseballs. The "ghosts" appear to visitors on the last Sunday of the month from June through September.

The baseball diamond is open free of charge from April through November, 9:00 A.M. to 6:00 P.M. From Dyersville take Highway 136 to the north edge of town and follow the signs to the farm. Call the Dyersville Area Chamber of Commerce at (319) 875–2311 for more information.

From Dyersville head north for 25 miles on Highways 136 and 52 to the Mississippi River port of Guttenberg. For information on the Mississippi's lock and dam system plus insight into local history, visit the

Lockmaster's House Heritage Museum. The museum is located in the former lockmaster's house, where the lockmasters and their assistants were required to live prior to 1972. The house is the last remaining lockmaster house on the upper Mississippi and is listed on the National Register. The museum is located next to the lock and dam; call (319) 252–2068 for information and hours.

Afterward, stop by *The Old Brewery,* an art gallery, beer and wine room, and bed-and-breakfast housed in an 1858-built limestone brewery. Artists Naser and Pat Shahrivar purchased the building in 1987 and have done most of the extensive renovation work themselves. Their two guest rooms are cozy and beautifully decorated, and downstairs you

Sandhill Cranes

Sandhill cranes migrate to and from their winter campground in Florida over a large portion of the upper Midwest in the spring and fall. Spring is a more popular time to watch for them because their Fall migration is much more relaxed and leisurely than the businesslike one they make in the spring. This is because they have to make accommodations for their young who cannot fly either as fast or as far. (I'm sure at least a few of you know what I'm talking about!) They may fly as much as 300 miles a day at an altitude below 5,000 feet. You can recognize them by their appearance during flight—long necks stretched out in front, longer legs trailing behind—and their bugling calls can be heard for miles. During migration the birds "paint" themselves, preening mud into their gray feathers for camouflage. When you see them in the Midwest they will appear to be brown.

Younger birds form "bachelor flocks," feeding and nesting together until they settle down. Males and females mate for life at about four years of age. Their

nests are adequate, yet plain (just a bunch of marsh plants piled on the ground), but they seem content. Sandhill cranes are most active just before sunrise and just after sunset. Listen for their unison calls during these times, the one-noted male and the two-noted female singing together. The female usually lays two eggs in April or early May and incubation takes about a month. When one bird leaves the nest to forage, the other takes over incubation duties. Unison calls, I am told, are particularly loud at this time. Cranes, like people, have difficulty deciding what to have for dinner.

*The International Crane Foundation sponsors the **Midwest Sandhill Crane Count** every year. Volunteers take to the fields on a designated morning in April to count cranes. If you are interested in participating, contact the foundation at (608) 356–9462. What a great way to learn about some fly-by-night neighbors. (Just kidding. These cranes almost always travel by day—no "red-eye flights" here!)*

can enjoy their award-winning artwork while sipping Iowa-made beer or wine.

The Old Brewery

Guest rooms at The Old Brewery are $55 and $65 and include a full breakfast. The beer and wine room and gallery are open from 10:00 A.M. to 6:00 P.M. May through October and from 10:00 A.M. to 5:00 P.M. November through April. For more information call (319) 252–2094.

From Guttenberg head north on County Road X56 to the small river port of Clayton, where you'll find the ***Cklaytonian Bed and Breakfast Inn*** (and yes, there is a "k" in Cklaytonian). Its owner is Karen Hagan, a native of nearby Garnavillo who lived in New York City for eighteen years before returning to her native state in 1981. In 1987 she purchased what used to be the Wilderness Motel along the riverfront in Clayton and spent the next few months completely refurnishing and remodeling it, inside and out.

Today the old motel is hardly recognizable to those who knew it in the old days. The rooms are individually and tastefully decorated with antique furniture, and guests also have the use of a hot tub and comfortable "gathering room." Five of the inn's six rooms enjoy a panoramic view of the Mississippi and surrounding bluffs—and Karen even provides complimentary bicycles for those who want to explore the nearby area.

The Cklaytonian Bed and Breakfast Inn is located on the river in Clayton. Rates range from $55 to $65, which includes a seven-course breakfast (319–964–2776).

Just east of Clayton, visit the charming town of Elkader, at the junction of state Highways, 13, 56, and 128. Take a stroll on the river walk, along the bank of the Turkey River. The walk connects the downtown area with the city park. Stop at the Keystone Restaurant at 107 South Main Street and enjoy a meal or a beverage while you sit at one of the riverside tables and enjoy the view of the ***Keystone Bridge***, one of the prettiest bridges in the state, built more than one hundred years ago and still holding its own. If you want a more active river visit, one of the town's canoeing outfitters will be happy to provide everything you need for some time on the Turkey—not a bad way to spend a beautiful summer or fall afternoon!

Spend a delightful (and informative) hour or two at the **Osborne Nature Center,** 5 miles south of Elkader on Highway 13. This place is really one of Iowa's best kept secrets. Set on 300 acres of diverse and well-maintained grounds along the Volga River, the Osborne is an educational treasure. The center itself houses natural exhibits galore. If you can't learn about Iowa wildlife here, you won't learn about it anywhere! On the grounds is one of Iowa's largest wildlife farms, with more than fifty species of animals and birds, even a couple of (not native) peacocks! In addition, there is a nature trail, a conifer trail, a conservation trail, and trails for hiking and cross-country skiing. Still not tired? Take a look around the pioneer village. Call (319) 245–1516 for more information.

The Story of Motor Mill

*N*o one knows why the three men who formed a partnership to build a town on the site of an old sawmill chose the name of Motor. But there are a few things we do know. The town of Motor was growing and prosperous until a flood in 1875 drowned its hope of a rail connection with McGregor. Residents had already battled chinch bugs, once in 1867 and again in 1871. These infestations had destroyed nearly every acre of wheat in this part of the state. Another infestation in 1887 led to the abandonment of the mill—almost the last remaining structure of this besieged little town. With no grain to grind, the mill was sold sometime during the 1880s. It settled into disrepair and was gutted, its equipment sold for junk. It managed to survive as a dairy barn from the 1930s until 1982.

Today it stands as a magnificent old building, some 90 feet tall, six stories high, with foundation walls more than 5 feet thick. It is reputed to be the tallest structure of its kind in the Midwest. Take some time to admire the mill and its interior (the machinery within is not original, it was donated from an old mill near St. Ansgar) and try to imagine it in action. Buckwheat was ground into pancake flour, wheat milled into fine bread and pastry flour, oats and rye ground for stock feed. Save some time to visit the other remaining buildings: the cooperage (where barrels were made to ship the cornmeal and flour), the stable, the inn (where farmers spent the night waiting for their grain to be ground), and the ice house (where ice was cut, harvested, and stored, to be used for refrigeration at the inn).

The short route to the mill is currently closed due to flood damage at the Turkey River Bridge but you can get there by taking a 7-mile detour. From the Highway 13 bypass take County Road C1X over three concrete bridges; at the top of the next hill take a gravel road to the right. This will lead you to the mill. For more information contact the Clayton County Conservation Board at (319) 245–1516.

BLUFFS AND VALLEYS

North of Clayton is McGregor, a river town that's one of the loveliest in the state. The area is especially popular during the fall, when the wooded bluffs along the Mississippi put on a spectacular color show. At other times of the year, people come here to enjoy fishing and boating on the river, antiques hunting in McGregor and the surrounding area, riverboat gambling aboard the *Miss Marquette,* which docks nearby in Marquette, and side trips to a number of historic sites and natural attractions.

One of those spots is **Pike's Peak State Park,** 2 miles southeast of McGregor on Highway 340. Here you can stand on one of the highest points along the entire Mississippi, a 500-foot bluff overlooking the meeting of the Mississippi and Wisconsin Rivers. This is also the place where the explorers Marquette and Joliet first set foot on land west of the Mississippi. Nearby are hiking trails and picnic and camping facilities.

In McGregor itself check out the many antiques and specialty stores on its main street. One store in particular is worth a visit: the **River Junction Trade Company.** The atmosphere inside is like that of an old general store from a century ago, with a tinplate ceiling, potbellied stove, and counters stacked with bolts of cloth and all kinds of implements and articles of clothing. Its owner is Jim Boeke, a man who has been fascinated by the Old West since he was a boy. When he grew up, he started collecting western gear and memorabilia but found that there were few sources from which to buy them—so he starting making things himself. Soon he began marketing his work to others, and eventually his business became so successful that he left his corporate job in Des Moines to set up shop in McGregor.

All the items in the store are replicas of nineteenth-century clothing and equipment: Riverboat gambling vests, Abe Lincoln hats, gun belts, sunbonnets, Shawnee tomahawks, mackinaws, leather boots, and calico dresses are just a few of the items that fill the store. The company has a thriving mail-order business in addition to its McGregor store and counts among its clients historic sites and museums, performing groups across the country, and even working cowboys in today's West. Jim reports that his overseas business is steadily increasing as well.

River Junction Trade Company is at 312 Main Street in McGregor (319–873–2387). An illustrated catalog is available for $10.

Before you leave McGregor, stop by for a meal at the **White Springs Night Club** on Highway 18 on the west end of town. The atmosphere inside is that of a 1950s roadhouse, and every time I've been there it has always been packed with people—nearly always a sign of a good restaurant. The food is good, standard Iowa fare, and my husband swears they have the best fried catfish he's ever eaten.

White Springs (319–873–9642) is open from 11:00 A.M. to 11:00 P.M. Monday through Saturday and from 4:00 to 10:00 P.M. on Sundays. Prices are inexpensive to moderate.

Next head to **Spook Cave,** 7 miles west of McGregor near the junction of Highways 52 and 18. Here you can take what's billed as "America's longest underground boat tour." Bring your sweater (the temperature is forty-seven degrees) and take a half-hour guided cruise. The tour is the perfect activity for a hot Iowa summer afternoon.

Spook Cave tours are $6.00 for adults and $3.00 for children. The cave is open daily from 9:00 A.M. to 5:30 P.M. from Memorial Day through Labor Day and from 9:00 A.M. to 3:30 P.M. in May, September, and October. Call (319) 873–2144 for more information. Camping and swimming are available nearby.

Five miles north of McGregor you'll find one of northeast Iowa's premier attractions, **Effigy Mounds National Monument.** This 1,500-acre area preserves outstanding examples of more than 2,000 years of prehistoric Indian mound building. Within its borders are nearly 200 known burial mounds, 29 of which are in the shape of bears or birds (most of the rest are conical or linear in form). The Great Bear Effigy is one of the most impressive mounds, stretching 70 feet across the shoulders and forelegs, 137 feet long, and more than 3 feet high. The mounds are all the more impressive when you realize that their builders didn't have the ability to see the giant shapes from the air but instead worked out all the shapes from ground level.

The visitor center at the monument has exhibits explaining the mounds and the artifacts found within them, plus a film on the culture of the Indians who lived here. Hours are 8:00 A.M. to 6:00 P.M. from Memorial Day through Labor Day and 8:00 A.M. to 4:30 P.M. during the remainder of the year. Guided tours are given during the summer months at 10:30 and 11:30 A.M. and at 1:30 and 3:00 P.M. The tours cover 2 miles of walking and last an hour and a half. Admission is $2.00 for adults, $4.00 maximum per family. There is no extra fee for the guided tour (319–873–3491).

From Effigy Mounds continue north on the river road (Highways 76 and 364) through the towns of Waukon Junction and Harpers Ferry. A few miles north of Harpers Ferry, the scenic river road takes you to one of the loveliest spots in the state, the tiny *Wexford Immaculate Conception Church.* Inside the exquisite stone building covered with ivy are simple wooden pews, a floor of colored mosaic tile, and an altar of lovely murals and statues. The church was built in the 1860s by a group of immigrants who journeyed here from County Wexford, Ireland. On the back wall of the church is a framed photocopy of the passenger list from the boat that brought the Wexford immigrants over the ocean, their names written in a beautiful flowing script. A peaceful cemetery surrounds the building, and just north of the church there's a shrine with a statue of Mary surrounded by blooming flowers.

Continue north on County Road X52 to the town of Lansing, where you can enjoy a lovely view of the Mississippi from Mt. Hosmer, a city park perched atop a high bluff.

Six miles north of Lansing off Highway 26 are the *Fish Farm Mounds,* a smaller cousin of Effigy Mounds to the south. Hiking trails and tent camping are available.

Located between Lansing and Waukon on Highway 9 and situated along the Lansing Ridge, one of the highest points in Allamakee County, you'll find *The Landmark,* a great place to stop for a meal or just to take a break. This beautiful restored building was built in 1851 as a residence for Colonel John Wakefield after he received this land as a military grant for his service during the "Indian Wars." It has seen action as a brewery, general store, tearoom, dance hall, and hotel, among other things. Take a look at the rock gun tower located in the rear—it was built for protection during the Sioux uprising in Minnesota in the 1850s. Inside The Landmark you'll find an oak and mahogany bar, believed to have been taken from an old Mississippi riverboat. Call owners Dick and Diane Prestemon at (319) 568–3150 for more information and be sure to ask about Barney, the ghost.

Immigrant Heritage

From Lansing take Highway 9 east for 35 miles to Decorah, a picturesque community that was the first Norwegian settlement beyond the Mississippi. About half of the residents are of Norwegian ancestry, and most of the half that aren't pretend that they are. Throughout the town you'll see evidence of Decorah's ethnic past, from the Norwegian *nisse* (gnomes) peeking out of windows to shops decorated with rosemaling, a type of Norwegian flower painting. Each year on the last full weekend in July the town celebrates its heritage with **Nordic Fest,** a three-day festival featuring parades, ethnic foods and music, historical displays, arts and crafts demonstrations, and antiques shows.

As a native of Decorah and a full-blooded Norwegian, I must admit to growing up with a somewhat skeptical view of the whole proceedings. My friends and I called the summer festival "Nordic Fester" and used to amuse ourselves by wandering the crowded streets talking gibberish in a sing-song voice to make people think we were speaking Norwegian. Today, however, I can't help but admire the immigrants who ventured from the old country to make a new life in Iowa. Even though they did afflict their descendants with such culinary abominations as *lutefisk* (cod soaked in lye), they also left a rich heritage that's well worth celebrating.

To learn more about Decorah's past, visit **Vesterheim,** a local museum that tells the story of Norwegian immigrants from their lives in Norway to their assimilation as Americans. The name means "home in the west," and throughout the facility you'll see the clothes, tools, household objects, and everyday items used by the immigrants, as well as replicas of homes and displays on the arduous sea crossing the settlers endured. There are also many examples of Norwegian folk crafts on display, as well as a gallery of paintings by Norwegian-American artists. This is considered one of the best ethnic museums in the country, so plan to spend several hours touring the entire thirteen-building complex.

Vesterheim is located at 502 West Water Street (319–382–9681). From May through October hours are 9:00 A.M. to 5:00 P.M. daily; from November through April hours are 10:00 A.M. to 4:00 P.M. daily. Admission is $4.00 for adults from November through April, $5.00 the rest of the year, with reduced rates for families, children, and senior citizens.

Next to the museum is the **Dayton House,** a cafe that specializes in Norwegian ethnic foods. In addition to a daily special of an American dish, the Dayton House serves such items as *lapskaus* (Norwegian stew), *rommegrot* (a thickened cream porridge), and *lefse* (a tortilla-like bread made from potatoes). Guests are not subjected, however, to the dreaded *lutefisk*, a dish whose aroma could clear the sinuses of someone a quarter of a mile away. The Dayton House is open during museum hours, and prices are inexpensive.

A new attraction in Decorah is the **Farm Park,** which is located in a huge, nineteenth-century barn on the ege of the Luther College campus.

The Farm Park is a mixture of zoo and museum that seeks to preserve near-extinct farm animals such as the Norwegian fjord horse, the Navajo-Churro sheep, and the mulefoot hog. As part of the Institute for Agricultural Biodiversity, the farm park is an ark for domesticated species that are now rarely bred, as well as an educational institution that seeks to educate the public about the importance of conserving our agricultural heritage. The Farm Park (319–387–2150) is open from May 1 to October 31 10:00 A.M. to 5:00 P.M. daily. Admission is $3.00 per person, $10.00 per family.

Dayton House Norwegian Cafe

Another Decorah attraction is the *Porter House Museum,* a Tuscan villa built of native brick in 1867. Inside you'll find an impressive collection of rare butterflies, moths, and insects as well as artifacts from around the world. The Porter House (319–382–1867) is open on weekends from Memorial Day through Labor Day, and a small admission is charged.

While you're in Decorah you might want to take a stroll around the lovely campus of Luther College, which is one of the most scenic in the Midwest. The Decorah area also has many fine parks, including Dunning's Spring, which has a beautiful waterfall, and Phelps Park, which offers hiking along a network of trails. The Upper Iowa River, which runs through the center of town, is popular with canoeing enthusiasts, and the area also has many well-stocked trout streams. For more information about Decorah attractions, call the Winneshiek County Tourism Council at (800) 463–4692.

If you're spending the night in Decorah, you should book a room at the *Montgomery Mansion* at 812 Maple Avenue. The impressive Victorian home was built in the 1870s and offers four guest bedrooms. Rates range from $45 to $55. Call (800) 892–4955.

From Decorah take Highway 52 north for 6 miles to North Winn Road (also known as County Road W34) to find *Seed Savers Heritage Farm,* the headquarters of the Seed Savers Exchange. This unique 173-acre farm is a living museum of historic varieties of endangered fruits and vegetables. The farm is set beside limestone bluffs and century-old stands of white pine woods. Seeds—for example, 300 varieties of tomatoes, 330 of beans, 125 of peppers—are multiplied and gathered from the organic gardens and offered for sale in the barn's cathedral-like loft, which was built by Amish carpenters. In the Preservation Gardens 15,000 rare vegetable varieties are maintained, including 2,000 traditional varieties from eastern Europe and Russia. The Cultural History Garden displays culturally rich vintage flowers and vegetables. In the Historic Orchard 160 hardy grapes are grown, as well as 650 nineteenth-century apple varieties. Don't miss the ancient White Park cattle while you're here! They're from the British Isles, and are distinguished by their white coats, black-tipped lyre-shaped horns, and black noses, ears, and hooves. There are only 300 in the world today and thirty of them reside at the Heritage Farm. The gardens and gift shop in the barn are open from 9:00 A.M. to 5:00 P.M. daily. For more information call (319) 382–5990 and help save a little bit of the living past from extinction!

Ten miles north of Seed Savers, just off Highway 52, you will find *Willowglen Nursery.* Owners Lee Zieke and Lindsay Lee have taken a giant step toward the creation of a little bit of paradise. You can view all the perennial plants offered for sale in their own incomparable gardens— no more guessing about what a plant will look like at maturity or how it grows and blooms. The selection of plants is large and varied and offers many hard-to-find varieties as well as those you've come to know and love. There is always someone on hand to help, whether you're just curious about a difficult primrose or have several acres to landscape. A real treat is offered on the third weekend of the month from June through September, when Willowglen hosts "Weekends in the Garden," occasions for area gardeners to meet, talk, and answer questions from visitors. Willowglen's hours are 10:00 A.M. to 6:00 P.M. from May 1 to September 15. The days of the week on which they are open vary with planting times. Please call (319) 735–5570 for more specific schedule information or to set up an appointment for the off-season.

Continue north on Highway 52 to the town of Burr Oak, site of the *Laura Ingalls Wilder Museum.* This National Historic Landmark was once home to the author of the famous *Little House* series of children's books. In the fall of 1876, the Ingalls family moved to Burr Oak following disastrous grasshopper plagues in Minnesota. Laura's father man-

FESTIVALS IN BLUFFS AND VALLEYS

Volga Voyage Cross Country Ski,
Fayette, first weekend in January

Snow Fest in Cresco,
last weekend in January

Fabulous February Fest,
Monona, second weekend in February

Smelt Fry,
Maynard, last Friday in March

Strawberry Days,
Strawberry Point, second weekend
in June

*Sturgis Falls Celebration/Cedar Basin
Jazz Festival,*
Cedar Falls, last full weekend in June

Woodcarvers Celebration,
Spillville, first weekend in July

Nordic Fest,
Decorah, last full weekend in July

Sweet Corn Days,
Elkader, fourth weekend in July

International Dvořák Festival,
Spillville, first weekend in August

Mississippi River Music Fest,
McGregor, first Sunday in August

Italian Heritage Days,
Oelwein, last weekend in August

German Fest,
Guttenberg, fourth Saturday
in September

Fayette County Fall Foliage Festival,
first full weekend in October

aged the hotel that is now the museum, while Laura, her mother, and her sister waited tables, cooked, and cleaned. The Ingalls family lived here for one year before moving back to Walnut Grove, Minnesota.

Local Ingalls fans borrowed $1,500 to purchase the hotel in 1973 and launched a campaign to raise money for its restoration. With public dances, benefit auctions, book sales, donations, and a "Pennies for Laura" campaign, enough funds were raised to open the old hotel as a museum. Today it's open daily from May through September, 9:00 A.M. to 5:00 P.M. Admission is $3.00 for adults and $1.50 for children. Call (319) 735–5916 for information.

Prairie lovers will want to take a detour east of Burr Oak to see one of the state's largest remaining sections of native grasslands, **Hayden Prairie.** The 240-acre tract is located 3 miles south of Chester on County Road V-26 and shows what much of Iowa looked like before it was broken by the plow. Owned and managed by the state of Iowa, Hayden Prairie contains more than a hundred species of wildflowers and attracts a variety of birds and wildlife. The best way to see it is slowly, pausing every few feet to savor the profusion of life growing here.

Southwest of Decorah on Highway 325 lies the ethnic enclave of Spillville. While Decorah is known for its Norwegian heritage, Spillville was settled by Czech immigrants. The little town takes great pride in one of its former residents, the famed Czech composer Antonin Dvořák, who spent a summer here in 1893. Homesick for the companionship of his countrymen after a year's work as director of the New York Conservatory of Music, Dvořák came to Spillville and spent the summer completing his most famous work, the *New World* Symphony.

The building where Dvořák lived that summer is now the home of **Bily Clocks,** a museum filled with the hand-carved clocks of brothers Frank and Joseph Bily. The two were local farmers who whiled away long winter days and evenings by carving. In thirty-five years they created twenty-five intricately carved clocks ranging in height from a few inches to 10 feet, using woods from various foreign countries as well as butternut, maple, walnut, and oak from America. Among the outstanding clocks on display

How to Play Pony Express

*F*irst you must have some great cousins who live on a farm (mine lived between Postville and Luana). They must have ponies! A saddle and bridle are not necessary, but at the very least you must have a halter. Your headquarters should be in a culvert under the gravel road that leads to town and you should have a network of stops where the ponies can eat. (Ponies don't like to hang out in culverts even if you have oats.)

These stops can be anywhere you choose: a neighbor's barn or an old oak tree, anywhere you can pick up mail and check out the "Wanted" posters. The posters are important, otherwise you would have no occasion to gallop (or trot, if that's all your pony will do—some of them are very fat). "Wanted" posters must have at least three things: a face (either an eye patch or a mask are obligatory), a name (Deadeye is always popular and never goes out of style), and, of course,

a reward (you may want to print up some money for this). The general rule is simple: the more desperate the desperado, the higher the reward. The posters should be taped to the culvert walls and delivered to your outposts at specified times. It is always important to keep things moving.

There will be times when these desperadoes may look suspiciously like a grown-up, say a mother or father, aunt or uncle. It is vital to outrun them— remember, they are probably in disguise! Keep this up at least until dinnertime or until they reveal, usually by a particular tone of voice you will soon come to recognize, that they really are who they say they are. It's just as well at this time—no earlier!—to return to the farmhouse, stable your pony, and sit down and eat as much sweet corn and pie as you possibly can, because tomorrow will be another very long day, and the mail must get through.

are an apostle clock from which the twelve apostles parade every hour, an American pioneer clock showing important historical events, and a clock built to commemorate Lindbergh's crossing of the Atlantic in 1928.

Bily Clocks is located on Main Street in Spillville and is open from May through October, 8:30 A.M. to 5:00 P.M. daily, with shortened hours in March, April, and November. Phone (319) 562–3569 for more information or to arrange a visit during the winter months. Admission is $3.50 for adults and $1.25 for children.

Before you leave Spillville, pay a visit to the lovely St. Wenceslaus Church where Antonin Dvořák played the organ for daily Mass during his stay in the village. Then head to the *Old World Inn,* an 1871 general store that houses guest rooms and a fine restaurant serving moderately priced meals, including many Czech specialties. You'll find the Old World Inn (319–562–3739) on Main Street near the Bily Clocks museum.

South of Spillville on Highway 24 is the town of Fort Atkinson, site of the *Fort Atkinson State Preserve.* Here you'll find a partial reconstruction of the only fort in the country built to protect one Indian tribe from another. It was constructed in 1840–42 to keep the Winnebago Indians on Neutral Ground (a 40-mile-wide strip of land established by the Treaty of 1830) and to protect them from the hostile Sioux, Sac, and Fox tribes. The state of Iowa acquired the property in 1921, and reconstruction of the old fort was started in 1958. Part of the original barracks is now a museum housing documents relating to the history of the fort.

A good time to visit Fort Atkinson is during its annual Rendezvous, held on the last full weekend in September. The event draws buckskinners from several states who re-create the days of the frontier. Events include cannon drills, skillet- and tomahawk-throwing contests, anvil shooting, and melodrama performances—and when you get hungry you can sample such frontier treats as venison stew and Indian fried bread.

Fort Atkinson is open on weekends from noon to 5:00 P.M. mid-May through September. Admission to the fort and its annual Rendezvous is free (319–425–4161).

On a country road near the town of Festina, east of Fort Atkinson, is the St. Anthony of Padua Chapel, better known as the *World's Smallest Church.* The stone chapel is only 14 by 20 feet and holds four tiny pews. It was constructed to fulfill a vow made by Johann Gaertner's mother, who promised God she would build him a chapel if her soldier son survived Napoleon's Russian campaign. The son did indeed return home unharmed, and the chapel was built of locally quarried stone in 1885. A small, peaceful graveyard filled with old cedar trees is located in back of the little church and includes the grave of Johann Gaertner (who died a natural death, one hopes).

To reach the chapel, follow the signs from Festina. The building is open during daylight hours with no admission charge.

Drive 4 miles north of Festina on Highway 150 and then east on Highway 53 if you want to take a trip back in time and get fed while you're doing it, plan a visit to **Green's Sugar Bush,** 3 miles south of Frankville. This is one of Iowa's longest continually operating and unique industries: maple syrup production the old-fashioned way. They just tap it! Since 1851, when current owner Dale Green's great-grandfather started his maple sugar and syrup business, the Greens have remained in business, weathering fads and fashions. On the last Sunday in March and the first Sunday in April (dates move up a week if Easter falls on one of the two Sundays), they host a Maple Fest, featuring horse-drawn wagon rides through the timber, followed by a pancake and sausage breakfast. Dale says, "People call and ask me if it's muddy. I tell them if they want to eat pancakes in a church basement they should go there instead!" In other words, be prepared. People begin to gather at "the Bush" around 10:00 A.M. The price is currently $3.50 for adults, less for children. Call Dale at (319) 567–8472 for more information. The Greens also sell maple syrup out of their home year-round.

Take Highway 18 south of Frankville to Clermont where you'll find **Montauk,** a lovely mansion that was home to Iowa's twelfth governor, William Larrabee. Larrabee built the Italianate house in 1874 high on a hill overlooking the Turkey River valley, and his wife, Anna, named it after the lighthouse on Long Island that guided her sea-captain father home from his whaling voyages.

The fourteen-room home is built of native limestone and local brick kilned in Clermont, and it is surrounded by forty-six acres of flower gardens and trees. Inside are the home's original furnishings, including Tiffany lamps, Wedgwood china, statues from Italy, onyx tables from Mexico, a large collection of paintings, and thousands of books. The elegant and cultured mansion reflects the character of its owner, a man of boundless energy and ambition as well as great intelligence and charisma. He ran for governor on a platform that called for tighter control of the railroads, women's suffrage, and strict enforcement of Prohibition (his campaign slogan was "a schoolhouse on every hill and no saloons in the valley").

Montauk is located 1 mile north of Clermont on Highway 18. Hours are noon to 4:00 P.M. daily from Memorial Day through October 31. Admission is $2.50 for adults and $1.00 for children. Call (319) 423–7173 for further information.

In nearby Clermont you can visit the Union Sunday School, which houses a rare pipe organ donated by William Larrabee, and also the Clermont Museum in the former Clermont State Bank building. On display in the museum are collections of china, crystal, coins, fossils, and seashells, as well as antique furnishings and native American artifacts.

Rural Treasures

Southeast of Montauk at the junction of Highways 3 and 13 lies the town of Strawberry Point. Though the town has only 1,500 residents, it's difficult to miss, for a huge strawberry has been erected at its city hall. The name was given to the town by soldiers, traders,

What Is a Famous Gunderburger?

Visit the community of Gunder (population 32), northwest of Elkader off County Road X16 and find out! Gunderburgers make their home at **The Shanti,** *a restaurant owned by Brenda and Jeff Pfister since 1992. Bring your appetite with you—or better yet, a friend (or two or three) to help you eat one. Please believe me when I tell you that this burger is one full pound of specially seasoned ground beef—that's right, one full pound— that comes smothered with Swiss cheese, sautéed mushrooms, green peppers, and fried onions. At least, that's one variation; you can pick and choose your toppings. This is not a fast food place. Each Gunderburger is shaped and made by hand (Brenda says she uses a metal plate as a guide), and a burger this size needs about twenty minutes to cook.*

Oh yes, I should add that a Gunderburger does come with a bun. The bun is obviously here for decorative, not practical purposes. You couldn't lift this burger if you tried! Most diners never make it to the bottom half of the bun, but are amused by the way the top half perches on this gigantic burger like a beanie on an elephant. How much will you pay for this behemoth of a burger? $4.50. For a little over a dollar more you can also get a small mountain of hash browns or American fries. There are plenty of other choices on the menu as well, but really, someone in your party is going to have to order this monster of a meal. For more information call The Shanti at (319) 864–9289.

and railroad workers who enjoyed the bountiful wild strawberries once found along the area's trails and hillsides. Each year in June the town holds **Strawberry Days,** a community celebration that culminates with the serving of free strawberries and ice cream on the last day of the festival.

Strawberry Point is also home to the **Wilder Museum,** which is best known for its collections of dolls and of Victorian glass, porcelain, lamps, and furniture. Much of its collection was donated by Marcey Alderson, a local music teacher and avid antiques collector who spent his lifetime acquiring exquisite pieces. Dresden, Limoges, and Haviland porcelains, beautiful glassware and lamps, and ornately carved furniture are all on display here. (A favorite with many visitors is a lamp once used on the set of *Gone With the Wind*.) The Wilder Museum is located on Highway 3 and is open daily from 10:00 A.M. to 5:00 P.M. from Memorial Day through Labor Day, and on weekends only in May and September. Admission is $2.50 for adults and 75 cents for students. For more information call (319) 933–4615 or (319) 933–2260.

Keep This One under Your Hat . . .

*H*ats, hats, hats! If there was one thing Faith Mitchell had it was hats. If you like hats (or if you just like collections that have gone totally out of control), the **Faith Mitchell Hat Collection** is one you will have to see to believe! At first Mrs. Mitchell stored her hat collection in the basement of her farm outside Arlington. When that was full to overflowing she started keeping them in an old house on her property. They moved again when she and her husband moved to town, and the collection just kept growing and growing. By the end of her lifetime Mrs. Mitchell had collected well over 3,000 hats. She left them to the Castle House in Arlington with the stipulation that the collection never be broken up. They are all there still, and the collection is still growing!

There are men's hats and women's hats, hats from all over the country and all over the world, hats from the last decade, hats from the last century, hats from Dior and hats made at home. There are now close to 5,000 hats. People just keep sending them! Included is the famous (or at least unusual) hat collection of Doyle Felton, once known as the "Hat Man" of Eldora. You may visit the hats by scheduling an appointment with Bertha Schuchmann, who is also a fine local historian, at (319) 633–3385. Castle House is not heated, so you may want to plan your visit between Memorial Day and Labor Day. Arlington is located on Highway 167, northwest of Strawberry Point. There is no admission fee but donations are warmly appreciated.

Just south of Strawberry Point on Highway 410 is one of Iowa's loveliest nature preserves, **Backbone State Park.** The park's most prominent feature is an unusual spinelike rock formation that is known in local lore as the devil's backbone. Legend has it that the devil lost his nerve one day and left his backbone behind as he slithered east to the Mississippi River. The park has camping sites, hiking trails, and wonderful views of the Maquoketa River and surrounding countryside.

From Strawberry Point travel south to the small town of Quasqueton, where you can visit one of the state's most significant architectural landmarks. *Cedar Rock* was designed by famed architect Frank Lloyd Wright and was built between 1948 and 1950. The house was commissioned by wealthy businessman Lowell Walter and his wife, Agnes, who later bequeathed their home to the Iowa Conservation Commission and the people of Iowa.

Nearly every item in the Walter house bears the imprint of the famous architect. The overall design is strongly horizontal, lines that Wright felt reflected prairie landforms. The long, low structure is skillfully integrated into the landscape and sits on a limestone bluff overlooking the Wapsipinicon River. Inside, Wright designed the furniture, selected the carpets and draperies, and even helped pick out the china, silverware, and cooking utensils. In addition to the house, the wooded eleven-acre site has a river pavilion, a fire circle, and an entrance gate that were all designed by Wright. The Walter house is one of the most complete designs Wright had the opportunity to create in his long and productive career.

Cedar Rock is located on the northern edge of Quasqueton. The house (319–934–3572) is open from May through October from 11:00 A.M. to 5:00 P.M. Tuesday through Sunday. Admission is free.

From Quasqueton go west on Highway 20 to the adjoining cities of Waterloo and Cedar Falls.

Cedar Falls is best known as the home of the **University of Northern Iowa,** a school founded in 1876 to fill the need for qualified public school teachers in the state. Today it enrolls about 13,000 students in a wide variety of undergraduate and graduate degree programs. One of the most prominent landmarks on campus is the UNI Campanile, a 100-foot-tall structure built to commemorate the school's fiftieth anniversary. The UNI-Dome is the other most recognizable landmark on campus. The bubble-topped building houses various sports facilities and also hosts many nonathletic events. For more information on activities at the university, call (319) 273–2761. A campus map and walking-tour guide are available at the Office of Public Information Services, 169 Gilchrist Hall.

Also in Cedar Falls is the *Ice House Museum,* a structure containing artifacts of the ice-cutting industry as well as other historical items. In the days before mechanical refrigeration, natural ice was cut from the Cedar River and stored year-round in this unusual circular building constructed in 1921. Each year some six to eight thousand tons of ice were stacked within its 100-foot diameter (the circular shape allowed only one wall to touch the stacked blocks rather than two, thus slowing the melting process). In 1934 the icehouse owner lost his business, and the structure was used for a variety of purposes in the following years. In 1975 it escaped demolition when a group of local citizens raised money to restore it and open it as a museum. Today you can see the array of equipment once used in ice cutting plus photographs of the entire process from harvesting to selling. A visit here is certain to make you appreciate your refrigerator and freezer at home.

The Ice House Museum is located at First and Franklin Streets in Cedar Falls. Hours are from 2:00 to 4:30 P.M. on Wednesday, Saturday, and Sunday, May 1 through October 31. Call (319) 266–5149 or (319) 277–8817 for more information.

Another fascinating museum to visit is the *Iowa Band Museum* at 203 Main Street. This historic band hall houses the memorabilia and history of the Cedar Falls Municipal Band, which has been entertaining this area since 1891. It is open Wednesday and Sunday from 2:00 to 4:00 P.M. and on Monday from 7:00 to 9:00 P.M. during June and July, or you can call (319) 266–1253 for an appointment.

Two other museums operated by the Cedar Falls Historical Society are the Victorian Home and Carriage House Museum, a historic Civil War–era home, and the 1907 George Wyth House, once the family home of the founder of the Viking Pump Company. The society also preserves the Little Red School, a turn-of-the-century country school moved in 1988 to a location near the Ice House Museum. For more information call (319) 266–5149 or (319) 277–8817.

In Waterloo begin your tour of the city with a visit to the *Rensselaer Russell House Museum,* which is considered to be the best example of Italianate architecture in Iowa. The lovely brick structure is one of the oldest homes in the county. It was built by Rensselaer Russell, a Waterloo businessman who completed the house in 1861 at the then princely cost of $6,000. Today it has been restored to its original Victorian splendor and is open to the public for tours.

The Rensselaer Russell House is located at 520 West Third Street. Admission is $2.50 for adults and $1.00 for children. Call (319) 233–0260 for hours.

Not far from the Russell House is the *Grout Museum of History and Science* on the corner of West Park Avenue and South Street. Here you can wander through an impressive variety of exhibits describing local history and the natural environment. On the lower level are five full-scale dioramas depicting a log cabin, toolshed, blacksmith shop, carpenter shop, and general store. On the upper level are displays that will inform you about the geology of Iowa, its first inhabitants, and the plant and animal life of the state. There's also a gallery for changing exhibitions.

A highlight of the museum is its planetarium, where public programs are offered each Saturday at 2:00 P.M. and daily during the summer. The facility features a 17-foot dome and a star projector that dramatically displays the stars, moon, and planets seen in an Iowa night sky. Topics range from the seasonal constellations to the chemical composition of space.

The Grout Museum (319–234–6357) is open Tuesday through Saturday. Admission is $2.50.

Other attractions in the area include the Waterloo Museum of Art at 225 Commercial Street, the Waterloo Greyhound Park off I–380, and the award-winning Black Hawk Children's Theatre, which holds performances at the city's recreation and arts center. One of the area's largest employers, the John Deere Company, provides free two-hour tours of its tractor assembly division each weekday. More than a dozen antiques stores can be found in the area as well. For more information on any of these attractions, contact the Waterloo Convention and Visitors Bureau at (800) 728–8431. The bureau can also provide information on the many fine bed-and-breakfasts in Waterloo and Cedar Falls.

South of Waterloo you'll find the *Heritage Farm and Coach Company,* located 3 miles south of Hudson on County Road D35. At Dick and Marie Brown's 80-acre working farm you can pile into a horse-drawn wagon or sleigh and enjoy a trip down to their cabin in the woods, where you can either be served a meal or bring one in with you. The Browns' nineteen Percheron draft horses pull you in the right direction. They were all raised on the farm and, as Marie says, "they are like part of the family." The vehicles hold about twelve people each and cost $125 for the afternoon or evening. People usually stay at the cabin for about three hours. The Browns will be happy to build a bonfire for you, and the inside of the cabin is warmed by a potbellied stove. There are scheduled events throughout the year like a Fall Fest and a "Breakfast with

Santa" (the three Saturdays before Christmas), which cost $10 a person. Call (319) 988–3734 for more information or to make reservations.

From Waterloo and Cedar Falls head north on Highway 218 for 15 miles to Waverly, the site of the *Waverly Midwest Horse Sale.* Twice a year this event draws buyers and sellers from around the country and the world. With a sale bill that includes more than a thousand horses and mules, plus hundreds of harnesses, saddles, wagons, carriages, cutters, and sleighs, the sale is the largest event of its kind in the country. The majority of the horses sold here are draft horses, the massive Percherons, Shires, Belgians, and Clydesdales that once farmed the country. Today they're bought and sold by a varied clientele—Amish farmers, lumber companies that use them in areas inaccessible to machines, ranchers who buy them to haul hay, and places like Disney World that use horses in parades and to pull trolleys. Even if you're not in the market for a Belgian or Clydesdale, the sale is a fascinating slice of rural life. The sales are held each year in March and October on the grounds of the Waverly Sales Company on Highway 218 on the northwest side of Waverly. For more information call (319) 352–2804.

Finally, complete your tour of northeast Iowa with a visit to perhaps the most famous church in Iowa, the *Little Brown Church in the Vale.* The church was immortalized in the hymn "The Church in the Wildwood," written by William Pitts in 1857. The story behind the writing of the hymn is part of the charm of a visit to the church. Pitts, a young music teacher, was traveling west from Wisconsin to visit his fiancée, who lived in Iowa. On the way he stopped to take a stroll along the Little Cedar River and came across a place that he thought would make a lovely location for a church. On his return home he sat down to write a hymn describing what he had imagined, a song with a refrain of "Oh, come to the church in the wildwood, Oh, come to the church in the vale."

The years passed, and eventually Pitts returned to the area to teach music at a local academy. He was stunned by what he found, for a small church was being built at the very spot he had visualized in his hymn. On dedication day in 1864, Pitts's vocal class sang the song in public for the first time, and the church and the hymn became inseparable. The song later gained wider fame when it became the theme of a popular gospel group that toured the country in the early 1900s.

Today the church is best known as a wedding chapel. Hundreds of couples come each year to be married in this simple Congregational church, and on the first Sunday in August, many of them return for the chapel's annual Wedding Reunion. The Little Brown Church is located 2 miles east of Nashua on Highway 346. The church is open from early morning until evening each day of the week. For more information (or to arrange a wedding), call (515) 435–2027.

Adjacent to the Little Brown Church is the **Old Bradford Pioneer Village,** a reconstruction of what was once a thriving village in the area. The thirteen-building complex includes log cabins, a railroad depot, a country school, and the building where William Pitts had his office. The village (515–435–2567) is open daily from May through October. Admission is $4.00 for adults, $1.00 for children.

PLACES TO STAY IN
BLUFFS AND VALLEYS

DUBUQUE
Juniper Hill Farm Bed and Breakfast,
15325 Budd Road, (800) 572–1449,
E-mail: jhbandb@aol.com,
$70–$145

Redstone Inn,
504 Bluff Street, (319) 582–1894,
$49–$175

MCGREGOR
Little Switzerland Inn,
126 Main Street, (319) 873–2057,
$48–$128

LANSING
Fitzgerald's Inn Bed and Breakfast,
160 North Third Street,
(319) 538-4872,
$65–$75

DECORAH
Villager Lodge Motel,
Highways 9 and 52, (800) 632–5980,
$25–$54

SPILLVILLE
Old World Inn,
331 South Main, (800) 924–3739,
$50–$75

WATERLOO
Fairfield Inn,
2011 LaPorte Road, (319) 234–5452,
$49–$79

CEDAR FALLS
Holiday Inn–University Plaza,
5826 University Avenue, (319) 277–2230,
$59–$79

PLACES TO EAT IN
BLUFFS AND VALLEYS

DUBUQUE
Bishops Cafeteria,
555 John F. Kennedy Road,
(319) 588–2031

Garden Room Cafe,
801 Davis Avenue, (319) 582–5100

The Toll Bridge Inn,
2800 Rhomberg Avenue
(319) 556-5566

DYERSVILLE
Country Junction Restaurant,
Highways 20 and 156,
(319) 875–7055

GUTTENBERG
Kanndle Restaurant and Lounge,
106 Schiller, (319) 252–3494

SPILLVILLE
Old World Inn,
311 South Main,
(800) 924–3739

CEDAR FALLS
The Broom Factory,
110 North Main Street,
(319) 268–0877

INDEPENDENCE
Station House and Co.,
1304 First West,
(319) 334–6018

ST. DONATUS
Kalmes Restaurant,
100 North Main Street,
(319) 872–3378

Cultural Crossroads

E ast central Iowa is truly a cultural crossroads. Here you'll find two of Iowa's largest metropolitan areas, the Quad Cities and Cedar Rapids, as well as the cosmopolitan charms of Iowa City, home of the University of Iowa. This region also includes the state's most popular tourism attraction, the Amana Colonies, which were founded as a religious communal society and where German traditions still remain strong. Here in east central Iowa you can also explore the legacies of two of Iowa's most famous native sons, President Herbert Hoover and artist Grant Wood.

Village Charm and City Sophistication

I f I had to name my favorite destinations in Iowa, the **Amana Colonies** would certainly be near the top of my list. Part of the reason is sheer gluttony: The restaurants in these seven picturesque villages are among the best in the state, each serving bounteous portions of hearty German food. If I ever get to heaven, I hope the cafeteria there is staffed by Amana natives.

But the food is not the only reason to visit this community, located 20 miles southwest of Cedar Rapids on Highway 151. Its rich history alone makes it a fascinating stop. The villages were settled by a group of German immigrants, bound together by a common religious belief that has its roots in the Pietist and Mystic movements that flourished in Germany during the early 1700s. The group fled religious persecution in Germany in 1842 and settled in New York State, but eventually they sought a larger and more isolated location for their community.

They came to Iowa in 1855 and built their new home on 26,000 acres of timber and farmland in the rolling countryside of eastern Iowa. Soon they had established a nearly self-sufficient communal society, sharing work, meals, and all worldly goods. This system continued until 1932, when the pressures of the modern world and the Depression combined

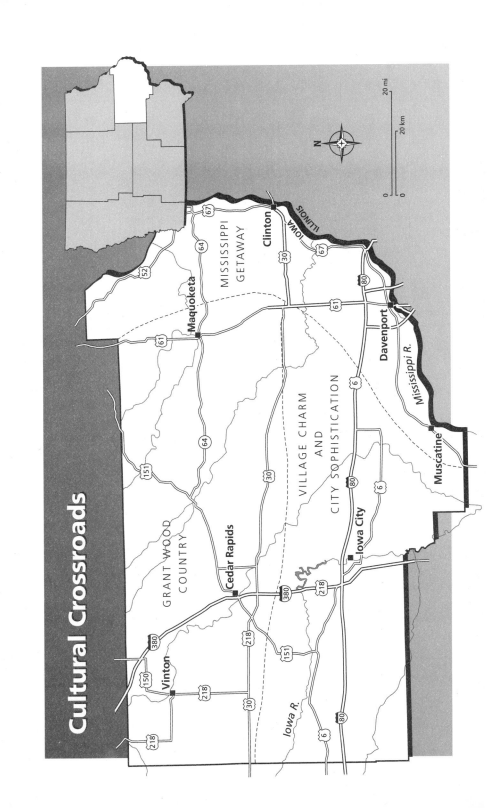

Cultural Crossroads

MISSISSIPPI GETAWAY

Clinton

Maquoketa

VILLAGE CHARM AND CITY SOPHISTICATION

Davenport

Mississippi R.

Muscatine

GRANT WOOD COUNTRY

Cedar Rapids

Iowa City

Vinton

Iowa R.

IOWA

ILLINOIS

N

20 mi

20 km

52

67

64

61

30

61

67

80

6

64

151

30

380

218

218

151

218

150

218

218

30

380

6

80

80

6

CULTURAL CROSSROADS

AUTHOR'S FAVORITES - CULTURAL CROSSROADS

The Amana Colonies

Butterfly Garden

The Black Angel

Stone City

Drollinger's Amusements

Zimmerman Lawn Ornaments

Rochester Cemetery

Cornell College

"The Tug"

Czech Village

to convince the villagers that changes were needed. A profit-sharing corporation was formed to manage the farmland and businesses, and the community kitchens served their last meal. So ended one of America's longest-lived and most successful experiments in utopian living.

Visit the Amanas today, however, and all around you'll see reminders of the past. These tidy brick villages look more European than midwestern, with their houses clustered in the center and weathered barns on the periphery. For a better understanding of their history, visit the ***Museum of Amana History*** in Main Amana, housed in three nineteenth-century buildings set on spacious grounds. There you can view exhibits on the history of the Amana Colonies, its culture and religious life, and the various crafts and industries of the society. The museum also operates a Communal Kitchen and a Cooper Shop in Middle Amana, where you can better understand the work and organization needed to feed the villagers before the "Great Change" of 1932. The museum is open from April 15 through November 15, Monday through Saturday 10:00 A.M. to 5:00 P.M. and Sunday noon to 5:00 P.M. Admission is $2.50 for adults and $1.00 for children. Call (319) 622–3567 for more information.

While you're in Main Amana, take the time to stroll through its streets and browse in the many shops filled with the handcrafted items that have made the Amanas famous. The ***Amana Furniture Shop*** sells beautiful walnut, cherry, and oak furniture and has a room devoted entirely to grandfather clocks, which create a delightful cacophony of ticks and chimes. Another popular spot is the ***Amana Woolen Mill Salesroom,*** an outlet that carries blankets, sweaters, jackets, mittens, and other items. Free factory tours are available Monday through Friday. Across the road is the ***Millstream Brewing Company,*** where premium local beers are brewed. Elsewhere in the village are wineries, gift shops, bakeries, and enough specialty shops to keep you occupied for several hours.

Though Main Amana has the most shops and visitor attractions, don't confine yourself to just one village. A leisurely drive through the countryside will take you on a tour of the other villages, most of which have their own shops, restaurants, wineries, and historical sites. In Middle Amana you'll drive past the villages' best-known industry, Amana Appliances. The business was founded by Amana native George Foerstner and is the largest employer in Iowa County.

From any of the seven Amana villages—Main, East, Middle, High, West, South, and Homestead—it is easy to get on the Amana Colonies Trail, the roads that link the seven villages. Each village has its own unique flavor, and a pleasant day or two can be spent exploring them. Take your time admiring the houses and buildings of brick, stone, or wood. If you are planning a picnic during the summer months make sure you stop at the *Lily Lake,* located on Highway 220 on the outskirts of Middle Amana. This small lake is literally covered with water lilies during mid- to late summer and offers a luxuriant display of green, gold, and creamy white foliage and flowers.

And before you leave the Amanas, enjoy a meal in one of the village restaurants, known for such German specialties as sauerbraten, Wiener Schnitzel, smoked pork chops, and pickled ham. Most serve their meals family style, with overflowing bowls of salads, potatoes, and vegetables, plus delicious homemade pies and desserts. In the words of one Amana native, "If you leave here hungry, it's your own fault."

Although I've made a glutton of myself at most of the Amana restaurants, one place I'd recommend in particular is *Zuber's Dugout Restaurant* in Homestead, a cozy spot filled with Amana antiques and baseball memorabilia relating to the major-league career of its founder. Back in the days when the Amanas were still a communal society, organized games like baseball were forbidden by the church elders. Word of young Bill Zuber's athletic abilities eventually spread, however, and one day a scout for the Cleveland Indians showed up and found the seventeen-year-old helping with the onion harvest in the kitchen gardens. With no baseball available, the scout selected a large onion and asked Bill if he could hit a nearby barn. The obliging young man promptly threw the onion over the barn roof—and an illustrious baseball career was launched.

After six years in the minors, Bill went on to pitch for ten years in the majors, until his arm was injured in 1948. After returning to his home, Bill and his wife, Connie, established a restaurant in a hotel built in Homestead in 1862. Though Bill died some years ago, the restaurant is still owned by the Zuber family. It is open Monday through Saturday 11:00 A.M. to 2:00 P.M. and 4:30 to 8:00 P.M. and Sundays and holidays 11:00 A.M. to 8:00 P.M. Prices are moderate. Phone (319) 622–3911 for more details.

Two newer attractions in the villages may also strike your fancy. One is the *Amana Colonies Nature Trail,* located at the junction of Highways 151 and 6 near Homestead. The trail winds for more than three miles through hardwoods and along the Iowa River and reaches its turnaround point on a scenic bluff overlooking an Indian dam built some 250 years ago.

The *Amana Colonies Golf Course* is set in 300 acres of forest and was named by *Golf Digest* as one of the top new courses in the country. Care has been taken to preserve the natural features of the land, and each hole is unique. For information call (800) 383–3636.

Overnight guests to the Amanas can choose from a variety of accommodations, from motels and campsites to intimate bed-and-breakfasts. *Die Heimat Country Inn* (319–622–3937) in Homestead offers nineteen rooms with private baths and is furnished with Amana antiques. In the late 1850s, Die Heimat (which is German for "The Home Place") was an inn for travelers, and later the building became a communal kitchen. Today it is a gracious small hotel offering a mixture of old-fashioned style and modern amenities.

Another delightful spot is the *Dusk to Dawn Bed and Breakfast* (319–622–3029) owned by Brad and Lynn Hahn in Middle Amana. Here you'll also find a pleasing mixture of traditional Amana furnishings and modern conveniences, including an outdoor Jacuzzi. Seven bedrooms are available for guests, each with a private bath.

The Amana Colonies Visitors Center, located between Main Amana and Middle Amana, will give you a complete listing of attractions in the area as well as hotel accommodations. The center also has an informational video presentation on the Amanas and a gift shop. It is open from 9:00 A.M. to 5:00 P.M. Monday through Saturday and from 10:00 A.M. to 5:00 P.M. Sunday. Call (319) 622–6034 or (800) 245–5465 for information about the Amana Colonies.

If you like to shop, one more destination should be on your itinerary before you leave this part of the state: the *Tanger Factory Outlet Center* near the town of Williamsburg off I–80 (exit 220). Here you'll find more than sixty shops selling merchandise from nationally known manufacturers at savings up to 70 percent off retail prices. From Liz Claiborne dresses to Mikasa dinnerware, this is the place to find bargains. Call (319) 668–2811 for information.

FESTIVALS IN CULTURAL CROSSROADS

Maifest,
Amana, first weekend in May

Houby Days,
Cedar Rapids Czech Village, third weekend in May

Grant Wood Art Festival,
Stone City, third weekend in June

Jazz Fest,
Iowa City, July 3–4

Hoover Fest,
West Branch, August

The Tug,
Le Claire, first weekend in August

Durant Polka Fest,
Durant, September

Oktoberfest,
Amana, first weekend in October

While you're in the neighborhood of Williamsburg make sure you stop at *Emma's Tea Room,* located at 519 Court Street. This charming spot, opened in 1994 by Elaine Wardenburg and named after her mother, offers a new menu daily and all of the foods are fresh and homemade. Whatever you order, make sure you save room for one of their justly famous desserts—there are usually only nine or ten to choose from. Their unique Sawdust Pie is served daily. Emma's is open Monday through Friday from 11:00 A.M. to 3:00 P.M. Prices are inexpensive.

Next head east on I–80 for 20 miles to Iowa City, a lovely university town that I'm delighted to claim as my home. Iowa City is home to the University of Iowa, a Big 10 school with some 27,000 students. Most Iowans have at one time or another attended a Hawkeye football or basketball game or else visited the other major draw in Iowa City: the University of Iowa Hospitals and Clinics, where more than a half-million patients are seen each year. Thanks to the hospital complex, Iowa City has the second highest concentration of physicians per capita of any place in the country—which means that Iowa City is a great place to get sick.

But there are other, more enjoyable things to do in this tranquil college town. Aside from the Saturdays when the football team has a home game, the pace here is as relaxed as the leisurely current of the Iowa River, which flows through the center of town. The university sits in the heart of Iowa City and is the focus of much of its life, but stroll just a few blocks from downtown and you'll find yourself on tree-lined, peaceful residential streets. One neighborhood you shouldn't miss is Summit Street, a stately parade of Victorian homes and beautifully kept lawns about $1/4$ mile from downtown.

Iowa City's nickname is "The Athens of the Midwest," and though the title may seem a bit exalted, there are an extraordinary number of cultural attractions here for a town of its size. Hancher Auditorium presents visiting artists and touring Broadway shows; the Museum of Art showcases a fine collection of American, European, and African art; Riverside Theatre (Iowa City's very own professional company) and the University Theatres present stimulating productions year-round; and the university's famed Writers' Workshop draws the nation's top literary talent for readings that are open to the public. Check the university's *Daily Iowan* newspaper for arts and entertainment information, or stop by the Campus Information Center on the first floor of the Iowa Memorial Union.

Prairie Lights Books, Iowa's largest independent book store, also offers readings throughout the year, as well as a great place to stop if you just want to have a good cup of coffee and browse through a book or a newspaper. But watch out! It's easy to spend more time here than you think. Located downtown at 15 South Dubuque Street, Prairie Lights is open from 9:00 A.M. to 10:00 P.M. during the week and from 9:00 A.M. to 6:00 P.M. on weekends. Call (319) 337–2681 or (800) 295–BOOK for scheduled readings.

The best way to see the University of Iowa is to take a stroll along the river walk that runs through its center. If you're an animal lover, be sure to bring along some bread crumbs, for you're likely to encounter the determined ducks that waddle down the sidewalks here with all the swagger of frontier cowboys. Frequent feedings have made them bold and sassy, and their raucous conversations are a steady accompaniment to the bustle of university life.

Just up the hill from the river is the *Old Capitol,* a lovingly restored Greek Revival structure that served as the state's first capitol from 1842 until 1857. Its golden dome can be seen throughout Iowa City; thus if you're given directions by local residents they're likely to begin, "From the Old Capitol it's about...."

Breaking the Time Barrier

*M*ake sure to take time on your stroll up the river to cross Park Avenue (opposite Hancher Auditorium) into City Park. If you walk far enough through the park between May 10 and October 10, you might begin to hear the laughter of children, the hoot of a train whistle, the antique music of a distant carousel. Before you know it, you will have entered the magical world of **Drollinger's Amusements,** situated along the western bank of the Iowa River. This is one of the best kept secrets of Iowa City.

In operation for almost fifty years, this tiny amusement park has been run by members of the Drollinger family for three generations. It is home for seven small but wonderful rides, ranging from teacups to airplanes to antique cars—and these are not reproductions! On some summer nights Guy Drollinger, who owns the amusements with his wife, Sue, will play some old fifties tunes, and you'll agree with Guy when he says, "Sometimes I think we break the time barrier."

Residents of Iowa City almost lost Drollinger's to the Flood of 1993, but Guy and his family were able to save it for the rest of us to enjoy. If a visit to Drollinger's doesn't bring back recollections of your childhood, it will, at the very least, create a new memory you will treasure. Drollinger's operates daily from May 10 to approximately October 10, opening at 11:00 A.M. and closing at 9:00 P.M. (or maybe a little bit later). If the weather is bad the Drollingers take a well-earned day off.

Old Capitol

Designed by John Francis Rague, the building served as the first permanent seat of Iowa's territorial and state governments until 1857, when the capitol was moved to Des Moines. For the next 113 years the building was used for various university purposes, until a restoration effort was begun in 1970. Today the centerpiece of the Old Capitol is a magnificent self-supporting spiral staircase that leads to the restored legislative chambers upstairs. This National Historic Landmark (319–335–0548) is open Monday through Saturday from 10:00 A.M. to 3:00 P.M. and on Sundays from noon to 4:00 P.M. Admission and guided tours are free.

Next door to the Old Capitol is the venerable Macbride Hall, home for many years to the university's natural history collections. In 1985 *Iowa Hall,* its new gallery, was opened, offering a comprehensive look at Iowa's geology, archaeology, and ecology. As you move through the gallery's three interrelated exhibits, you'll witness the passage of five billion years. One of the most impressive exhibits is a diorama depicting the arrival of Europeans into the state in 1673, seen from the perspective of two Ioway Indians looking out over the Mississippi River from tall bluffs on the Iowa shore. Another highlight is a life-size recreation of a giant ground sloth, a sight that never fails to draw a gasp from young children. The museum's lobby features a small gift shop, plus displays on the pioneering work of Iowa's early naturalists. Iowa Hall is open Monday through Saturday from 9:30 A.M. to 4:30 P.M. and on Sundays from 12:30 to 4:30 P.M. Admission is free. Phone (319) 335–0480 for more details.

Though the University of Iowa tends to overshadow the rest of Iowa City, there are many other attractions to explore here. The walking mall downtown is the perfect place to people-watch, and during the summer months various food vendors peddle their wares. Stop by any of the food carts on the pedestrian mall or at any of the downtown area's numerous restaurants or, if you're looking for a wonderful meal in a unique location, give **Fitzpatrick's** a try. Home of Iowa City's only brew pub, owner Gary Fitzpatrick offers sandwiches and pizza, as well as five different brews (usually a lager, a wheat, an ale, a sweet stout, and something seasonal) in the Irish-style bar. Prices are moderate. If you're in the mood for something fancier, try **The Brewery** next door, his newly opened restaurant. Here you can have an elegant dining experience in breathtakingly beautiful surroundings. Take note of the magnificent copper brew kettles behind the bar. The Brewery is open from 11:00 A.M. to 11:00 P.M. Monday through Saturday; Sunday features a brunch from 10:00 A.M. to 2:00 P.M. as well as the usual dinner hours. Reservations are recommended; prices are expensive. Fitzpatrick's and The Brewery (319–356–6900) are located at 525 South Gilbert Street.

Another popular place is right down the street at 505 South Gilbert Street. **The Sanctuary** serves some of the best pizza in town (as well as a

The Black Angel

*N*o visit to Iowa City is complete without a visit to the enigmatic **Black Angel,** a grave marker that is a source of local tradition and speculation. Dozens of legends cling to the marker: One of the most popular says that a grieving husband spent his savings to place a white angel over the grave of his wife, only to have it turn black overnight because of her unrevealed infidelity to him.

Another cheery story says that anyone who touches the angel will die within the year. There's a happier bit of folklore associated with it as well—college students say that you're not a true University of Iowa coed until you've been kissed in the shadow of its wings.

The real story behind the angel is a bit more prosaic, though it has its share of intrigue as well. The statue was com- missioned in 1911 by a Bohemian immigrant named Teresa Feldevert for the graves of her son and second husband. When the statue arrived in Iowa City, however, Teresa refused to pay for it, saying that it wasn't what she had ordered. The dispute ended up in court, and the woman was ordered to pay the Chicago sculptor $5,000. The disgruntled Teresa decided to have the statue erected in spite of her dislike of it—and ever since it's been a source of fascination for Iowa City residents.

This hauntingly beautiful grave marker, located in the Oakland Cemetery (the entrance is at the intersection of Brown and Dodge Streets), stands 9 feet tall and really has to be seen to be appreciated—I can promise you she is not what you will expect. Does her posture admonish or beckon, forbid or entreat? I leave it for you to decide.

good variety of other choices) and has a huge selection of international beers, in addition to offering entertainment on the weekends—usually a folk singer or a small band. The ambience is delightfully bohemian and the Pizza Fontina (a pizza covered with broccoli, tomatoes, mushrooms, and Fontina cheese) is a personal favorite. The Sanctuary (319–351–5692) opens daily at 4:00 P.M. and serves dinner until midnight.

If you follow Gilbert Street south across Highway 6 it will become Sand Road and you will be well on your way to **Bock's Berry Farm,** a wonderful place to stop and pick berries: strawberries during the month of June, blueberries in July, and raspberries from August until frost, or you can pick out that perfect pumpkin in October. The Bocks have tried to make this a real family place and they have definitely succeeded. There is a farm animal petting zoo and a recently opened barn that has been transformed into a gift shop. Their season runs from late May or early June through December 25. Bock's Berry Farm (319–629–5553) is open seven days a week; hours vary, depending on growing conditions and weather.

During the autumn months make sure you stop at the **Sand Road Orchards,** where the Kroeze family produces and sells not only a wide and distinguished variety of apples, but in my opinion, some of the best apple cider the state has to offer. The orchard is located at 4552 Sand Road; call (319) 351–4999 for more information.

Don't pass up a visit to **Plum Grove,** at 1030 Carroll Street. The Greek Revival structure was once the home of Robert Lucas, Iowa's first territorial governor from 1838 until 1841. Called Plum Grove after a thicket of plum trees on the property, the home was a showplace in frontier Iowa. In the late 1930s the state of Iowa agreed to purchase it, thanks to a local preservation effort led by a grandson of Lucas. Today it's fully restored and furnished with period antiques.

Interesting for those who garden, and even for those who don't, are the heritage garden plots on the grounds of Plum Grove. Planted with only the flowers, vegetables, and herbs that would have been used before the 1850s, these plots re-create a different, growing kind of history. On Sundays a Master Gardener is available to answer questions. You may also, during the first several weeks of June, watch archaeologists at work on open and active digs. Finds have ranged from arrowheads to a 1950s Iowa Football Homecoming pin. Plum Grove is open from Memorial Day weekend through October from 1:00 to 5:00 P.M. Wednesday through Sunday. Admission is free. Call (319) 351–5738 for more details.

A newer attraction in the Iowa City area owes its existence to a natural disaster. During the Flood of 1993, massive amounts of water surged over the emergency spillway at Coralville Lake and eroded a 15-foot-deep channel. When the waters receded, a geologic treasure emerged: an ancient seabed filled with thousands of fossils. The ***Devonian Fossil Gorge*** has become a popular spot for anyone interested in geology—and a good spot to see firsthand the awesome power of a flood. The gorge is located 3$^4/_{10}$ miles north of I–80 on Dubuque Street (turn right at West Overlook Road).

The visitor center run by the Army Corps of Engineers provides a brief but interesting video of the Flood of 1993, which describes the uncovering of the gorge and includes some incredible footage of the flood itself. Also available are maps and guides to the numerous campgrounds and hiking, biking, and cross-country ski trails in the Coralville Reservoir/Lake Macbride area. One recommended trail is the Veterans' Trail, a wonderful barrier-free raised walkway with interpretive signs. Close to the visitor center, it is about $^1/_4$ mile long and is accessible for everyone.

Iowa City's neighboring city is Coralville, a town named after the coral formations left behind by the same sea that created the Devonian Fossil Gorge. Coralville's ***Heritage Museum of Johnson County*** is housed in an 1876 former school and features exhibits that bring to life the history of the area, including a turn-of-the-century schoolroom. The Heritage Museum (319–351–5738) is at 310 Fifth Street and is open Wednesday through Sunday afternoons.

A new attraction in Coralville is the ***Iowa Firefighters Memorial.*** The monument recognizes the sacrifices of those who have lost their lives while fighting fires. The larger-than-life bronze statue depicts a firefighter rescuing a child and the memorial wall at the end of the plaza lists the names of Iowa firefighters killed while rescuing others. The memorial is located at exit 242 off of I–80.

Those wishing to stay overnight in the area should book a room at ***The Golden Haug Bed and Breakfast,*** which is run by Nila and Dennis Haug and features four guest rooms with names that include "Swine and Roses" and "Sir Francis Bacon." The 1920s Arts and Crafts style home has been whimsically decorated and offers cozy accommodations close to Iowa City's downtown. Rates range from $65 to $90; call (319) 354–4284 for reservations.

For more information about attractions in the Iowa City and Coralville area, call (800) 283–6592.

Eight miles east of Iowa City lies the historic small town of West Branch, birthplace of President Herbert Hoover and the location of the **Herbert Hoover National Historic Site.** Here you'll find his official presidential library, a museum detailing his life, the cottage where he was born, a blacksmith shop, an 1853 schoolhouse, and the Quaker meetinghouse where the devout Hoover family attended services. All are set on expansive, beautifully kept grounds, making this a favorite picnic spot for many visitors.

If you're like me, the thought of visiting the Hoover site might not fill you with excitement. My only memory of Hoover before I visited was a vague knowledge of "Hooverville" shanty towns and the grim man who plunged the country into the Great Depression. After I spent a fascinating afternoon in West Branch, however, I came away surprised and impressed. The much-maligned Hoover, I learned, was a complex man of extraordinary abilities.

Tour the newly renovated library and museum and you'll learn the history of his life. The son of an Iowa blacksmith, Hoover was orphaned at the age of ten and went on to become a noted mining engineer and businessman. He made his entry into public life during World War I as the director of food relief programs that fed an estimated 318 million victims of war and drought in Europe and the Soviet Union (take special note of the display of embroidered flour sacks sent to Hoover by grateful children). Later he became secretary of commerce and in 1928 was elected the thirty-first president of the United States—a position for which he refused to accept a salary. Defeated for reelection during the depths of the Depression, the indomitable Hoover continued his work as an active public servant until his death at age ninety. By the end of his life he had once again regained the respect of his fellow citizens, and his passing was marked by tributes from around the country and the world.

Be sure to visit the various buildings on the Hoover site, and don't miss the large statue near the library that was given to Hoover as a gift from the people of Belgium. The figure is a larger-than-life woman wearing a veil, a depiction of the Egyptian goddess Isis. Her air of mystery is irresistible.

The Hoover Library-Museum complex is open from 9:00 A.M. to 5:00 P.M. daily, and admission is $2.00 for adults. A particularly fun time to visit is during "Hooverfest," held the first weekend in August. Call (319) 643–5301 for more information.

Before you leave West Branch, take the time to tour its charming downtown, an area that has been named a National Historic District.

A number of antiques and craft shops line the streets, and one that you shouldn't miss is *Main Street Antiques,* located at 110 West Main. Not only will you find an eclectic and unique assortment of antiques, but in the back of the shop is a gallery of paintings by proprietor Lou Picek. Noted for their colorful and "primitive" style, they offer a unique depiction of the artist's experiences or, as Lou says, his "everyday life with a touch of humor and fantasy." Main Street Antiques (319–643–2065) is open Monday through Saturday from 10:00 A.M. to 5:00 P.M.

You might want to take a road trip along the historic *Herbert Hoover Highway,* which runs from the Old Capitol in Iowa City (see page 35) and ends where it meets the old Lincoln Highway in Lowden. This 42-mile route, designated as the Hoover Highway in 1923, was once heralded as a "shortcut"—first between Iowa City and Lowden (which was the supply station stopping point for the Chicago, Iowa, and Nebraska Railroad) and later between Des Moines and Chicago. This route will take you through the heart of Cedar County and is well marked by the distinctive "three H" signs, some of which are still attached to the utility poles as they were in 1923.

Wildflowers and Gravestones

*I*f you're traveling the Herbert Hoover Highway, make sure you plan a stop at the **Rochester Cemetery,** located just southeast of the Cedar River bridge in Rochester. Particularly during the spring and summer months, this remarkable cemetery, set as it is on thirteen acres of natural prairie, comes alive with wildflowers and prairie grasses. Around Mother's Day the cemetery is filled with swirling galaxies of shooting stars and mayapples. Later, false dandelion predominates, punctuated by prairie phlox and golden alexanders. In late June and July there are beautiful patches of black-eyed Susans sprinkled among the other flowers, and in August the prairie grasses glow with their subtle

inflorescence. All told, more than fifty species of wildflowers have been counted here.

Don't miss the grave of Mary King in the southwest portion of the cemetery. This grave is the source of a Cedar County legend. that claims that Mary King was the mother of the great actress Sarah Bernhardt. Once, immediately before Miss Bernhardt took the stage in Iowa City in 1904, a gigantic bouquet of red roses was placed on the grave. The rumor has it that "the divine Miss Sarah" was in reality little Sarah King who had run away earlier with an acting troupe and was never heard of—at least under her own name—again.

From West Branch head south on County Road X30 for 4 miles to Downey, where the town's 1903 bank has been renovated by artists Judith Spencer and Richard King into the **Custom Surfaces Gallery.** Inside the airy and inviting gallery is an eclectic mixture of works: King's mixed-media paintings and collage, a variety of tile murals and pottery pieces created by Spencer, amber jewelry imported from Poland, and reproductions of neolithic goddess figurines that are a collaboration between the two artists. Among the gallery's more dramatic pieces are a dining room table that is already "set" with outlines of plates and silverware underneath a glass top, and a phone booth filled with the tiled images of Venus and Cupid floating in the clouds. The gallery also stocks imported tile from around the world and is filled with examples of how tile can be used in innovative ways. Custom Surfaces Gallery (319–643–5683) is at 110 Front Street in Downey and is open by appointment during the week and on Saturday from noon to 5:00 P.M. and Sunday from 1:00 to 5:00 P.M.

East of Downey on Highway 6 you'll find another Iowa treasure: the **Wilton Candy Kitchen,** the oldest continuously operating ice-cream parlor in the nation. This old-fashioned soda shop and ice-cream parlor was built in the small town of Wilton in 1856 and has been owned by the Nopoulos family since 1910. George Nopoulos began working in his family's business in 1926 at the age of six, when he was given the job of winding the record player. Today he and his vivacious wife, Thelma, continue the establishment's long tradition of serving scrumptious homemade ice cream and soda treats as well as a selection of sandwiches. Among the dignitaries who have visited the Wilton Candy Kitchen are actor Gregory Peck (who made himself a cherry Coke behind the counter) and Governor Terry Branstad. In the back of the building you'll find a museum of Wilton history. The Wilton Candy Kitchen is at 310 Cedar Street and is open from 7:30 A.M. to 5:30 P.M. daily. For information call (319) 732–2278 or (319) 732–2871.

Mississippi Gateway

egin your tour along east central Iowa's portion of the Mississippi River in Muscatine. Life in this river port has always been dominated by the Mississippi River. In 1835 an influx of white settlers came to the area, and two years later James Casey started a trading post here to service the flourishing riverboat industry. Soon people began calling the area "Casey's Wood Pile"—though by 1850 the growing town had adopted the more elegant name of Muscatine. The word was taken (depending on whom you believe) either from the Mascoutin Indians who lived here or from an Indian word meaning "burning island." (It's interesting, however, to speculate on what the town's sports teams would have been called had the original name been kept. Casey's Wood Pile Termites, perhaps?)

Although the first major industry in Muscatine was lumber, by the late 1890s button making had become the city's major source of revenue. By 1905 the area was producing more than one-third of the world's buttons, which were made from the shells of clams harvested from the Mississippi River. Muscatine's *Pearl Button Museum* chronicles the development of the industry and is the only museum in the world dedicated to this unique enterprise. Here you can see the complete button-making procedure, from collecting shells from the bottom of the Mississippi River through processing, cutting, and dyeing. The Pearl Button Museum (319–263–8895) is located in downtown Muscatine at the corner of Iowa Avenue and Second Street and is open from 1:00 to 4:00 P.M. on Saturdays.

You can find out more about Muscatine's history at the *Muscatine Art Center,* a combination museum and art gallery located at 1314 Mulberry Avenue. The museum is housed in a 1908 mansion donated to the city by the Laura Musser family. The first floor is furnished in the fashion of the Edwardian era, and upstairs is gallery space for various exhibits and an art library. Connected to the elegant mansion is a modern three-level facility with gallery space for the art center's collections. Outside is a small but nicely landscaped area featuring a Japanese garden and native Iowa wildflowers.

The Muscatine Art Center is open Tuesday through Friday 10:00 A.M. to 5:00 P.M., Thursday evenings 7:00 to 9:00 P.M., and Saturday and Sunday 1:00 to 5:00 P.M. Call (319) 263–8282 for more details. Admission is free.

Once you've enriched your mind at the art center, exercise your imagination at Muscatine's *FantaSuite Hotel* on Highway 61. The idea may seem a bit juvenile at first, but the "fantasy suites" contained within are a great opportunity to get completely away—to ancient Rome, for example, or Sherwood Forest. Each of the hotel's seventeen suites is decorated in a different theme, and each comes with a spacious whirlpool spa. My personal favorite: Caesar's Court, a room with pink marble columns and a whirlpool big enough for a small dinner party.

FantaSuite Cantebury Hotel is located 2402 Park Avenue, Highway 61 (319–264–3337). Rates for fantasy suites range from $99 to $179 per night. Standard hotel rooms are also available.

If you visit Muscatine during the summer months, don't leave without buying one of the region's renowned melons. I've yet to taste any watermelons or cantaloupes that can compare with those grown here. Open-air markets are held on Muscatine Island from mid-July through October.

You may also want to plan a stop at Pearlcity Perennial Plantation and the *Karkosh Korners Display Gardens,* located just outside Muscatine on scenic Highway 22. The display gardens offer more than 7,000 varieties of bulbs in the spring, as well as 200+ hosta species and more than 800 varieties of daylilies in the summer. Winding trails will lead you through shady corners and sun-soaked meadows. Different areas are devoted to a grasses garden, a water garden, an orchard, a pine grove, wildflowers, and many others. There is also a delightful children's zoo with domestic animals, peacocks, and even a llama! Admission to the display gardens and zoo is free. You may well be tempted, after seeing all this abundance, to cross the highway to the "perennial plantation" and try out a few of the plants you've seen for yourself! The staff is as friendly and as helpful as any you are ever likely to find. Located at 2821 Highway 22, the plantation opens on April 15 and closes sometime in the fall. Call (319) 262–5555 for hours, which are long but varied, depending on the growing season.

If you're headed to the Quad Cities, take Highway 22 east to the small community of Fairport. On the riverbank next to the Fairport Landing Marina there is a wonderful restaurant and bar with fine river views. The *Chart House,* best known for catfish sandwiches, offers a casual but varied menu. There is nothing more delightful than sitting on the wide screened-in porch watching the Mississippi slide by and chatting with people at the adjoining tables. The Chart House is a fun-filled place, noisy with the laughter of boaters, especially during the evening hours when the porch twinkles with hundreds of tiny white lights. It is very relaxed, very informal. If you want a taste of a "real" Mississippi experience this is the place to go. The Chart House, located at 2142 Water Street, is open only during the boating season. Call (319) 264–6862 for hours.

Close to the Chart House on Highway 22 is Wildcat Den State Park, a beautiful area with winding trails and some spectacular river views. Here you will also find the *Pine Creek Grist Mill.* The mill, originally built in 1848 at a cost of ten thousand dollars, was bought by the state of Iowa in 1927 for $87.50 after it had gone out of business. It is currently undergoing a thorough restoration so that it can once again become a fully working mill. The mill is open to visitors on Sunday afternoons from 1:00 to 5:00 P.M., from the second Sunday in June through the second Sunday in September. For more information call (319) 263–4337.

If you're looking for a place to stay, chug on up Highway 22 to Montpelier, home of *Varners' Caboose,* a genuine Rock Island Lines caboose, which now sees service as a unique bed-and-breakfast. It has a self-contained bath and shower, a complete kitchen, and can accommodate up to four people. If rented by the day, a fully prepared breakfast is left waiting for you in the kitchen. For stays of more than five days the caboose may be rented as a "housekeeping" cabin. Varners' Caboose is open year-round at 204 East Second Street. For reservations call (319) 381–3652.

Highway 22 will lead you to the largest metropolitan area in Iowa, the Quad Cities. The name is misleading, for there are five cities that come together here on the Mississippi: Davenport and Bettendorf line the Iowa side, while Rock Island, Moline, and East Moline hug the Illinois bank.

The first thing to realize is that these are river towns, with a rich history that stretches back some 200 years. The area was a trading center for the American Fur Company and a battleground during the War of 1812. Davenport was the first city in Iowa to have railroad service, and it was here that the first train crossed the Mississippi in 1856. (The railroad bridge was later the cause of a historic lawsuit between the river trade and the railroad. Successfully defending the railroad interests was a young Illinois lawyer who would later make quite a name for himself—Abraham Lincoln.) During the Civil War, a prison camp for Confederate soldiers was located in the area, and nearly 2,000 Southern soldiers are buried here far from their homes. In the years following the war, the area became a major port for river travel between New Orleans and St. Paul.

Arsenal Island, the largest island in the upper Mississippi, is an excellent place to learn more about the history and military importance of the Quad Cities. The arsenal was established by the U.S. Army in 1862 and continues to manufacture weapons parts and military equipment. With 9,000 civilian and military workers, the Rock Island Arsenal is the area's largest employer.

There are a number of attractions here worth a visit. The Rock Island Arsenal Museum is the second oldest U.S. Army museum after West Point and contains one of the largest military arms collections in the nation. The building is open daily from 10:00 A.M. to 4:00 P.M., and admission is free (309–782–5021). Also of historical interest on the island are the Confederate Cemetery and the Colonel Davenport House, built in 1834.

The Mississippi River Visitors Center is located at the west end of the island at Lock & Dam #15 and offers a bird's-eye view of the workings of the dam, plus interpretive displays on river navigation and the work of the U.S. Army Corps of Engineers. The Channel Project was developed in the 1930s to maintain at least a 9-foot depth in the Mississippi River channel. The result is an "aquatic staircase" created by twenty-six locks and dams on the river. The visitor center is open daily from 9:00 A.M. to 9:00 P.M. May through September. Hours vary at other times of the year. Call (309) 788–6412 for more information.

Arsenal Island lies in the Mississippi River channel between Davenport and Rock Island and can be reached through three entrances, one on the Iowa side and two on the Illinois.

Davenport's **Putnam Museum of Natural History and Science** offers additional insight into the area and its history. The museum's $5 million expansion has greatly increased its space. Inside you'll find exhibits on the region's heritage and the wildlife of the Mississippi River valley as well as Asian and Egyptian galleries and a hands-on science lab. The Putnam Museum (319–324–1933) is at 1717 West Twelfth Street and is open Tuesday through Sunday.

Next door to the Putnam you'll find another fine museum, the **Davenport Museum of Art,** which features nineteenth- and twentieth-century American art, European old masters, Mexican colonial and Haitian art, and an extensive regionalist collection. The museum (319–326–7804) is at 1737 West Twelfth Street and is open Tuesday through Sunday.

The Family Museum of Arts and Science in Bettendorf is a fun stop whether or not you have young children in tow. I recommend borrowing one for the day if you don't have one of your own; watching kids explore the exhibits within is as much fun as looking at them yourself. The museum features exhibits designed with curious young children in mind. While most museums say, "Don't Touch," this one says, "Please Do!" During your visit you can go down a rabbit hole, visit an old-fashioned farm kitchen from 1940, and turn into a bird in the "Kinder Garten."

The Family Museum is open Monday through Thursday from 9:00 A.M. to 8:00 P.M., Friday and Saturday from 9:00 A.M. to 5:00 P.M. and Sundays from noon to 5:00 P.M. Admission is $3.00 for children and adults and $2.00 for those over 60.

Vander Veer Botanical Center at 214 West Central Park in Davenport is a peaceful place to recover from all your sightseeing. The Rose Garden is considered one of the finest in the Midwest, with 1,800 roses representing nearly 145 varieties. The peak blooming period normally begins in early June and continues through the summer. The recently enlarged conservatory presents five special floral displays throughout the year, and at any time it's a lush and quiet place to wander through and enjoy.

One stop you shouldn't miss during your visit here is the *Iowa Machine Shed,* one of the state's best restaurants. The walls are filled with old farm implements and antiques (including a large collection of seed corn hats), and the food is home-style midwestern cooking at its best: dinners of crispy fried chicken, thick pork chops and tasty stuffed pork loin, savory soups, and mouthwatering desserts, all served family style with big bowls of vegetables and freshly baked bread.

The Iowa Machine Shed is open for breakfast (don't miss their huge cinnamon rolls), lunch, and dinner and is located off I–80 at exit 292. Prices are moderate; call (319) 391–2427 for reservations.

Another attraction in the Quad Cities is the Village of East Davenport, an area of historic shops and homes that date back to 1851. Here you'll find nearly sixty unique shops and boutiques. Riverboat gambling is also a big draw here, with three boats—the *President, Lady Luck,* and *Casino Rock Island*—offering a wide variety of gaming options. For more information about area attractions, contact the Quad Cities Convention and Visitors Bureau at (800) 747–7800 or (309) 788–7800.

While you're in East Davenport you may want to grab a *Channel Cat Water Taxi* ride. This wonderful transport functions as a "water bus," departing from and returning to four different landings at various spots along the river. Each landing is visited approximately every half hour. It serves as a watery link between Quad Cities bicycle trails (each taxi has space for twenty bicycles), but nonbikers are welcomed as well. Tickets are for all-day unlimited use and cost $3.50 for adults and $1.50 for children, those under two ride for free. The Channel Cats run from Memorial Day to Labor Day. Call (309) 788–3360 for schedule information.

Walnut Grove Pioneer Village, located 9 miles north of the Quad Cities near the town of Long Grove on Highway 61, is a pleasant place to unwind after visiting the Quad Cities. Walnut Grove was a crossroads settlement in the pioneer days of Scott County in the 1860s. Today, the three-acre site contains fourteen historic buildings, including a blacksmith shop, schoolhouse, church, and pioneer family homes. The surrounding *Scott County Park* offers nature trails, camping facilities, playground equipment, and a nature center.

Walnut Grove Pioneer Village is open daily from 8:00 A.M. to sundown April through October. Admission is free.

A beautiful place to stay in the Quad Cities area is *The Woodlands Bed and Breakfast,* a modern-style home set amid twenty-six acres of forest and meadows in a private wildlife refuge. The Woodlands's many windows seem to bring the trees inside the house, and owner Betsy Wallace has filled the home with items collected on her extensive travels around the world. Two suites are offered to visitors, and the entire house is also available for retreats and meetings. The Woodlands (800–257–3177) is located 15 miles north of the Quad Cities, and rates are $75 to $115, which include a full breakfast.

A few miles north of the Quad Cities lies the charming river town of Le Claire. Founded in 1833, Le Claire was once a boat-building center and home to many steamboat captains, who used to hire on with riverboats traveling past the treacherous rapids near the Quad Cities. Today it's a pleasant town of 3,000 people who take great pride in Le Claire's history and historic homes and buildings.

The town's most famous son is "Buffalo Bill" Cody, who was born on a farm near Le Claire in 1846. Cody became a pony express rider at the age of fourteen and later gained fame as a buffalo hunter who supplied meat for the workers building the railroad lines. In 1872 he began his long career as a showman, taking his Wild West Show to all parts of the United States and Europe.

There are several sites to visit in the Le Claire area if you're interested in the life of this colorful man. The *Buffalo Bill Cody Homestead* is located about 10 miles northwest of Le Claire near the town of McCausland. Buffalo, burros, and longhorn cattle graze the land around the homestead, and the house is furnished with nineteenth-century items. The site is open from 9:00 A.M. to 5:00 P.M. daily from April 1 to October 31 (319–225–2981).

In Le Claire visit the *Buffalo Bill Cody Museum* on the bank of the river next to the dry-docked stern-wheeler *Lone Star.* Along with memorabilia relating to Cody's life, the museum also has exhibits on Indians, early pioneers, and the history of Le Claire. The museum is located at 20 North River Drive and is open from 9:00 A.M. to 5:00 P.M. daily May 15 through October 15. Winter hours are 9:00 A.M. to 4:30 P.M. on Saturday and Sunday. Phone (319) 289–5580.

For a brochure highlighting these and other local sites relating to Cody's early life, as well as a wide variety of other tourism material, visit the

Mississippi Valley Welcome Center at 900 Eagle Ridge Road in Le Claire. Located high on a bluff overlooking the Mississippi, the center also features educational displays, a gift shop, and a multimedia slide presentation.

Le Claire is also home to the *Twilight,* a paddle wheel riverboat that offers a two-day cruise along one of the prettiest sections of the entire Mississippi. I've taken a number of cruises on the Mississippi, and I consider the trips offered by the *Twilight* to be among the very best. The food is delicious, the scenery magnificent, the live entertainment enjoyable, and the boat itself lovely. River cruises on the *Twilight* depart from Le Claire in the morning, travel upriver all day, and dock at Galena, Illinois, where guests spend the night at Chestnut Mountain Resort. The next day you can tour Galena and then board the boat again at noon for a leisurely trip back to Le Claire. Cruises run from mid-May through mid-October, and reservations are required. Tickets are $225 (double occupancy) and include all meals, entertainment, and lodging. For a free brochure write to River Cruises, P.O. Box 406, Galena, IL 61036, or call (800) 331–1467.

An excellent restaurant in Le Claire is the *Faithful Pilot* (319–289–4156), overlooking the river at 117 North Cody Road. Here you'll find a changing and creative menu, along with homemade breads and desserts. Prices are moderate to expensive.

The Tug!

*T*he states of Iowa and Illinois have been fighting it out every first Saturday in August since 1987 in a rip-roaring tug-of-war contest. What line defines the loser? Why, the mighty Mississippi, of course! That's right—contestants from Le Claire on the Iowa side and from Port Byron on the Illinois side pit their strength against one another with ropes stretched across the width of the river. These will have to be the longest ropes you've ever seen, for the river is a half mile across at this point. I am informed that there used to be weight restrictions for the participants but in the fierce heat of rivalry, these restric-

tions have collapsed. I am also informed (by an Illinois resident) that Illinois holds the edge in these competitions and that the traveling trophy currently resides in Illinois. It's time to step up to the plate and cheer on the Iowa team. There are fun things to do in both communities before and after the tug—boat flotillas, craft exhibits, and food vendors abound—and the evening explodes in fireworks when the two sides join together to host a gigantic fireworks display from barges moored in the middle of the river. This is competition and cooperation at its finest—come and join the fun!

From Le Claire head north to the river port of Clinton. Like the Quad Cities, Clinton is a town dominated by the Mississippi River. During the late nineteenth century, Clinton became an important transportation and lumbering center, and today it continues to be an active industrial area.

Clinton takes great pride in its history as a river town, and you can enjoy an echo of that past at the *Clinton Area Showboat Theatre.* This is a theater group that performs each summer aboard the *City of Clinton* showboat—an authentic paddle wheeler permanently dry-docked on the riverbank in Clinton's Riverview Park. Recalling the days when lavish showboats plied their way up and down the river, the theater is the perfect place to complete a day's touring along the Mississippi.

These aren't amateur productions, either. Each spring the theater recruits nationally to produce its June-through-August summer stock season. Performances are given in a 225-seat air-conditioned theater and include contemporary works as well as old standards. Musicals, comedies, and dramas are offered each season.

The *City of Clinton* showboat is docked at Riverview Park, Sixth Avenue North along the Mississippi. Tickets to the performances range from $10 to $11; call (319) 242–6760 for more information.

To experience the river firsthand, board the *Mississippi Belle II,* a floating casino with accommodations for 1,000 passengers. The boat docks at Showboat Landing in Riverview Park and offers gambling cruises from 1:00 to 3:00 P.M. on weekdays from May through October. Dockside gambling is offered daily, year-round. Call (800) 457–9975 for information.

Travel to the north end of Clinton and you'll find *Eagle Point Park and Nature Center,* a recreation area perched high on a bluff overlooking the river. The park itself contains 200 acres with numerous hiking trails and picnic areas. Be sure to see the 35-foot observation tower built of locally quarried stone that stands on a promontory above the river.

The nature center adjacent to the park will help you appreciate the beauty and ecology of the area. During the summer and early fall, the center manages various animal exhibits and a petting zoo, plus a pond for fish and waterfowl. Nearby is the Flannery School, a restored one-room schoolhouse, and just to the east is a prairie demonstration area with native prairie flowers and grasses. Although schoolchildren make up a good part of the nature center's clientele, adults are always welcome.

The Eagle Point Park and Nature Center is located on North Third Street on the northern edge of Clinton. Call (319) 242– 9088 for more information.

Costello's Old Mill Gallery

Another lovely nature area is the **Bickelhaupt Arboretum** at 340 South Fourteenth Street. This thirteen-acre horticultural showplace features more than 2,000 plants and 600 trees and shrubs. It is open from sunrise until sunset, year-round, and no admission is charged.

A fun place to eat in Clinton is **Holiday Harry's** at 226 Fifth Avenue South. The restaurant draws its name from a 1920s-era gangster who is said to have been a "Robin Hood" character who used much of his loot from gambling and bootlegging to help out people in his neighborhood. The restaurant is housed in the bank building that was robbed by Harry's gang on several occasions. Holiday Harry's (319–243–5736) is open Wednesday through Saturday from 5:00 to 9:00 P.M. Prices are inexpensive to moderate.

From Clinton travel north on Highways 67 and 52 to Bellevue, one of the Mississippi River's most charming towns. Begin your tour at Lock & Dam #12 in the middle of town, and then wander through Bellevue's shopping district, an area lined with century-old stone and brick buildings. Many now house stores selling antiques, collectibles, and arts and crafts.

For a treat of a different sort, visit the **Butterfly Garden** at Bellevue State Park. And just what is a butterfly garden, you ask? From a butterfly's point of view, it's heaven. This one-acre garden is carefully planned to provide for the care and feeding of nature's most beautiful and delicate creatures. In it is a mixture of plants that range from radishes and carrots to milkweeds and stinging nettles—plants that play host to some sixty species of butterflies that hover here each spring, summer, and fall. Interspersed among the plants are large rocks that make ideal basking spots for butterflies, plus a small pond where they can get water.

This serene oasis is the product of thousands of hours of volunteer labor done by Bellevue citizens, and in particular Judy Pooler, who in 1986 received the Governor's Award for volunteer service to the state of Iowa. Pooler first came across the idea for a butterfly garden in a magazine in 1984 and soon persuaded the park to develop a former meadow into a garden. Since then she has traveled to Newfoundland and South America to study butterflies and has corresponded with lepidopterists around the country in her quest to expand and improve the garden.

Pooler says that the best time to visit the garden is on a sunny day with little wind. The Butterfly Garden is located in Bellevue State Park, ½ mile south of town off Highway 52.

One of Bellevue's magnificent old mansions is now *Mont Rest,* a bed-and-breakfast inn built in 1893. Nestled into a wooded hillside overlooking the town and river, Mont Rest is owned by Christine Snyder, who has restored the house to its original elegance. Six bedrooms are open to guests, each beautifully decorated and furnished with antiques. The most unusual is located in a tower that was once a gambling den for the home's original owner. The bedroom has a panoramic view of the Mississippi and a deck right outside its door. Be forewarned, however: In order to go to the bathroom you have to walk outside and down a steep set of stairs. I think that adds to its charm, though a visitor may think differently on a frigid January night. "The owner wanted to make the room as inaccessible as possible so that he'd have plenty of warning if the place was raided for gambling," explains Christine Snyder.

Mont Rest is located at 300 Spring Street in Bellevue (319–872–4220). Prices for double occupancy range from $64 to $94 a night, with a full country breakfast and evening dessert included.

Snyder also owns the *Springbrook General Store* in the nearby small town of Springbrook, 7 miles south of Bellevue. The National Register structure was built in 1874 and now houses a gift shop, restaurant, and dinner theater. Call (319) 872–4220 for more information.

In Bellevue another attraction you shouldn't miss is the *Spring Side Inn,* a stunning example of Gothic Revival architecture that overlooks the town of Bellevue and the Mississippi. Owned by Mark and Nancy Jaspers, the inn has six rooms, each named after an American author who was writing at the time the house was built in 1850.

In addition to a full breakfast, the Jaspers serve a complimentary evening dessert to guests. Rooms range from $120 to $160 per night. The inn is located on Ensign Road; call (319) 872–5452 for information.

Travel north on Highway 52 for 10 miles and you'll reach **St. Donatus,** a small village famous for its Old World architecture and traditions. Its settlers were immigrants from Luxembourg who tried to duplicate the architecture, dress, and customs of their native land in their new home.

One of the village's main attractions is the Outdoor Way of the Cross, the first of its kind in America. Built in 1861, it consists of fourteen brick alcoves scattered along a winding path behind the St. Donatus Catholic Church. Each alcove contains an original lithograph depicting Christ's journey on Good Friday. At the top of the hill is the Pieta Chapel, a replica of a church in Luxembourg.

Other attractions in St. Donatus include **Gehlen House and Barn,** a house built in 1848 that is listed on the National Register of Historic Places. Call (319) 773–8200 for more information.

Grant Wood Country

owa's most famous native artist, Grant Wood, drew rich inspiration from this part of eastern Iowa, depicting its rolling countryside in many of his paintings. You'll find this region easy to explore on the **Grant Wood Scenic Byway,** a series of county roads and highways that takes you past many attractions relating both to Wood's life and to Iowa history. The byway stretches between Bellevue and Anamosa and is marked by special signs. For a brochure describing the route, call the Iowa Division of Tourism at (515) 242–4705.

On your tour of this part of the state, follow the winding roads of the byway to Maquoketa. One mile east of town you'll find **Costello's Old Mill Gallery.** The 1867 stone building was bought and restored by nationally known wildlife artist Patrick J. Costello, who displays and sells both his work and that of other artists. Many days you can find Costello working in his studio at the back of the mill, where visitors are invited to watch him as he sketches. "At times it's distracting," he admits, "but I think it helps people be more appreciative of the work I do."

Costello's Old Mill Gallery is located just east of Maquoketa on Highway 64 (319–652–3351). From January through March the mill is open Wednesday through Sunday from 10:00 A.M. to 6:00 P.M.; from April through December it's open daily from 10:00 A.M. to 6:00 P.M.

Two miles north of Maquoketa on Highway 61 are the **Hurstville Lime Kilns,** once the site of the old company town of Hurstville. Built in the

1870s, these formerly active kilns crushed the limestone quarried nearby and heated it with wood fires to produce a lime resin. Preceding the development of concrete, this was one of Iowa's most important early industries. Thanks to a large community volunteer effort, these kilns are open to visitors year-round. You can call the Jackson County Welcome Center for more information at (800) 342–1837.

In Maquoketa itself several attractions are worth a visit. North of town on Highway 61 is Banowetz Antiques, the Midwest's largest antiques shop, with more than two acres of merchandise. And for an introduction to the history of the area, tour the Jackson County Historical Museum on the Jackson County Fairgrounds.

A nice place to stay in Maquoketa is the *Squiers Manor Bed and Breakfast* located at 418 West Pleasant Street. Built in 1882, this lovely Queen Anne–style mansion offers a beautiful antique decor that is set sparkling with fireplaces and special candlelight desserts. Morning delivers a full gourmet breakfast. Rates range from $75 to $185 for a grand suite. Squiers Manor may be reached at (319) 652–6961.

Then take Highway 428 west of town to the *Maquoketa Caves,* one of Iowa's most unusual geologic formations. This 272-acre state park contains a labyrinth of underground caverns and woodland trails. You can reach the thirteen caves scattered throughout the park by well-marked and sometimes rugged trails. Although two of the main caves are lighted, flashlights are needed in the others.

Indian pottery, arrowheads, spears, and other artifacts found in the caves provide proof that they were used by native tribes for hundreds of years. When the caves were first discovered before the Civil War, lovely stalactites and stalagmites were found, but unfortunately, souvenir hunters have robbed the caves of most of these. Two monuments that remain are a balanced rock and a natural bridge.

Camping and picnic sites are available in the park. Call (319) 652–5833 for more information.

For some local color and hearty food, visit *Bluff Lake Restaurant,* 1 mile from Maquoketa Caves at the end of a long and winding gravel road (follow the signs once you leave the park). This bustling establishment sits surrounded by a pond in which visitors used to catch their own dinners. On weekends hundreds of people flock to its all-you-can-eat fish fries. On Fridays fresh, pond-raised catfish is served; on Saturdays the menu features haddock. Its owner is the friendly Linda Wells, whose father built the restaurant in 1971.

Bluff Lake is open Thursday through Saturday from 4:00 to 10:00 P.M. and on Sunday from 11:00 A.M. to 8:30 P.M. Prices are moderate. Call (319) 652–3272 for more information.

From Maquoketa travel west on Highway 64 to the town of Anamosa, site of the *Grant Wood Tourism Center and Gallery.* At the center you can see Grant Wood prints and murals and view a movie about Wood's life and art, as well as a large display of "American Gothic" caricatures. The center also stocks tourism information and sells a large selection of Grant Wood prints, books, notecards, T-shirts, and other memorabilia. The gallery (319–462–4267) is at 124 East Main Street and is open Monday through Saturday from 10:00 A.M. to 4:00 P.M. and Sunday from 1:00 to 4:00 P.M.

Before leaving Anamosa take note of the impressive architecture of the *Iowa State Men's Reformatory* located at the west end of the downtown. Beginning in 1873 prisoners labored to construct the prison using stone quarried from the nearby Stone City area. Upon its completion, Iowans dubbed it the "White Palace of the West," a tribute to its imposing architecture, beautiful stone walls, and immaculate landscaping. The prison today looks much the same as it did a hundred years ago, down to the regal stone lions guarding its entrance. During the summer months a formal garden in front of the prison is filled with blooming flowers. Although visitors are not allowed inside the prison, they are invited to enjoy the outside grounds.

West of Anamosa lies lovely *Stone City,* once a thriving quarry area and later the site of several summer art colonies run by Grant Wood during the early 1930s. The best time to visit the village is on the second Sunday in June, when Stone City hosts the *Grant Wood Art Festival.* Area artists come to demonstrate and sell their work, tours of the town's historic ruins are offered, and strolling entertainers perform throughout the village. For more information call (319) 462–4267.

North of Anamosa on Highway 51 lies the small town of Langworthy, the site of one of my favorite off-the-beaten-path destinations in Iowa. If you're looking for a concrete rhino for your front lawn, or perhaps a life-size buffalo for your patio, *Zimmerman Lawn Ornaments* is the place for you. Even if you're not in the market for statuary, Zimmerman's is a fun place to browse and marvel at what can be done with concrete. Owned by former farmer Don Zimmerman, the business stocks thousands of statues that range from small turtles and birdbaths to 2,500-pound lions. Zimmerman Lawn Ornaments (319–465–3987) is located on the north end of Langworthy and is open Monday through Saturday from 9:00 A.M. to 5:00 P.M.

The Cherry Sisters

The famous Cherry Sisters spent most of their lives in Cedar Rapids. The name doesn't sound familiar? The Cherry Sisters (Effie, Addie, and Jessie) were stage performers at the turn of the century whose act was so bad that it sometimes had to be "presented behind nets to protect the sisters from vegetables, fruit, and other missiles hurled at them," according to one Iowa history book. Nevertheless, their performances were so popular that they enabled the Oscar Hammerstein Theatre in New York to pay off its mortgage in one season. The Cherry Sisters then returned to Cedar Rapids, where they spent the rest of their lives.

Next head south to the major city in this part of the state, Cedar Rapids. A number of famous Iowans are associated with Cedar Rapids: artist Grant Wood made his home here for many years and Mamie Doud Eisenhower lived here as a child. Even native Iowans are likely to be surprised by the variety and wealth of attractions in Iowa's second largest city. One of my favorites is the *Czech Village,* a 3-block area of Czech shops and restaurants on Sixteenth Avenue SW. One-third of the population in Cedar Rapids is of Czech origin, making it the dominant ethnic group in the city. The village area is a center for preserving that heritage and is the site of several ethnic festivals and businesses.

Stop by the Sykora Bakery for an authentic taste of Czech culture—one of their specialties is *kolaches,* a fruit-filled pastry. Then visit the *National Czech and Slovak Museum,* located on the banks of the Cedar River in Czech Village. The new $2.9 million museum is five times the size of the original museum, which opened in 1974. Designed in the style of traditional Prague architecture, the facility preserves more than 5,000 artifacts—the largest collection of such items to be found anywhere outside of the Czech Republic and Slovakia. Included are rare maps, Czech glass and porcelain, and more than forty traditional costumes (*kroje*) from all regions of the two countries. Another highlight is an early immigrant home restored to the 1880–1890 period. For those who want to take some ethnic artistry home, the museum's gift shop sells elaborately decorated Easter eggs, blown-glass Christmas ornaments, and imported dolls along with other unique gifts. The National Czech and Slovak Museum (319–362–8500) is at 30 Sixteenth Avenue SW. It is open from 9:30 A.M. to 4:00 P.M. Tuesday through Saturday; admission is $2.50 for adults, $1.00 for children.

There are a number of good restaurants in the village. A fun place to eat is the *Little Bohemia Tavern* at 1317 Third Street SE. The building, recently named to the National Register of Historic Places, is filled with Cedar Rapids memorabilia, collected over the years by the Melsha family, and some of it is decidedly "funky." Don't stop here without trying the Czech goulash.

Also in the Czech Village area are a number of gift shops, as well as Polehna's Meat Market, a shop that smokes its own meat and sells various ethnic sausages and meats.

Another worthwhile attraction in Cedar Rapids (especially if you have children) is the **Science Station** at 427 First Street SE. The station is located in the historic former Central Fire Station and is a delightful hands-on museum of science and technology. Here you can make giant bubbles or become a television weather reporter, as well as explore major traveling science exhibits. The Science Station (319–366–0968)

The Days of Corn and (Sunburned) Noses

*I*magine this: *The beautiful cloudless days of an Iowa July, a good hot sun, plenty of fresh country air, plenty of friends, gallons and gallons of lemonade, the song of meadowlarks and red-winged blackbirds, the low whir of cicadas, the distant lowing of grazing cows, the smell of green things growing. Perfect working conditions, right? The ideal job, right? Wrong. At least, that is, if you're corn de-tasseling.*

I am lucky to have the hardest job I hope I will ever have to do behind me. From the time I was twelve until I was fifteen (at the age of sixteen I became eligible, under then current Iowa law, to get a "real job"), I spent ten to fourteen of these beautiful cloudless July days out in the country, with plenty of fresh air, plenty of friends, gallons and gallons of lemonade, etc., pulling tassels out of field corn. Those of us foolhardy enough or greedy enough (why, you could make at least a hundred dollars for only ten days work!) climbed on board a school bus at our local high school at six or seven in the morning and bounced out to a farmer's field where the corn awaited us. One person to a row, we marched

(or strolled or crawled, whimpering) pulling tassels out of (I think) the "female" rows. This had something to do with pollination or fertilization or something. (I'm afraid I wasn't that interested in biology in those days. At least not that kind of biology.)

There were days the temperature reached a hundred degrees or more, days it poured rain and we slogged through mud up to our ankles, days we had aphid-infested corn and had to pull tassels out of their black jelly, gagging. We got blistered, sunburned, and stung. We worked ten-hour days. We worried about our "farmers' tans." We got to know one another, our weaknesses and strengths, well. We had tassel fights—which were forbidden—mud fights, and water fights; we sang songs, some of them not very nice. We ate lunches our moms had packed and that have never tasted better and drank barely cool lemonade that has also never tasted better. I will admit there were probably days we could have smelled better. At night, a bed had never felt better. All in all, I suppose it could have been a lot worse . . . but not much.

is open Tuesday through Friday from 9:00 A.M. to 4:00 P.M., Saturday from 10:00 A.M. to 4:00 P.M., and Sunday from 1:00 to 4:00 P.M.

Other attractions in Cedar Rapids include the new **Cedar Rapids Museum of Art,** a $10 million structure that houses an outstanding regional collection, including the nation's largest collection of works by Grant Wood and Marvin Cone. Don't miss the dramatic Winter Garden! The museum (319–366–7503) is at 410 Third Avenue SE and is open Tuesday through Sunday.

For a relaxing end to a day of touring, visit the **Cafe de Klos,** located in a Victorian brick home built in 1870 on the city's southeast side. Its owner, Gary Dvorak, traveled to Holland some years ago and came across a restaurant in Amsterdam with a delicious secret marinade. He persuaded the owner to give him the recipe, and eventually he and his wife, Joan, opened their own restaurant based on the one in Holland.

If you like the sauce, you'll love Cafe de Klos. Nearly everything they serve—ribs, chicken, pork loin, seafood, steak—is seasoned this way, including garlic bread and French fries. (Though the Dvoraks won't reveal the recipe, the sauce has a definite curry flavor to it.)

Cafe de Klos is located at 821 Third Avenue SE (319–362–9340). Evening dining is from 5:00 to 10:00 P.M. Tuesday through Saturday. Reservations are recommended and prices are expensive.

Cedar Rapids has many varieties of ethnic cuisine, a reflection of its wide ethnic diversity and the pride its residents take in their heritage. Another restaurant that is definitely worth a visit is **The Vernon Inn,** located at 2663 Mount Vernon Road SE. A favorite of Cedar Rapidians, owners Basil and Lynn Hadjis offer an outstanding Greek menu as well as exciting and eclectic American food; they are famous throughout the area for their artichoke pizza. The Vernon Inn is open for lunch and dinner and their prices are moderate. After you've finished your meal here you may want to step across the street to Eddie Piccard's, a bar that offers live jazz nightly.

Other sites of interest in Cedar Rapids include the restored Brucemore Mansion, Indian Creek Nature Center, Seminole Valley Farm, Ushers Ferry Historic Village, and Duffy's Collectible Cars, a car dealership with dozens of restored automobiles dating from the 1940s to the 1960s. For more visitor information on Cedar Rapids, call (319) 398–5009, or visit the Cedar Rapids Web site at *http://www.cedar-rapids.com.*

Before you leave the Cedar Rapids area, check out the **Cedar Valley Nature Trail,** a 52-mile route that follows a former railroad line between Cedar Rapids and Waterloo. Opened officially in 1984, the trail is the longest one of its kind in Iowa and the longest one in the country connecting two metropolitan areas.

One advantage of the trail is that its grade is never more than 3 percent, making it an easy place to hike, bike, or cross-country ski. The path winds through grasslands, woods, wetlands, and farms, with abundant wildlife along the way, from wild turkeys to white-tailed deer. It also passes through the towns of Gilbertville, La Porte City, Brandon, Urbana, Lafayette, and Center Point. Water and rest rooms are available at various locations along the trail.

To enter the trail from Cedar Rapids, drive north on I–380, take exit 25, and follow the signs to the trailhead. A daily pass is available for $2.00 at county parks and from local businesses and trail park rangers. Call (319) 398–3505 for more information.

No visit to this part of Iowa is complete without a visit to Mount Vernon, the home of *Cornell College.* Cornell boasts the fact that it is the only college in the nation whose entire campus is on the National Register of Historic Places. A very pleasant afternoon may be spent wandering through this lovely old hilltop campus and the adjacent downtown area, where there are several antiques shops and places to eat. In the winter make sure you bring your sled along because when there's snow, Third Avenue North's "Pres Hill" is blocked off and left unplowed for some winter fun. For more information about Mount Vernon and its environs call (319) 895–8214.

Take Highway 30 West out of Mount Vernon to end your trip to this region with a visit to the *Palisades-Kepler State Park,* located 10 miles east of Cedar Rapids. During the autumn months especially, this beautiful park skirting the banks of the Cedar River makes an ideal picnicking spot and a wonderful place to while away a Sunday afternoon. You may even wish to rent a cabin here (from May through mid-October). For more information call (319) 895–6039.

PLACES TO STAY IN CULTURAL CROSSROADS

HOMESTEAD
Die Heimat Country Inn,
4434 V. Street,
(319) 622–3937,
$45–$70

IOWA CITY
Holiday Inn,
210 South Dubuque Street,
(800) 848–1335,
(319) 337–4058,
$79–$95

Radisson Highlander Inn,
Highway 1 and I–80,
(800) 728–2000,
(319) 354–2000,
$60–$100

MUSCATINE
Hotel Muscatine,
101 West Mississippi Drive,
(800) 339–0998,
(319) 263–8231,
$55–$135

CLINTON
Ramada Inn,
1522 Lincoln Way,
(319) 243–8841,
$58–$64

DAVENPORT
Jumer's Castle Lodge,
I–74 at Spruce Hills Drive,
(800) 285–8637,
(319) 359–7141,
$78–$142

MAQUOKETA
Decker House Inn,
128 North Main,
(319) 652–6554,
$45–$75

ANAMOSA
Shaw House,
509 South Oak Street,
(319) 462–4485,
$45–$75

CEDAR RAPIDS
Collins Plaza,
1200 Collins Road NE,
(800) 541–1067,
(319) 393–6600,
$99–$125

Crowne Plaza Five Seasons Hotel,
350 First Avenue NE,
(800) 2–CROWNE,
(319) 363–8161,
$89–$115

PLACES TO EAT IN CULTURAL CROSSROADS

MAIN AMANA
The Ronnenberg,
4408 220 Trail,
(319) 622–3641

TIFFIN
The Lark,
Highway 6,
(319) 645–2461

IOWA CITY
Pagliai's Pizza,
302 East Bloomington Street,
(319) 351–5073

The Mill,
120 East Burlington Street,
(319) 351–9529

WEST BRANCH
L & B Steak House,
102 West Main Street,
(319) 643–5420

WASHINGTON
Winga's Restaurant,
Main Street,
(319) 653–2093

MUSCATINE
Mississippi Brewing Company,
107 Iowa Avenue,
(319) 262–5004

Riverbend Bistro,
101 West Mississippi Drive,
(319) 262–4030

DAVENPORT
The Freight House,
421 West River Drive,
(319) 324–4425

Front Street Brewery,
208 East River Drive,
(319) 322–1569

LE CLAIRE
Francescon's,
627 North Cody Road,
(319) 289–4721

MOUNT VERNON
Pizza Palace,
106 First Street,
(319) 895–6971

CEDAR RAPIDS
Ced-Rel Supper Club,
Highway 30,
(319) 446–7300

Rural Charms

Southeast Iowa is rich in rural pleasures. In the Kalona area you'll find the largest Amish-Mennonite settlement west of the Mississippi, while a few miles south lies Mount Pleasant, home of the Midwest Old Threshers Reunion that celebrates the state's agricultural heritage. The southern part of this region has been shaped in countless ways by two great rivers: the mighty Mississippi and the scenic Des Moines. In this part of southern Iowa you'll find that many legacies from the nineteenth century still remain in the Villages of Van Buren and in the Mississippi River ports of Fort Madison and Keokuk.

Amish Country

Begin your tour of Amish country in Kalona, a place where buggies travel the highways next to cars, Amish farmers work the land with horse-drawn equipment, and on the downtown sidewalks women in black dresses and bonnets mingle with those in blue jeans and T-shirts. Seven Amish congregations (with about 700 members) are located in the area, along with seventeen Mennonite churches.

Although the Amish live in the countryside and limit their contact with the outside world, Kalona itself welcomes visitors to its tidy and prosperous downtown. Here you'll find a wide selection of antiques, bakery goods, and locally made gifts and craft items, including the hand-stitched quilts for which the area is famous. In April the town hosts the *Kalona Quilt Show and Sale,* which is one of the Midwest's largest quilt shows. Each year more than 4,000 people attend this nationally advertised event featuring hundreds of new and antique quilts made by the local Amish and Mennonite women. The show is held at the Kalona Community Center, and a $3.00 admission fee is charged. Call (319) 656–2660 for information.

At any time of year you can tour the *Kalona Quilt and Textile Museum.* Each year the museum presents three or four shows that

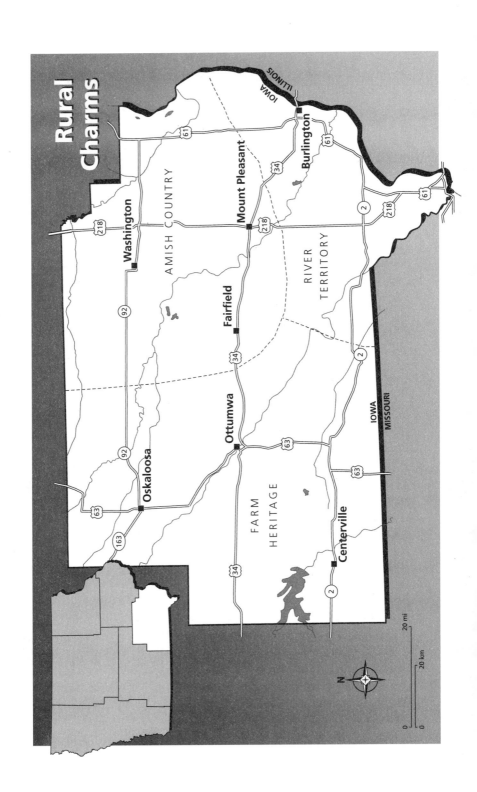

Rural Charms

AMISH COUNTRY

RIVER TERRITORY

FARM HERITAGE

Washington

Mount Pleasant

Burlington

Fairfield

Ottumwa

Oskaloosa

Centerville

IOWA
ILLINOIS

IOWA
MISSOURI

N

20 mi

20 km

AUTHOR'S FAVORITES - RURAL CHARMS

Museum of Repertoire Americana

Hotel Manning

American Gothic House

Mars Hill

Snake Alley

Liz Clark's

Columbus Junction Swinging Bridge

Fort Madison Farmington & Western Railroad

Toolesboro Indian Mounds

The Skean Block

showcase the creativity of generations of women. Past exhibits have included "feed sack quilts" made during the Depression and crazy quilts made of tiny scraps of material. The museum (319–656–2240) is at 515 B Avenue and is open Monday through Saturday from 9:00 A.M. to 5:00 P.M.

Quilt fanciers should also pay a visit to **Kalona Kountry Kreations** (319–656–5366), a store that is located 3 miles north of Kalona off Highway 1. As one of the largest quilt supply stores in the Midwest—and perhaps in the country—the establishment attracts busloads of customers from as far away as Texas, Louisiana, and Minnesota. Owner Sara Miller is a noted expert on quilting and its history, and the store always displays a quilt in progress.

Don't miss a stop at the **Kalona Cheese House** at the intersection of Highway 1 and 540th Street (north of Kalona). While you are here you can watch cheese being made and pay a visit to the tasting room (there are plenty of samples) and gift shop. Whatever you do make sure you buy a bag of their cheese curds. They may look funny and they may "squeak" when you bite into them, but they are absolutely delicious. If you continue east on 540th Street from the cheese house you will find the **Stringtown Grocery,** a fascinating Amish-run store featuring a huge variety of products sold in bulk. Don't leave here without getting some of their tomato rotini—it's great!

Continue east on 540th Street for almost 3 miles, turn right (south) on James Street, and drive $1\frac{3}{4}$ miles to the **Community Country Store,** another Amish-owned general store that sells such varied items as boots, handkerchiefs, cookware, canning supplies, and other necessities.

Another charming place to visit is **Sisters Garden**, about $2\frac{1}{2}$ miles north of the Cheese House on Highway 1. An old farmhouse has been converted into a shop that sells both the delightfully old and the delightfully new. During the spring and summer months you can also buy potted herbs, annuals, and perennials. Among the things you can find here are handcrafted willow furniture pieces and many unique items with a garden theme. There are also a few picnic tables scattered about the yard so you can relax and enjoy yourself in this rural setting. Call (319) 683–2046 for their schedule.

For further insight into the history and culture of the area, visit the **Kalona Historical Village** at Highway 22 and Ninth Street. The village contains seven restored nineteenth-century buildings that include a one-room schoolhouse, general store, log house, buggy shop, and an old railroad depot. Also on the grounds is the Iowa Mennonite Museum and Archives, a repository for the documents and history of the Mennonite community in the area (about half of Kalona's residents are Mennonites, members of a religious group who, like the Amish, are noted for their simple living and plain dress).

The best time to visit the village is during its annual **Fall Festival,** a down-home celebration with plenty of delicious food, homemade crafts, and demonstrations of old-time skills like spinning, weaving, cornmeal grinding, and wood sawing. For me the smells alone are worth the trip: big pots of bubbling apple butter send a heavenly aroma through the crisp air, a smell rivaled only by that of bread baking in the village's outdoor oven.

The Kalona Fall Festival is held the last Friday and Saturday in September, and the Historical Village is open Monday through Saturday from 10:00 A.M. to 4:00 P.M. April 1 to October 31. The rest of the year, hours are 11:00 A.M. to 3:00 P.M. Monday through Saturday. Admission is $4.00; $2.00 for children 7-12; call (319) 656–2519 for more information.

East of Kalona in the small town of Riverside lies an Iowa landmark of interest to all *Star Trek* fans: the **Future Birthplace of Captain James T. Kirk.** In 1985 the Riverside City Council voted unanimously to declare a spot behind what used to be the town's barbershop as the place where Captain Kirk of *Star Trek* fame would one day be born.

Riverside has some official proof to back up its claim. Gene Roddenberry's book, *The Making of Star Trek,* says that Kirk "was born in a small town in the State of Iowa." The town contacted Roddenberry and received a certificate confirming its birthplace status, and thus was born one of Iowa's most famous future historical sites.

On the last Saturday in June each summer, Riverside celebrates Kirk's future birthdate in the year 2228 by holding its **Trek Fest.** This gathering includes videos of the show, a swap meet, and fan club meetings, plus sports events, a beer tent, and a parade on Main Street. All proceeds from Trek Fest go to community projects and for constructing a permanent monument to mark Kirk's birth. In the meantime the town marks its future status with a 20-foot replica of the *Enterprise* on display in a downtown park. Captain Kirk will undoubtedly be proud. For more information about Trek Fest, call (319) 648–3501.

RURAL CHARMS

Southeast of Riverside at the junction of Highways 70 and 92 lies Columbus Junction, where you'll find the *Columbus Junction Swinging Bridge.* A 262-foot suspension bridge made of steel cable and wooden boards, it stretches across a deep wooded ravine and provides a suitably scary feeling as you stand in its center and sway back and forth.

The bridge's nickname is the "Lover's Leap Bridge," a reference to a local legend that says that an Indian maiden jumped to her death in the ravine after hearing that her warrior sweetheart had been killed in battle. The bridge itself was first erected in 1896 so that citizens could travel between Third and Fourth Streets in Columbus Junction without making a detour around the ravine. Since then the bridge has been replaced several times, most recently in 1921 when a professor of engineering at Iowa State University designed a new bridge for the town. To reach the bridge, follow the signs on Highway 92 on the west end of Columbus Junction.

Bald Eagle Appreciation Days, Keokuk, third weekend in January, (800) 383–1219

Bonaparte's Historic Cemetery Walk, Bonaparte, third Saturday in May, (319) 592–3400

Albia Restoration Days, Albia, second weekend in August

Old Fort Candlelight Tour, Fort Madison, first weekend in October, (319) 372–7700

Forest Craft Festival, Keosauqua, second weekend in October, (800) 868–7822

Halloween Hike, Ottumwa, third weekend in October, (515) 682–3091

South of Columbus Junction lies the aptly named town of Mount Pleasant. A prosperous community of 8,500, Mount Pleasant is an Iowa success story with a thriving economy and friendly small-town atmosphere.

But what makes this town well known throughout the state belongs as much to the past as it does to the present: the *Midwest Old Threshers Reunion,* a celebration of old-time agriculture that draws more than 100,000 visitors each Labor Day weekend. The event began in 1950, when a small group of enthusiasts got together at the Henry County Fairgrounds to exhibit steam-engine equipment. (Before the development of the gas-engine tractor in the 1920s, smoke-belching steam engines provided the power that ran America's farms.)

Today the reunion has grown into a five-day event that draws visitors from throughout the country. Many are drawn by the wonderful old behemoth machines on display here: antique tractors and trucks, electric trolleys, steam trains, and all kinds of engines. Other attractions include live entertainment by nationally known performers, a log village, craft demonstrations, and food tents staffed by local church and civic groups that serve platefuls of ham, fried chicken, mashed potatoes, and various fixings. Take a ride on a trolley, attend classes in a one-room school, learn how to make soap, and watch a horse-pull competition—activities all meant to recall a largely vanished way of life.

If you can't make it to the reunion, the Old Threshers 160-acre site is still worth a visit. The permanent **Heritage Museums** here house scores of steam engines, antique tractors, agricultural equipment, and tools. There are also a farmhouse, barn, and exhibits on farm women and the use of water and electricity.

The Midwest Old Threshers Reunion is held each year during the five days ending on Labor Day. Camping and motel accommodations are available. Admission is $15.00 for a five-day pass and $7.00 for a one-day pass. The Heritage Museums are open daily from Memorial Day through Labor Day from 9:00 A.M. to 4:30 P.M. Admission is $3.00 for adults; children under 14 are admitted free. Call (319) 385–8937 for more information on the reunion or museums.

Also on the Old Thresher grounds is the **Museum of Repertoire Americana,** one of my favorite museums in the state. The facility houses the country's largest collection of tent, folk, and repertory theater memorabilia—show business that's in the rural, rather than Hollywood, style. Before the days of radio, movies, and television, hundreds of traveling theater companies crisscrossed the nation, bringing live entertainment to even the smallest of towns. This museum provides a colorful introduction to that forgotten past.

The museum owes its existence to Neil and Caroline Schaffner, former owners of the Schaffner Players. The two are best known for their stage characters of Toby and Susie, the wise country bumpkin and his sharp-tongued girlfriend. For nearly forty years their company performed throughout the Midwest, and after they retired they dreamed of establishing a museum to save the memories of early popular theater.

Mount Pleasant and the Midwest Old Threshers Association came to their rescue, and in 1973 the new museum opened its doors. Inside is a fascinating collection of costumes, advertising sheets, scrapbooks, scenery, pictures, and newspapers relating not only to the Schaffners' careers, but to all forms of early American theater. (Don't miss the beautiful hand-painted opera house curtains that were used as scenery for plays.) If you're lucky, museum curator Caroline Schaffner will be on hand to regale you with stories of what it was like to be a traveling performer forty years ago.

The Museum of Repertoire Americana is open from Memorial Day through Labor Day, Tuesday through Sunday. Admission is $3.00. Call (319) 385–9432 for information.

From Mount Pleasant drive west on Highway 34 to the town of Fairfield, home to the state's most unusual institution of higher learning, *Maharishi International University.*

Steam-Powered Tractor, Midwest Old Threshers Reunion

Much of the university looks like any tranquil midwestern college campus—until you drive past its two huge, golden domes rising out of the Iowa prairie. The contrast symbolizes the interesting mixture at MIU, which combines traditional academic disciplines with the practice of transcendental meditation. Twice each day students and faculty gather in the domes to practice a meditation technique that they say reduces stress and increases their creativity and productivity.

When representatives of the Maharishi Mahesh Yogi bought the campus of bankrupt Parsons College in Fairfield in 1974, many locals worried that their peaceful community would become a haven for leather-fringed hippies. Instead, MIU has helped stimulate an economic boom in Fairfield that has made it one of the most dynamic small towns in the state. Many new businesses have been started by people associated with MIU, from health food stores and restaurants to financial consulting firms. One of the most successful enterprises is *The Raj,* a luxury hotel and health center that offers the indulgent delights of a full-spa experience. The center's treatments are based on Maharishi Ayurveda, an ancient system of preventive health care originally reserved for the royal families of India. Guests receive a consultation with the spa's on-staff medical doctor, who recommends a personalized treatment routine that includes massages, cleansing steam baths, and rejuvenation techniques. If you don't want to sample the spa, you can still visit The Raj Restaurant, which is open for lunch from Sunday through Friday. The vegetarian buffet is moderately priced. The Raj is located on Jasmine Avenue north of Fairfield; call (800) 248–9050 for information.

Farm Heritage

B egin your tour of this predominantly rural part of southeast Iowa with a visit to the small town of Eldon. There you'll find the *American Gothic House,* a home whose image is one of the most reprinted in the country, thanks to Grant Wood's having used it as a backdrop for his painting *American Gothic.* The picture of the grim, pitchfork-bearing farmer and his equally sour wife is one of the most familiar (and parodied) images in American art, and it has brought fame to the modest house that inspired it.

The home's brush with fame was entirely coincidental. While on a motor trip through southeastern Iowa in 1930, Wood saw the house and made a rough sketch on the back of an envelope of its Gothic-arched window and two long-faced people in front. Later he looked around his home of Cedar Rapids for a farmer who would fit his ideal, but none was quite right. Finally he persuaded his sister, Nan, and his dentist, Dr. B. H. McBeeby, to be his models. Nan must have had a sense of humor, however, because she collected parodies of this painting during her lifetime and donated them to the Davenport Museum of Art (see page 46).

Eldon takes great pride in its famous landmark, though the home is being restored by the State Historical Society and can be viewed from the outside only. Follow the signs through town to find it, and don't forget to pack your camera. (It helps if you have a friend along who can take your picture in front of it, and you might bring a lemon along so you can achieve the proper facial expression.)

From Eldon travel north on Highway 16 and then go west on Highway 34. Just before you reach the town of Agency, you'll see a sign for *Chief Wapello Memorial Park,* a little rest area that marks an important spot in Iowa's history. The park was once the site of an Indian agency (hence the town's name) where the 1842 Sac and Fox treaty was signed to complete the Indian cession of Iowa lands to the U.S. Government. This set the stage for the homesteading of Iowa in 1843.

The site is also a reminder of the unique friendship that sprang up between Chief Wapello, a principal leader of the Sac and Fox Nation, and General Joseph Street, director of the Indian agency. After being forced from his home along the Mississippi by the government, Wapello led his people to settle near the Indian agency out of his friendship with Street. The general died in 1840, and before Wapello died two years later he asked to be buried beside him. Their graves rest undisturbed in the park to this day.

Continue on Highway 34 and you'll come to Ottumwa. Whereas Riverside is the future birthplace of Captain James T. Kirk, Ottumwa can claim a famous citizen of its own: Radar O'Reilley of *M*A*S*H* fame. The city also boasts fine parks, several annual festivals, a number of historic sites, and a new water park complete with wave pool.

Ten miles south of Ottumwa off of Highway 63 lies the **Wilderness Kingdom Zoo,** a privately owned wildlife refuge that is home to lions, tigers, bears, wolves, an alligator, and harp and harbor seals. The zoo also includes a three-acre petting area with goats, llamas, sheep, deer, and potbellied pigs. The zoo (515–459–2224) is open from 10:00 A.M. to 6:00 P.M. daily from April 15 until October 15.

Southeast of Ottumwa and north of Floris (off County Road J15) and located on the Wapello-Davis county line is **Mars Hill,** the oldest log church in the United States still in use, as well as the state's largest remaining log structure. Built in 1857, it was one of Iowa's earliest religious buildings. It is constructed of hewn oak and walnut logs, some of them as large as 16 feet high and 8 inches thick, while others are as long as 28 feet. Services are held once each year on the third Sunday in June. Mars Hill was also a stop on the Underground Railroad. The adjoining cemetery has many old tombstones, the oldest dated 1846. This building is really amazing; go out of your way to pay it a visit.

Travel Highway 63 south to the town on Bloomfield, home of the **Davis County Historical Museum,** which is open from 1:00 to 4:00 P.M. on Saturdays during the summer. The museum complex contains a hand-hewn log cabin built by Mormons traveling west in 1848, a one room schoolhouse and a livery barn built in 1920. Inside the barn is a great mural painted by a local high school art teacher, which depicts the Civil War Guerrilla Raid of 1864 when twelve raiders marched across Davis County, stealing horses and guns and killing three men in the process. In addition, there is a unique feed sack display. Call (515) 664–1512 for more information or to schedule a tour.

Nearby (about 13 miles northwest of Bloomfield off Highway 273) is pretty **Lake Wapello State Park.** It has fourteen family cabins with bathroom and cooking facilities, which may be rented by making reservations with the park ranger. Call (515) 722–3371 for more information.

Another attraction in the area is the **Air Power Museum,** which is located west of Ottumwa near the town of Blakesburg. The museum is home to nearly fifty old-fashioned aircraft and is the site of an annual reunion of antique-airplane enthusiasts each Labor Day weekend. The museum is a labor of love for its founder and president, Bob Taylor, an

Antique Biplanes, Air Power Museum

aviation buff who soloed just before Pearl Harbor, served in World War II and Korea as a crew chief, and then returned to his hometown of Ottumwa to open a flying service in 1953. That same year he founded the Antique Airplane Association, an organization that claims members from throughout the United States and twenty-two foreign countries.

At the museum you can see airplanes from the 1920s through the 1940s, plus various flight memorabilia. Most of the planes are civilian craft, with a few home-built ones on display as well. There's also a library for people doing research and renovation on antique aircraft.

The Air Power Museum is at 22001 Bluegrass Road, on Highway H-41, 3½ miles northeast of Blakesburg. It is open from 9:00 A.M. to 5:00 P.M. on weekdays, from 10:00 A.M. to 5:00 P.M. on Saturday, and from 1:00 to 5:00 P.M. on Sunday. Call (515) 938–2773 for more information. Admission is by donation.

From Blakesburg travel north to Oskaloosa, which has always struck me as one of the prettiest-named towns in Iowa. It's named after the wife of Chief Osceola of the Seminole tribe, and its meaning is as lovely as it sounds: "Last of the Beautiful." Legend has it that Oskaloosa's husband believed that her beauty could never be surpassed.

A major attraction in Oskaloosa is the **Nelson Pioneer Farm Museum,** a complex of restored buildings developed around the original pioneer homestead of Daniel Nelson, who acquired the land from the U.S. Government in 1844. The land was farmed by the Nelson family until 1958, when it was given to the Mahaska County Historical Society. The Nelson home and barn are both designated as National Historic Sites, and there are also a number of other buildings open for tours, including a log cabin, summer kitchen, meat house, post office, voting house, school, and Friends meetinghouse. Guided tours are available.

This is also the site of the only mule cemetery in Iowa, the final resting place of Becky and Jennie, two white mules owned by Daniel Nelson that served in the U.S. Artillery during the Civil War. They lived out the rest of their days on the farm and now have a special plot near the museum.

A good time to visit the Nelson museum is during its annual Pioneer Farm Festival held on the third Saturday in September. More than thirty pioneer skills are demonstrated each year, along with special exhibits and musical entertainment. The Nelson Pioneer Farm Museum is located on Glendale Road, 2 miles off Highway 63 (515–672–2989). It is open May 1 to October 12, Tuesday through Saturday 10:00 A.M. to 4:30 P.M. and Sunday 1:00 to 4:00 P.M. Admission is $4.00 for adults and $1.00 for children.

From Oskaloosa head south on Highway 137 to *Albia,* which at one time had the dubious distinction of being known as the ugliest town in Iowa. What once had been the center of a prosperous coal-mining region had gradually slipped into decay and neglect, and years of grime and coal dust coated the downtown's once-elegant Victorian buildings.

Then came Operation Facelift in the early 1970s, when the community banded together to save its historic buildings using funds that came almost entirely from local sources. Visit Albia today and you'll see a town square far different from the shabby district of years past. Brightly painted, refurbished storefronts, tree-lined sidewalks, and a general air of prosperity announce that Albia is a town that intends to survive and grow. In 1985 the town received a sweet reward for all its restoration efforts when the entire ninety-two–building business district was named to the National Register of Historic Places—the largest such district in the state.

There are a number of particularly impressive restorations in town that should be on your architectural tour of the city. The Perry House at 212 Benton Avenue West is an outstanding example of Victorian Gothic style; Kendall Place at 209 Benton Avenue East was the home of Nate Kendall, governor of Iowa from 1921 to 1925; and the Elbert-Bates House at 106 Second Avenue West is one of four sister homes built in the beautiful Italianate style. Another outstanding renovation is the Barbary Coast Opera House, now used for movies, concerts, recitals, and community theater. And at the Monroe County Historical Museum, housed in a restored trolley barn, you can browse through displays that tell the story of Albia's coal-mining and farming past. Of course, you can't miss the Davis County Court House in the middle of the town square. And you may want to visit the Hickory Grove Cemetery where you'll find three 15-foot pyramids, built as a shrine in the early 1900s.

Make sure to have lunch or dinner (or Sunday brunch) at *The Skean Block,* located on the town square at 11 Benton Street. The building itself is absolutely gorgeous—it was completely restored in 1996. Note the beautiful stained glass windows above the storefront and the elaborate ceilings. But don't forget about the food! They use the freshest ingredients and finest products with a real midwestern flair. For dinner try the snapper, grilled over apple and hickory with a fresh thyme and fish broth, or sample the lamb soubise served on a bed of caramelized onions, asparagus, and artichoke hearts, and topped with a caper cream sauce. The beef dishes are fabulous and there are plenty of exceptional pasta-and-seafood, poultry, and pork entrees as well. Please don't miss the lobster corn bisque! The menu is enormous and diverse. The Skean Block is open Tuesday through Saturday for lunch and dinner; reservations are recommended. Call (515) 932–2159.

Each year on the weekend before Labor Day, the town celebrates its rebirth during *Albia Restoration Days.* A parade, talent show, antiques auction, art show, and ethnic food booths are all part of the festivities, along with guided tours of many of the restored buildings. For more information about Albia or Restoration Days, contact its chamber of commerce at (515) 932–5108.

From Albia head south to Rathbun Lake, the state's largest lake, which was created in the 1970s as part of a flood-control project on the Chariton River. Seven parks line its banks, and there are swimming areas, boat ramps, campgrounds, and picnic areas available for public use.

The *Rathbun Fish Hatchery* was the first hatchery in the country to raise fish under intensive culture techniques. That means that the fish are raised in concrete tanks in which fresh water is continually circulated. The method is undoubtedly successful: The hatchery produces some 160,000 pounds of fish each year. Catfish, walleye, largemouth bass, and northern pike are all raised here and then released into Iowa's lakes and rivers.

The visitor center at the hatchery is located 7 miles northwest of Centerville and has an elevated observation walkway, a theater with audiovisual presentations on production methods used at the hatchery, and a nature trail. The hatchery (515–647–2406) is open from 8:00 A.M. to 3:45 P.M. daily.

South of Rathbun Lake lies the town of Centerville. During the late nineteenth century this part of southern Iowa was home to a thriving coal-mining industry, a period that is commemorated at Centerville's **Historical and Coal Mining Museum.** The town's 1903 post office houses a coal mine replica on its lower level, with mining tools and equipment that show the hard working conditions endured by the early miners. The museum also includes information on the Mormon exodus that passed through here in 1846 as well as other aspects of southern Iowa history. The museum (515–856–8040) is at 100 West Maple Street and is open on weekends from 1:30 to 4:30 P.M. Memorial Day through Labor Day.

River Territory

Next travel to scenic Van Buren County. Keosauqua, its county seat, has a grand total of one thousand people (when everyone is home), and the pace in the county's other towns is just as slow. Visitors agree that the quiet is part of the area's allure—that and an old-fashioned atmosphere that's authentic, not manufactured.

Back in the mid-nineteenth century, however, life was more hectic in Van Buren County. The meandering Des Moines River that flows through the center of the county was a busy passageway for steamboats, and the villages on its banks were bustling ports. Mills, stores, and hotels filled the towns, and an active social life kept both locals and visitors entertained. Unfortunately, the years of prosperity ended abruptly when the U.S. Congress decided that the locks and dams along the river would no longer be maintained, thus making the river unnavigable by the larger boats. Soon the towns settled into faded obscurity, as all but a few residents packed up their bags and moved away.

Within the past twenty years, the area has experienced a renaissance that has preserved its historical character and charm while still making it a favorite destination for growing numbers of visitors. **Keosauqua** is a good place to begin your tour. The name comes from an Indian word meaning "great bend," a reference to the loop the Des Moines River takes around the town. Keosauqua was once a stop on the Underground Railroad and was also a fording spot for the Mormons on their westward trek in the late 1840s.

Also in the area is Lacey-Keosauqua State Park, one of the state's largest parks, with more than 1,600 acres. The great horseshoe bend the river makes here offers beautiful vistas for hikers and campers.

Next travel east to *Bentonsport,* a tiny village with a number of restored buildings and stores on its main street. Take special note of the Greef General Store, a structure built in the Federal style in 1853 that now serves as a showcase for local antiques and crafts. The town also is home to a growing community of artists, including potter Betty Printy. She has established a regional reputation with her distinctive "Queen Anne's Lace" pottery. Using hand-dug local clay, Printy molds the pottery and then presses the wildflower Queen Anne's lace into the clay while it's still wet. The result is a beautiful tracery of lines and flowers.

Another landmark in town is the *Mason House Inn,* which like the Hotel Manning was built in the 1800s to accommodate steamboat passengers. Furnished with antiques, the house contains nine guest rooms. Call (800) 592–3133 for reservations. Prices range from $54 to $74 per night, which includes a full breakfast.

Down the river from Bentonsport is the village of *Bonaparte,* also the site of historic preservation efforts. In 1989 its downtown area was named a National Historic District, a tribute to the hard work of the vil-

The Hotel Manning

*T*oday the best-known landmark in Keosauqua is the **Hotel Manning,** a two-story brick structure with wide verandas for watching the Des Moines River flow by. The hotel was built in 1899 and through the ensuing years has withstood no less than four floods. (During the flood of 1947, the owner and her guests were forced to live on the second floor and had to use a rowboat to traverse the downstairs lobby.)

I enjoy staying at the Hotel Manning because it's like slipping into an old, comfortable shoe. The floors creak, the doors don't always match, and there's a

delightful air of faded gentility about the place that makes it easy to imagine how it must have been when river travelers stayed here a hundred years ago.

The hotel's eighteen rooms are furnished with antique furniture and brightly patterned quilts, braided rugs line the floor, and steam radiators keep the building toasty warm in winter. Downstairs is a cozy bar, and off the main lobby is the hotel's dining room where breakfast, lunch, and dinner are served. Rates at the Hotel Manning range from $35 to $72 a night; call (800) 728–2718 for reservations.

RURAL CHARMS

Did You Know?

The great poet T. S. Eliot was one of the Hotel Manning's famous guests. He signed the hotel register on September 13, 1919.

The town of Pittsburg was the birthplace of Phil Strong who's best remembered for writing the play State Fair, *on which three movies and a Broadway play were based. The state fair referred to, of course, is the Iowa State Fair.*

lage's citizens. Stop by the Aunty Green Museum, which was once a hotel and now houses historical displays.

The best-known restoration in Bonaparte is *Bonaparte's Retreat,* a fine restaurant housed in a nineteenth-century gristmill. Owned by Ben and Rose Hendricks, the restaurant is known for both the quality of its food and its decor, and a pleasing mixture of steamboat and gristmill relics. The restaurant's menu includes steak, pork, and seafood.

Bonaparte's Retreat is open Monday through Saturday for lunch and dinner. Phone (319) 592–3339. Prices are moderate to expensive.

For more information about other attractions in the area, call the Villages of Van Buren at (800) 868–7822.

From Van Buren County travel to Keokuk, a city that lies at the southeastern tip of the state. Keokuk was once known as the "Gate City" because of its position at the foot of the Des Moines rapids on the Mississippi. In the early days of settlement, steamboats were unable to go beyond this point, and all passengers had to disembark here to either continue their journey on land or board another boat upriver. The city played an important role in the Civil War, when seven hospitals were established here to care for the wounded transported up the Mississippi from southern battlefields.

The *Keokuk National Cemetery* was one of the first twelve such cemeteries designated by the United States Congress and is the resting place for both Union and Confederate soldiers. It was also the first national cemetery west of the Mississippi and is the only one in Iowa. It's located at Eighteenth and Ridge and is open from dawn to dusk daily.

The city's most famous citizen was Mark Twain, who worked here as a young man in the printing shop of his brother, Orion Clemens. Most of the type for the city's first directory was set by Twain, who listed himself in its pages as an "antiquarian." When asked the reason for this, he replied that he always thought that every town should have at least one antiquarian, and since none had appeared for the post, he decided to volunteer.

The **George M. Verity** *Riverboat Museum* will take you back to those days when Keokuk was a busy river port. Built in 1927, the *Verity* was the first of four steamboats built to revive river transportation on the Mississippi. In 1960 it was retired and given to the city of Keokuk for use as a river museum. Today it contains many old-time photographs of riverboats and the river era, as well as other artifacts and historical items.

The *Verity* is berthed in Victory Park at the foot of Main Street on the Mississippi River. It is open April through November. Admission is $3.00 for adults and $2.00 for children. Call (319) 524–4765 for hours.

More history comes to life during the **Battle of Pea Ridge Civil War Reenactment,** which includes a mock battle, a military ball, period music and dancing, and many other events. The event is held each year

The (Not So Famous) Honey War

*I*n December of 1839 troops gathered in Farmington, Iowa, and in Waterloo, Missouri, prepared to go to war—against each other. Like a lot of other wars, this one was set off by a seemingly innocuous incident: A Missourian had cut down three bee trees on what was thought to be Iowa land. But honey was very important to the early settlers and bee trees were valuable.

The problem behind the bee trees was this: Surveys since 1819 had confused the boundary between the two states. Some marked it from the Des Moines River rapids, some from the so-called Des Moines rapids of the Mississippi. At issue was a 2,600-square-acre region, and both states wanted it. A further complication was the fact that the Missouri Compromise of 1820–21 had allowed Missouri into the Union as a slave state while Iowa remained a free state. Of course, there was also the issue of taxation; taxes were as important to the governors of each state as the honey was to the settlers. Iowa settlers had resisted paying taxes to Missouri. Next, Iowa's Van Buren County

sheriff arrested Missouri's Clark County sheriff during one of his tax collection rounds. As a result, Missouri's governor called for militia support and Iowa's governor responded by summoning volunteers. Fortunately, war never actually erupted, but the problem was getting stickier and stickier and things continued to buzz on both sides of the border until the U.S. Supreme Court finally decided the issue in favor of Iowa in 1851.

You can call the Honey War a foreshadowing of the Civil War, you can call it a mere footnote in the history books, you can call it anything you like, but in 1839 it was definitely one honey of a problem. But all's well that ends well, and I have read, though I haven't been able to confirm, that it did end happily for one farmer whose land was in the disputed territory. She is reputed to have said that she was glad her land turned out to be in the state of Iowa after all, because she had heard that the Iowa climate was much better for crops than the climate of Missouri. So there!

Did You Know?

on the last weekend in April in Rand Park, and most events are free. Call (800) 383–1219 for more information.

The statue in Rand Park honoring Chief Keokuk, the famous leader of the Sac/Fox tribe, was modeled after the style of the Sioux chiefs, some of Keokuk's most hated enemies.

While you're in Keokuk, take a walk. *On the Avenue* is a self-guided walking tour that takes in thirty beautiful old houses (and ends at the lovely Rand Park), built at the end of the nineteenth and the beginning of the twentieth centuries. The houses are all located on Orleans and Grand Avenues along the river and were built for the elite of this once booming town. Don't miss 925 Grand Avenue (#21 on the tour). This house was built in 1880 by Howard Hughes Sr., father of the famous junior and the inventor of the oil well drill. Hughes built the house for his mother, and constructed it entirely without closets because she was panicked by the fear that they were breeding grounds for disease. To get a wonderfully detailed map and brochure of this informative and lovely tour, contact the Keokuk Area Convention and Tourism Bureau at (800) 383–1219 or (319) 524–5599.

Also of interest in Keokuk are the Miller House Museum (once home to U.S. Supreme Court Justice Samuel Miller), an excursion trolley car company, and the Keokuk Hydroelectric Power Plant/ U.S. Lock #19. When the power plant was completed in 1913, it was the largest electric generating plant in the world. Later a 1,200-foot lock, the largest on the Upper Mississippi, was constructed to accommodate modern river traffic. Visitors are welcome to visit the lock anytime and can tour the power plant daily from Memorial Day through Labor Day. Call (319) 524–6363 for tour information.

Thanks to the lock and dam, Keokuk is one of the most important winter feeding areas for the American bald eagle. As the birds' primary feeding spots in Canada and Alaska begin to freeze, they fly south to find food. As many as 1,400 bald eagles winter along the Mississippi between Minneapolis and St. Louis. Keokuk enjoys one of the highest populations because the lock and dam keep the water below from freezing, thus enabling the birds to hunt for fish.

Eagles can be seen in the area from October to early April, but the best time for viewing them is from mid-December to mid-February. Early morning is the ideal time, when they can be seen soaring and diving for fish. During *Keokuk Bald Eagle Appreciation Days* each January, the Keokuk Area Convention and Tourism Bureau sponsors shuttle-bus service to and from observation areas, as well as seminars, lectures, exhibits, and films on the magnificent birds. It also puts out a brochure listing prime viewing areas; call (800) 383–1219. If you do go eagle viewing on your own, bring a pair of binoculars and stay either in or next to your car. It's important that resting eagles not be disturbed; when they fly off, they burn up energy badly needed during the cold weather.

Overnight visitors to Keokuk should make reservations at the **Grand Anne Bed and Breakfast,** which overlooks the Mississippi at 816 Grand Avenue. The twenty-two-room showplace was built in 1897 and offers four guest rooms furnished with period antiques. Freshly baked desserts and beverages are served at bedtime, and a full breakfast is served each morning. Rates are $65 to $90; call (319) 524–6310 for information.

Another Keokuk treasure is **Liz Clark's,** a gourmet restaurant and cooking school run by (you guessed it) Liz Clark. Born and raised on a farm in the area, Liz has studied cooking in Italy and France and has been named by various publications as one of the Midwest's best chefs. Her cooking school offers courses for students from beginners to advanced, on topics as varied as Parisian bistro classics to traditional barbecue.

You can sample Liz's expertise at a seven-course meal in her restaurant, which is open by reservation only. The prices are considerably higher than you'd pay at a local steak joint, but it's definitely worth it for anyone who appreciates fine food. A typical menu may include such delicacies as French country pâté, shrimp in wine and butter, rice and pine nuts, stuffed tomato, mushroom salad with lemon cream dressing, and raspberry crepes with almond cream sauce. Prices run about $35 per person, far less than you'd pay for a comparable meal in New York or Chicago.

Another treat at Liz Clark's is the setting. In 1971 she purchased one of Keokuk's oldest homes, an Italianate house built by a lumber magnate in the mid-1800s. She has completely renovated the elegant structure at 116 Concert Street, and both her cooking school and restaurant are housed here. For more information call (319) 524–4716.

A less formal culinary treat can be found at The Cellar, located next to the Mississippi River at the intersection of Second and Johnson Streets. The Cellar is well known for its mammoth half-pound hamburgers, and the homemade onion rings are light and delicious.

From Keokuk travel north on Highway 61 to Fort Madison, a river town first established in 1808 as a government trading post and one of three major forts guarding the Northwest frontier. Rozanna Stark, the first white child to be born in the state, was born here in 1810. In 1813 the fort was attacked by Indians and its settlers were forced to flee, burning the fort as they left so that all that remained was a blackened chimney (the chimney is now a monument on Avenue H and Highway 61).

On the riverfront in Riverview Park you'll find **Old Fort Madison,** a reconstructed replica of the frontier fort. Costumed interpreters lead visitors on a tour of buildings that include officers' quarters, enlisted men's barracks, and blockhouses. The fort hosts a number of living-history events during the year. Old Fort Madison (319–372–7700) is open daily from 9:00 A.M. to 5:00 P.M. Memorial Day through September.

Can't You Hear the Whistle Blowin'?

*Y*ou will at the **Fort Madison, Farmington & Western Railroad** located west of Fort Madison, near the town of Donnellson. The railroad specializes in carrying its passengers back in time. This chugging and tooting "museum" covers fifteen acres and includes 2 miles of track, an antique full-size train, an authentically replicated depot, as well as a village of the 1920s. Recently added (in 1997) were the general store, the print shop (in actual operation), and the music house, which features phonographs, radios, and mechanical music machines antedating World War II.

Besides the working train that passengers ride through the woods and over a trestle, there are plenty of other antique railroad cars and engines to admire, and even a working hand pump car (formerly the track workers' only form of transportation). Look for the "Doodlebug," a self-propelled passenger coach.

This museum began with only the abandoned roadbed and is the result of one man's passion for trains and everything connected with them. One of the most remarkable things about this place is the people who work here. Staffed solely by volunteers, the "employees" range from ticket takers to conductors, engineers, and brakemen. This railroad is run the old-fashioned way, by hand signals and ticket punching and dedication to preserving a piece of the past. Many of the volunteers are retired or current railroad employees; many of them are just hooked on trains or history. Join the fun!

Trains depart on the half hour. The $4.00 fare for adults and the $3.00 fare for students ages 5 to 18 (children under five travel free) includes admission to the museum grounds and a ride. The FMF&W is open from noon to 5:00 P.M. on weekends and holidays from Memorial Day weekend through October. There is also a "Santa Train" the first three Sundays in December that includes a train ride, a return trip in a horse-drawn sleigh (or wagon if there's no snow), and a present! To get here take Highway 2 to County Road W78 to 220th Street; drive 1½ miles to the entrance. It is adjacent to Wilson Lake Park. Call (319) 837–6689 for more information.

Near the reconstructed fort are two other attractions: the **North Lee County Historical Museum,** which houses local history displays in the town's 1909 railroad station, and the **Flood Museum,** which contains exhibits on the 1993 Mississippi Flood that devastated much of the Midwest. Photos, newspaper articles, quotes from those who experienced the flood, and television footage help tell the story of the disaster. The museums (319–372–7661) are open daily from 10:00 A.M. to 5:00 P.M. April through October.

Don't miss the **Santa Fe Swing Span Bridge** built in 1927, at the foot of Second Street. It is the longest (525 feet) double-decker swing span bridge in the world.

Indulge yourself with a stay at the elegant **Kingsley Inn** located in the heart of the "original city" of Fort Madison. The inn's fourteen guest rooms pamper visitors with period antiques while providing the best in modern conveniences (notably in the private bathrooms). Right off the lobby is Alpha's Restaurant, named after Lieutenant Alpha Kingsley, who administered the construction of the fort in 1808. The restaurant has a bar, offers a full-service menu, and is loaded with memorabilia. Call the Kingsley at (800) 441–2327 or (319) 372–7074 for reservations.

For more information about Fort Madison attractions, call its convention and visitors bureau at (319) 372–5472.

From Fort Madison head north on Highway 61 to the Mississippi River port of Burlington. The Indians called the great bluffs bordering the river here *Shoquoquon,* a name meaning "flint hills." Many tribes gathered flint from area hillsides in the early 1800s for use in their weapons and hunting tools. Their days in the area were numbered, however, for in 1805 Zebulon Pike landed in what is now the city of Burlington, and within thirty years the territory was thrown open to white settlers. Burlington was the first capital of the Iowa territory from 1838 to 1840 and an important steamboat, lumber, and railroad center in the nineteenth century.

A good place to begin your tour of the city is the **Port of Burlington Welcome Center** at 400 North Front Street. Located on the bank of the river, the 1928 building once was a coal-loading site for barges. Now it houses an information center with historical displays and a video of local attractions. The center (319–752–8731) is open daily.

Next take a stroll along Burlington's most famous landmark, **Snake Alley.** Building a town along the steep hillsides surrounding the river required considerable ingenuity. In 1894 Snake Alley was constructed as an experimental street connecting the downtown business district and the neighborhood shopping area on North Sixth Street. This 275-foot-long, zigzagging street rises nearly 60 feet up the bluff and is constructed of tilted bricks designed to allow better footing for horses. The switchback design proved to be less successful than was hoped, however, as drivers often lost control of their horses on its steep curves, and plans to construct more streets on its model were abandoned.

Snake Alley nevertheless proved to be a useful landmark for the city. Horses were "test driven" up the winding curves at a gallop, and if they were still breathing when they reached the top, they were deemed fit enough to haul the city fire wagons. When cars were first offered for sale they had to endure the same test, as auto dealers used Snake Alley to

The Toolesboro Indian Mounds

*S*even Indian mounds are situated on a bluff overlooking the Iowa River near its junction with the mighty Mississippi. The largest one measures 100 feet wide and 8 feet high. Two thousand years ago, between 100 B.C. and A.D. 200, Native American peoples constructed these mounds as sacred burial sites for the highest-ranking members of their nation, probably the chiefs and priests. The names of the tribes are lost to us; no written language survives. They—or rather, their system of burial practices—are known only to the modern world as the "Hopewell tradition." No village site has ever been found, perhaps because of the shifting course of the Iowa River over the centuries. We only know that these cultures shared a widespread system of belief and worship. They probably lived along river flood plains and buried their dead on the high bluffs as they did here. They had an extensive trade network; artifacts including marine shells, Chesapeake Bay sharks' teeth, Rocky Mountain obsidian, Great Lakes cop-

per, Appalachian mica, and Gulf of Mexico pearls have all been discovered. After A.D. 500 the mound builders disappeared from the archaeological landscape. Many of these ancient peoples' mounds were damaged or ruined by European-American land clearing, plowing, and clumsy excavation techniques. Fortunately, this has been stopped in the last fifty years or so. Current archaeological exploration prefers nonintrusive studies, using such methods as aerial photography, surface surveys, and a technique known as "remote sensing," which takes pictures that function a lot like X rays.

Visitors are welcome to the mounds anytime. The admission is free. They are located on Highway 99 between Wapello and Oakville. The fine Educational Center is open from noon to 4:00 P.M. daily Memorial Day through Labor Day, and noon to 4:00 P.M. on Saturdays and Sundays from Labor Day through October. Call (319) 523–8381 for more information.

show off the vehicles' power, with prospective buyers clinging in terror to their seats. (Snake Alley is no longer open to vehicles.)

Ripley's *Believe It or Not* has dubbed Snake Alley the "Crookedest Street in the World," and each year it continues to draw many visitors. Today the alley and Victorian homes that surround it have been named to the National Register of Historic Places. You can approach the top of Snake Alley along North Sixth Street between Washington and Columbia Streets.

Burlington's three historical museums will give you more background on the city's past. At the top of Snake Alley is the 1851 **Phelps House,** once home to one of the city's most prominent families. On the bluff in Crapo Park where Zebulon Pike first raised the American flag is the **Hawkeye Log Cabin,** now filled with tools and household items from the pioneer era. The third museum, the **Apple Trees Museum,** is built on the site of the first apple orchards planted west of the Mississippi and houses the growing collections of the Des Moines County Historical Society. For information on hours call (319) 753–2449.

Burlington is also home to the *Catfish Bend Riverboat Casino,* a 1,300-passenger vessel that spends the winter in Burlington and the summer in Fort Madison. The boat offers dockside gambling from November through April; call (800) 372–2WIN for information.

A block down from the casino is a Burlington institution known as **Big Muddy's.** The 1898 structure was once a railroad freight station and now houses an excellent restaurant (prices are moderate to expensive). You'll find Big Muddy's (319–753–1699) at 710 North Front Street

Visit **Mosquito Park,** named for its size, not its bite! You will find this little gem tucked away at Third and Franklin Streets. Set on bluffs just north of the downtown district, it offers a captivating view of the rolling Mississippi below.

A jewel of a different cut is located at St. Mary's Catholic Church in West Burlington at 420 West Mount Pleasant Street. **Our Lady of Grace Grotto,** completed in 1931, was constructed of thousands of imported and native stones and features split rock sidewalks and crystal rock walls. Forty different varieties of trees are found in the garden. For more information call (319) 752–4035.

A new attraction in Burlington is **Zellmer's Stage Door Dinner Theatre,** a professional theater at 3001 Winegard that offers a variety of comedy and musical performances. Call (319) 753–2223 for information about current shows.

The biggest annual event in this river city is ***Burlington Steamboat Days,*** when nationally known rock, country, pop, rhythm and blues, jazz, big band, and oldies groups perform daily on outdoor stages. More than 100,000 visitors converge in Burlington for the event, which also includes fireworks, parades, a carnival, sports competitions, an art fair on Snake Alley, and plenty of good food and drink. Call the Burlington Area Convention and Tourism Bureau at (800) 82–RIVER for information.

Two other events are worthy of mention, both held in July. The ***Dragon Boat Festival*** features twenty-member teams from around the world paddling 40-foot, 2,000-pound boats in exciting contests. And then there is ***MADRAC*** (the Mississippi Annual Down River Adventure by Canoe), which draws canoe paddlers from far and near to participate in this fun-filled event on the Big Muddy. For more information and dates contact the Burlington Area Convention and Tourism Bureau at the number listed above.

PLACES TO STAY IN RURAL CHARMS

KALONA
Home on the Hill,
1208 J Avenue,
(319) 656–3500,
$65–$85

MT. PLEASANT
Heartland Inn,
Highway 218 North,
(800) 334–3277,
(319) 385–2101,
$48–$66

OTTUMWA
Parkview Plaza Hotel,
107 East Second Street,
(515) 682–8051,
$36–$85

MORAVIA
Lakeside Inn,
Lake Rathbun,
(515) 724–3212,
$55–$130

KEOKUK
River's Edge,
611 Grand Avenue,
(888) 581–3343,
(319) 524–1700,
$75–$110

FORT MADISON
Mississippi Rose
and Thistle Inn,
532 Avenue F,
(319) 372–7044,
$70–$90

BURLINGTON
The Schramm House,
616 Columbia Street,
(800) 683–7117,
(319) 754–0373,
$65–$95

PLACES TO EAT IN RURAL CHARMS

OTTUMWA
The Greenbriar,
1207 North Jefferson Street,
(515) 682–8147

KEOSAUQUA
Milky Way in the Old
Farmers Co-op Creamery,
901 1st Street,
(319) 293–6255

KEOKUK
Tailwater Towing Co.,
215 Mississippi River
Drive, (319) 524–DOCK

The Sampler House Tea
Room & Marketplace,
120 North Fourth Street,
(319) 524–1581,
By reservation only

FORT MADISON
The Palms Supper Club,
Highway 61 West,
(319)372–5833

Bridges Country

South central Iowa can be thought of as "bridges country" in two different ways. In Madison County you can discover the sites made famous by the popular novel and film *The Bridges of Madison County.* In Des Moines and its neighboring cities—a region sometimes called the "golden circle"—you can explore the metropolitan area that serves as a bridge between Iowa's rural communities and its increasingly urban central core. South central Iowa is also home to the ethnic enclave of Pella, where Dutch traditions remain strong, as well as other rural treasures along the southern border.

Golden Circle

There's no better place to begin your tour of this part of the state than the town of Grinnell. J. B. Grinnell, the founder of the town and the nationally acclaimed Grinnell College located here, was the recipient of Horace Greeley's famous dictum: "Go West, young man, and grow up with the country." Josiah Bushnell Grinnell was active in the early educational concerns of Iowa's legislature as well as an ardent abolitionist. He made Grinnell a stop on the Underground Railroad; more than 1,000 freedom-seeking slaves passed through Grinnell in the pre-Civil War years. In 1859 he gave refuge to John Brown following his raids in Kansas and Missouri. Learn more about this influential man and this community when you visit the ***Grinnell Historical Museum,*** which is housed in a ten-room late-Victorian residence at 1125 Broad Street. Besides the furniture and artifacts of an earlier era, there is a barbed-wire collection and several carriages (including a surrey with fringe on top) made by the old Spaulding Carriage Company of Grinnell.

For a real treat (and maybe even a few tricks) visit ***Carroll's Pumpkin Farm*** from late September through Halloween. There's so much to do here it's hard to go wrong. You can pick a pumpkin, get lost in a corn maze, climb into a tree house, burst with laughter as you slide into bales of straw, and see an honest-to-goodness pumpkin tree. If you have children along, you may want to devote an entire afternoon to Carroll's.

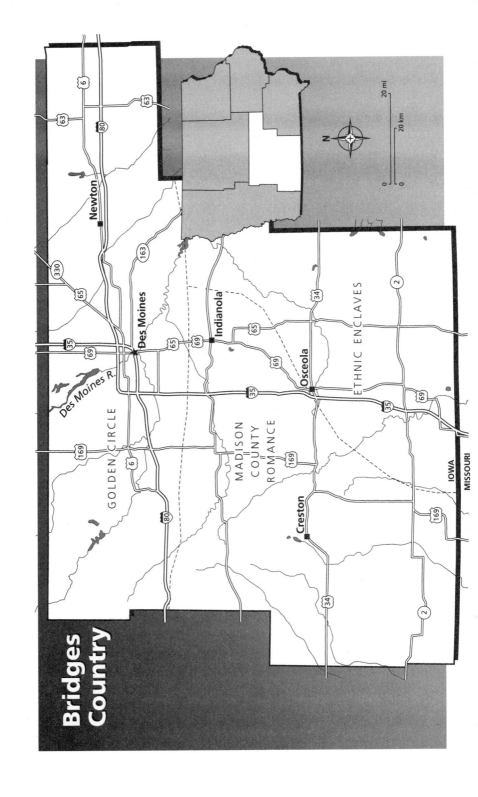

Bridges Country

Newton

6

63

63

80

330

65

35

69

169

6

80

Des Moines

Des Moines R.

GOLDEN CIRCLE

163

65

65

69

Indianola

MADISON COUNTY ROMANCE

169

Creston

34

34

69

Osceola

35

ETHNIC ENCLAVES

2

69

169

2

IOWA

MISSOURI

N

20 mi

20 km

0

0

BRIDGES COUNTRY

Author's Favorites –
Bridges Country

Walnut Creek National
Wildlife Refuge

Iowa State Fair

Inn of the Six-toed Cat

Great Cardboard
Boat Regatta

Valley Junction

Piper's Grocery Store

Cutler-Donahoe
Covered Bridge

Des Moines Metro Opera

Mount Pisgah

C. B. & Q. Railroad Depot

There's a small concession stand that serves seasonal treats like caramel apples, popcorn, and cider and you're welcome to bring in a picnic lunch. With advance notice a bonfire can be built so you can roast your hot dogs and marshmallows. On the weekends there are unlimited hay rides, shows in the barn loft (don't miss Bingo, the farm dog!) and if you were lucky enough to be born in October, you will be specially honored. Carroll's Pumpkin Farm, located at 244 400th Avenue, is open Monday through Saturday from 10:00 A.M. to 7:00 P.M. and on Sundays from 1:00 to 7:00 P.M. Admission during the week is $1.25 for ages three and up and $2.50 on weekends. Take Highway 146 south of Grinnell to 400th Avenue and turn right. For more information call (515) 236–7043.

Continue east to Newton, best known as the home of the Maytag Company, one of the world's largest appliance manufacturers. At the **Jasper County Historical Museum** you can view displays on local history, including the **Maytag Historical Museum,** which traces the development of Maytag washing machines from 1907 to the present. The machines' renowned reliability is supported by the fact that the museum frequently receives letters from people across the nation describing their turn-of-the-century washing machines still in use. The museum (515–792–9118) is at exit 164 off I–80 and is open daily from 1:00 to 5:00 P.M. from May 1 to October 1.

E. H. Maytag, son of the founder of the Maytag Company, established another of Newton's well-known industries, the **Maytag Dairy Farms.** The farms are home to a herd of award-winning Holstein-Friesian cows that produce the milk that goes into the farms' Maytag Blue Cheese, which is acclaimed by connoisseurs as one of the country's finest gourmet cheeses. Stop by the cheese shop to sample some of the tasty cheese, then take a guided tour of the farms' operations. The Maytag Dairy Farms (800–247–2458) are located north of Newton; call for directions. The farms are open Monday through Friday from 8:00 A.M. to 5:00 P.M. and on Saturday from 9:00 A.M. to 1:00 P.M.

A culinary treat in Newton can be found at **La Corsette Maison Inn,** a gourmet restaurant and country inn housed in an opulent Spanish Mission–style mansion built in 1909. Owner Kay Owen is a former farm girl who worked as a teacher and horse breeder before deciding to open her own business as a restaurateur. "I've always loved to cook and entertain," she says. "Eventually I decided to try making a living at what I enjoy most."

Guests at La Corsette are treated to a lavish dinner that's served with impeccable style. Several nights a week Kay prepares a six-course gourmet dinner for as many as forty-eight—or as few as two—scheduled guests, with the entree selected by the first caller to make reservations. The one-entree arrangement and single seating for each meal mean that guests can mingle between courses as they explore the home's art nouveau interior.

A meal at La Corsette lasts about three hours, with ample time to savor each course. The food is innovative and delicious. A typical menu might begin with an appetizer of mussels Provençal, followed by a chilled fruit soup and a beet salade mimosa topped with chopped egg. Entrees include medallions of pork in cognac sauce, French veal in cream, and beef tenderloin tips in tarragon butter. Next is a cheese and fruit course and then a truly decadent dessert such as triple chocolate mousse with Grand Marnier sauce or floating island with crème Anglaise and caramel sauce. Amid the strains of music provided by the pianist at the baby grand, each course is served by solicitous waiters in tuxedos, who also offer selections from La Corsette's wine cellar.

Twister Alert!

*O*n June 17, 1882, the state of Iowa almost lost the town of Grinnell. Storms had been raging across the state all day and were to meet with a furious uproar in Grinnell. Ten miles away in Kellogg, two black clouds united and formed a tornado that swept northeast to Grinnell. In the west, in Carroll County, another tornado was moving swiftly to the southeast.

As if by appointment, the two twisters met in the very center of the town of Grinnell. It was a clash of titanic proportions that sent at least six smaller tornadoes spiraling downward.

Thirty-nine people were killed and the college was in ruins. The only property salvaged was the college bell.

Seven years later in 1889, the downtown district was again almost destroyed by a devastating fire. We are lucky to have this town still on the map. J. B. Grinnell, the founder, was instrumental in rebuilding the town twice. Earlier he had given lots to the college, stating that they would have to be given back to him or his estate if liquor was ever sold on them. Could it be that the tornadoes knew more about what was going on than he did?

BRIDGES COUNTRY

FESTIVALS IN BRIDGES COUNTRY

Red Bud Festival,
Chariton, last Saturday in
April, (515) 774–4059

**Shear Entertainment
Weekend,**
Des Moines, first weekend in
May, (515) 278–5286

Jesse James Days,
Corydon, first weekend in
June, (515) 872–2512

Iowa State Fair,
Des Moines, third week in
August, (515) 262–3111

**Baxter Pedaling
Pajama Party,**
Baxter, second Saturday in
September, (515) 227–3502

La Corsette Maison Inn has seven bedrooms available for guests. The most unusual is a room in the tower dubbed "The Penthouse," with beveled-glass windows on all four sides and a balcony. Each room comes with breakfast served in gracious La Corsette style.

La Corsette is located at 629 First Avenue East in Newton. Reservations are required for dinner, with most entrees costing $34.50 and $38 per person. Rates for the rooms range from $70 to $170. Call (515) 792–6833 for reservations.

From Newton travel west to *Trainland U.S.A.,* a must-see for anyone who loves model railroading. Located a few miles north of the town of Colfax, Trainland is the fulfillment of a dream for its owner, Leland "Red" Atwood. After many years of collecting Lionel trains, Atwood tore down his family home in 1976 and replaced it with a building designed to house both a museum and living quarters. Friends and neighbors devoted hundreds of hours of labor to help him turn the building's ground floor into a huge display depicting the development of railroads in the United States.

The exhibit represents three eras of railroading: frontier, steam, and diesel. All the scenery is hand painted and includes details such as a miniature Mount Rushmore, White House, Statue of Liberty, and Kentucky coal mine, plus a drive-in movie with animated cartoons projected on a tiny screen. More than twenty electric trains operate simultaneously over nearly a mile of track, with the sound of steam locomotive whistles and diesel air horns playing in the background. It's all a monument to Atwood's lifelong passion, a love that began at the age of five when he received his first model train as a Christmas gift.

Trainland U.S.A. is located on Highway 117, $2^1/_2$ miles north of the Colfax exit on I–80. From Memorial Day through Labor Day it is open daily from 10:00 A.M. to 6:00 P.M. Admission is $4.50 for adults, $4.00 for seniors, and $2.00 for children. Call (515) 674–3813 for more information.

No visit to this area would be complete without a visit to the newly opened *Walnut Creek National Wildlife Refuge* near Prairie City, 8 miles south of Interstate 80 on Highway 163. More than 5,000 acres (with more to come as acquisitions are made) of land have been set aside to re-create the tall-grass prairie that covered most of the state of

Iowa 150 years ago. Undomesticated buffalo have been reintroduced to the land, as well as other birds and animals, prairie grasses, and native flowers. Several miles of paved road wind through the refuge so visitors can see the prairie up close. Make sure you stop at the **Neal Smith Prairie Learning Center** to learn more about this incredible and almost extinct part of the American landscape. Nestled unobtrusively amid the softly rolling plains, the center offers a closer look at the flora and fauna you will see when you travel through the refuge. There are animals to look at and plants to identify and many fascinating interactive displays. It is open from 9:00 A.M. to 4:00 P.M. Tuesdays through Saturdays and from noon to 5:00 P.M. on Sundays. Admission is free.

From Colfax head west to Des Moines, Iowa's capital city. Think of Des Moines, and the image that comes to mind is of a good, solid, and (yes, let's admit it up front) boring midwestern city. If that's your image of Des Moines, it's time you took a closer look at Iowa's capital. The city is full of historic sites, unique shops, fine restaurants, and other attractions that

Only in Iowa

*T*he story goes that the community of **Brooklyn,** *located two miles north of Interstate 80 on Highway V18 (take exit 197), got its name from one Dr. Rueben Sears who, having climbed the ridge pole of a building under construction, spied a brook lying to the north and said, "There lies a brook." Then, looking south, after much deliberation said, "There lies another brook. We shall name this new town Brookland."*

"Only in Iowa," I say to myself.

This town of 1,500 bills itself as the "Community of Flags," for its prominent display of the flags of every state along a well-maintained promenade. Stop and visit its restored opera house and flag store, where you can buy anything from flags and flagpoles to Iowa honey and popcorn. Or visit the charming local library or Brooklyn Hotel. Or take

a walk across the Brooklyn Bridge— not the one you've heard about.

When I stopped here on a raw, wet Sunday evening in February to take a few pictures, a gentleman in a pickup truck pulled over to see if I wanted to know anything about the flags and the community. In a day when people leave others pretty much to themselves, this was a welcome I hadn't expected.

We shivered and chatted for twenty minutes or so and when this unknown man (for I'd forgotten to ask him his name) jumped back into his truck to drive away, he invited me to come back and enjoy myself in more seasonable weather. We nodded and laughed and waved goodbye. "Only in Iowa," I thought, for what seemed to me to be the millionth time in my life.

will keep you entertained on your visit, and you're likely to leave Des Moines with plans to return.

Within the past two decades, downtown Des Moines has undergone a renaissance that has brightened its atmosphere and raised its skyline. A major project was the construction of a $3^1/_2$-mile skywalk system that links twenty blocks of the downtown area. Included on the skywalk route are hotels, restaurants, shopping centers, office buildings, residential complexes, and parking facilities, making it possible for you to travel throughout the downtown without ever going outside—an attractive alternative on one of Iowa's cold winter days. (The skywalk system is also the site of one of the state's most unusual sports competitions, the Skywalk Open, an indoor golf tournament held each February.)

A good place to begin your tour of Des Moines is at the ***Iowa State Capitol,*** one of the nation's most beautiful capitols. It dominates the city's skyline visually as well as politically, with its 275-foot-high gold-leaf dome flanked by four smaller domes. Inside it's a showcase for nineteenth-century craftsmanship and an impressive monument to the artisans who constructed it in the late 1800s. Its cornerstone (a huge prairie boulder from Buchanan County) was laid in 1871, and the building was finally completed in 1886 at a total cost of more than $2.8 million—a figure that must have made conservative farmers of the day shake their heads in disgust.

Some of the country's most highly regarded artists were commissioned to fill the building's marble, stone, and wood interior. Elaborate hand-painted ceilings, exquisite mosaics and murals, and intricate wood carvings have all been preserved, making this an elegant setting indeed for the workings of state government. Major features of the building include the legislative chambers, supreme court, governor's office, and a lovely law library with spiral staircases leading to the shelves of books. Outside, you're welcome to explore the acres of public gardens that put on a continuous show of color from spring through fall. Another good time to visit the capitol is when the legislature is in session, when you can see up close the lobbying and politicking that go on in the hallways of the grand old building.

The Iowa State Capitol is located at East Ninth Street and Grand Avenue off I–235. It is open from 8:00 A.M. to 4:00 P.M. Monday through Saturday,

Iowa State Capitol

and free tours are given each day. Call (515) 281–5591 for times and information.

Next to the capitol is another of Iowa's treasures, the *Iowa Historical Building.* Completed in 1987, this dramatic granite-and-glass structure is a stunning setting for the collections of the State Historical Society of Iowa. Visitors enter a soaring atrium-style lobby that ascends to a height of 65 feet. Oak floors, exposed pipes, and large skylights make for an inviting interior, which includes two floors of exhibits, a gift shop and auditorium, and the State Historical Library. The building's $25.4 million cost was met through private donations and $10 million from the Iowa State Lottery, so that no tax dollars were used in its construction.

Among the permanent exhibits in the museum is "The Delicate Balance," a look at how the animals, land, plants, and people of Iowa have coexisted throughout the state's history. "You Gotta Know the Territory," with displays that tell the story of the settlement of pioneer Iowa, is a permanent exhibit that illustrates the museum's new emphasis on interactive displays. Here you can churn butter, scrape animal hides, and play American Indian games. Temporary exhibits, some on loan from other institutions, fill much of the remaining space in the museum, making this a fascinating place to spend an afternoon browsing through Iowa's history.

The Iowa Historical Building is located at 600 East Locust Street. Its hours are Tuesday through Saturday from 9:00 A.M. to 4:30 P.M. and on Sunday from noon to 4:30 P.M. Admission is free. For more information call (515) 281–5111.

Two other stops should be part of your historical tour of Des Moines. The first is *Terrace Hill,* the official residence of the Iowa governor and one of the finest examples of Second Empire–style architecture in the country. The home was constructed at a cost of $250,000 in the 1860s and was home to a couple of the city's most prominent citizens for many years. It was built for the state's first millionaire, B. F. Allen, who sold it to the F. M. Hubbell family, who donated it to the state in 1971. Since then more than $3 million has been spent on its renovation. Much of the effort has gone into refurbishing the home's main-floor rooms to their original Victorian splendor. The lower two floors are included in the tour open to the public, with the exception of one room on the second floor used as quarters for visiting families and dignitaries. The third floor houses the offices and family quarters of the governor. Terrace Hill is open from Tuesday through Saturday, except during January and February, from 10:00 A.M. to 1:30 P.M. Call (515) 281–3604 for information.

Salisbury House is another Des Moines mansion that will bring you back in time—to Tudor England, not nineteenth-century Iowa. The home is modeled after a centuries-old Tudor dwelling in Salisbury, England, complete with a great hall with beamed and raftered ceiling, rich tapestries, Oriental rugs, stained-glass windows, and ornate wall paneling. It was built by a wealthy cosmetics manufacturer, Carl Weeks, who purchased many of the home's furnishings in England and who also collected art objects as well as a 3,500-volume library that includes such treasures as a page from the Gutenburg Bible and a copy of the Kelmscot Chaucer produced by William Morris. Call (515) 274–1777 for a tour schedule.

For a taste of modern Des Moines, a number of attractions are worth a visit. For a quiet treat on a frosty winter day, stop by the *Des Moines Botanical Center,* an 80-foot geodesic dome, 150 feet in circumference, filled with lush tropical and semitropical plants as well as a variety of major floral shows. Don't miss the bonsai collection, rated one of the ten best in the United States. Some of the plants have been in training for more than a hundred years! On pleasant days you can spend an enjoyable time wandering through the special outdoor gardens. Here you'll find the only outdoor cactus-and-succulent garden in the Midwest.

The *Blank Park Zoo* displays more than 800 animals from five continents in exhibits that simulate the animals' natural habitats. It's open from May 1 through October 15. Finally, the *Des Moines Art Center* is nationally recognized both for its art collection and for its futuristic architecture created by the internationally known architects Eliel Saarinen, I. M. Pei, and Richard Meier.

To recover from your sightseeing, stop by the **Taste of Thailand,** a local ethnic restaurant that has achieved fame in publications ranging from the *London Times* to *USA Today.* Its owner is Prasong Nurack, a Thai immigrant who was a lawyer in his home country before coming to the United States. Here he earned a master's degree in political science from Northeastern Illinois University and then moved to Des Moines in 1976 to open its first Thai restaurant. His lifelong passionate interest in politics has remained strong, however, and his restaurant has become a favorite gathering place for politicians, lobbyists, journalists, and political staffers, particularly during the Iowa caucus season that kicks off the presidential elections every four years. According to the *New York Times,* "the Taste of Thailand has become Des Moines's answer to Elaine's in New York."

The restaurant's reputation is based on its wonderful, authentic Thai food, a huge selection of imported beers, and its famous "TOT Poll." Nurack began polling his customers in 1986 about their political likes and dislikes, offering them ballots to complete as they dined. Since then his poll has expanded to cover such burning questions as whether his customers believe in reincarnation, which talk-show host they prefer, and whether they can touch their toes (76 percent said they could, 24 percent called it a silly question). In the front of the restaurant there's a polling booth for those who wish to make their choices in private; otherwise, you can fill yours out at your table. Each month results are tabulated and posted by the front door.

Even if you're not interested in politics, Taste of Thailand is a Des Moines institution you shouldn't miss. The restaurant is located at 215 East Walnut Street, and prices are inexpensive for lunch and inexpensive to moderate for dinner. Call (515) 243–9521 for reservations and more information.

For an afternoon of browsing, shopping, and munching, check out **Valley Junction** in West Des Moines. The area was settled by coal miners and was once a bustling railroad center with a wild reputation, but as the importance of the railroad faded, so did the town's spirit. Then in the late 1960s, the area began to come to life again, as small-business owners (many of them antiques dealers) opened their doors in the area's historic old storefronts. Today Valley Junction has become a popular shopping district filled with more than a hundred businesses, which include upscale restaurants, fancy boutiques, antiques stores brimming with mismatched treasures, and specialty stores selling everything from lace to jewelry to kitchen tools. On Thursday and Sunday evenings from mid-June through September, Valley Junction is also the site of a Farmers Market. Call the Valley Junction Foundation at (515) 222–3642 for more information.

While browsing through Valley Junction, stop by Winnie's Toy Orphanage for a present for the children, shop for homegrown Iowa gifts at a store called From the Heart of Iowa, and look for unique gifts for cat and dog lovers at Raining Cats and Dogs. Then relax in the friendly, Irish pub atmosphere of AK O'Connor's (I can personally recommend the tastiness of their chocolate-chip cheesecake).

The Valley Junction district is located on Fifth Street and the surrounding area in downtown West Des Moines. Take I–235 to the Sixty-third Street exit, and then go south and follow the Valley Junction signs.

One other stop is definitely worth a visit before you leave Polk County: *Living History Farms,* in Urbandale just west of Des Moines. This is a 600-acre agricultural museum that tells the story of farming in the Midwest, from a 1700 Ioway Indian village to displays on twentieth-century farming. In between, several eras are highlighted, including an 1850 pioneer farm, an 1875 town, and a 1900 farm. The artifacts come to life through the efforts of interpreters dressed in historical clothing who re-create the daily routine of early Iowans. On each farm the buildings, planting methods, and livestock are authentic to the time periods represented, and visitors are often invited to try their hand at old-time skills like wool carding and apple-butter making. Tractor-drawn carts transport visitors between the five period sites on a regular schedule, and walking trails through native woodlands are also open between the sites.

Living History Farms garnered national attention in 1979, when Pope John Paul II visited here to deliver a sermon on the bounty of the land before a crowd of some 400,000 people. Today the site has been commemorated with an interfaith Church of the Land.

Throughout the year special events and festivals are held at Living History Farms, from bobsled parties and hayrides to pioneer craft shows and turn-of-the-century plowing exhibitions. On July 4th there's an old-fashioned Independence Day celebration, and during the fall there are several events centered on the harvest. Another popular attraction at Living History Farms is the 1900 farm supper program. From November through April interpreters prepare and serve authentic meals based on turn-of-the-century recipes. Reservations are required (and the suppers are often booked well in advance).

To reach Living History Farms, take exit 125 (Hickman Road, Highway 6) off the combined Interstates 35 and 80. The farms are open daily

May 1 through the third Sunday in October from 9:00 A.M. to 5:00 P.M. Admission is $8.00 for adults, $7.00 for seniors, and $5.00 for children ages 4–12. Call (515) 278–5286 for more information.

A fun place to visit and to grab a bite to eat is the Bavarian Haus Restaurant located at 5220 NE Fourteenth Street. This is the home of the *Iowa Polka Music Hall of Fame.* It's a "can't miss" spot for polka fans and the food is good as well! Call the Bavarian Haus at (319) 322–5489 for their hours and more information.

Every April Des Moines hosts the Drake Relays, bringing together track competitors of all skill levels, from high school to professional, to compete with their peers. On a lighter note, Drake College, whose mascot happens to be a bulldog, hosts a *"Bulldog Beauty Contest"* in which fifty bulldogs compete for the title. But don't get your hopes up—it does not include a swimsuit competition. The contest serves as a kickoff to the Relays and is held the third week in April; call (515) 243–6625 for more information or an entry blank.

Finally, one more Des Moines–based event needs to be mentioned: **RAG-BRAI, the Register's Annual Great Bicycle Ride Across Iowa.** The seven-day bike ride is sponsored by the *Des Moines Register* newspaper and draws thousands of participants who toil up and down Iowa's hills for a week at the end of each July. The event began in 1973 and was the first statewide bicycle ride in the country. A mixture of endurance test, parade, and party, RAGBRAI has become an Iowa tradition that's well-loved both by its participants and by the small towns that feed and shelter the riders as they pass through. For information call (515) 284–8282.

For more information about attractions in the Des Moines area, call the Greater Des Moines Convention and Visitors Bureau at (800) 451–2625 or visit their Web site at *www.desmoinesia. com.*

From Des Moines head west on Highway 6 to the charming small town of Adel, which is home to a number of surprisingly sophisticated attractions. Begin your visit with a stroll around Adel's picturesque town square and then stop in at *Aubrey's Vintage Collection* (515–993–5057) at 815 Main Street. Inside are exquisite silk and dried floral arrangements created by Aubrey Dunbar, whose skills make him one of Iowa's most sought-after floral arrangers. Also for sale are unusual gifts and accessories, showcased amid reproduction period furniture, lamps, paintings, and crystal.

Just off the square at 202 South Ninth Street is the *Atherton House on the Boulevard* (515–993–2034), a turn-of-the-century cottage that houses a cornucopia of treasures from around the world. From Nigerian baskets and Ojibwe birdhouses to Pennsylvania harness bells and Russian lacquer boxes, the Atherton House offers retail delights that put the standard shopping mall to shame.

Next to the Atherton House is the *Old Depot Restaurant,* located in the town's renovated train depot. The Old Depot Restaurant is at 218 South Ninth Street. Call (515) 993–5064 for information.

North of Adel in the town of Perry is another exceptional restaurant: the *Thymes Remembered Tea Room.* Its dining room is a bright medley of floral prints, exquisite flower arrangements, and seasonal touches that range from Victorian valentine trees decorated with roses and cherubs to antique Christmas decorations that would make Charles Dickens feel right at home.

Owned by Ramona and Jim Birdsell, the tearoom and adjacent nine-room gift shop make this an irresistible stop for travelers. Each week the restaurant serves a different selection of four or five entrees ranging from a rich chicken cordon bleu to a hearty German cabbage roll with aspic sauce. The desserts are just as tempting as the entrees: Italian cream cake, rice pudding with raspberry sauce, and chocolate lace cheesecake are perennial favorites. "I think if you pay attention to the details, people will keep coming back," says Ramona, whose unerring good taste guides the entire operation.

The Thymes Remembered Tea Room (515–465–2631) is located at the corner of First and Otley Streets in Perry. Hours are Monday through Saturday from 10:00 A.M. to 4:00 P.M.; the shops remain open

Inside Pitch

*W*here will you find the **Bob Feller Hometown Exhibit** *you've been looking for? Well, in Van Meter, of course. You won't need directions because you can't miss the mural of "Rapid Robert" painted on the side of the museum devoted to this famous Hall of Fame pitcher for the Cleveland Indians. Dominated by Bob's smiling face, this mural depicts him in various stages of his pitch. Inside you'll be able to catch a glimpse of his old uniforms, special awards, and rare photos. Van Meter is deservedly proud of its native son. To get there take exit 113 off I–80 and proceed to 310 Mill Street. The exhibit is open Monday through Saturday from 10:00 A.M. to 5:00 P.M. and on Sundays from noon to 4:00 P.M. Adult admission is $2.00; seniors $1.50; $1.00 for children. Call (515) 996–2806 for more details.*

until 5:00 P.M. Lunch is served from 11:00 A.M. to 2:00 P.M., and entree prices are moderate.

For a memorable experience make reservations to stay at the *Hotel Pattee* in downtown Perry. This beautiful old hotel, originally opened in 1913, has been completely renovated by owner Roberta Ahmanson, and was reopened during the summer of 1997. Much of the original Arts and Crafts feeling has been retained; both the inside and the outside are gorgeous. There are forty rooms, all with private baths, four of which are suites and two of which are junior suites. (One of the latter is called "the kids' suite"—milk and cookies are served promptly at 8:00 P.M.!) The hotel boasts a whirlpool, sauna, steam room, and fitness room for its guests, and a library filled with books and videos to borrow for the night, free of charge. In the lower level there's even a two-lane bowling alley! Also on the premises are the Inter-Urban Lounge and Mike's Milwaukee Diner, which serves breakfast, lunch, and dinner. For dinner you may want to try one of their Oak Plank Platters. This includes either an eight-ounce filet of beef or a chicken breast served "Swedish style" on a bed of grilled onions and served on a sizzling oak plank with mashed potatoes and roasted vegetables. The Hotel Pattee is usually booked two months in advance for Saturday nights so make your reservation soon! Located at 1112 Willis Avenue, call (888) 424–4268 or (515) 465–3511 for more information. Prices range from $80 to $185 for a night's stay.

Madison County Romance

Author Robert James Waller's decision to set his first novel in Madison County, Iowa, has sparked a remarkable series of events that have helped revitalize this primarily rural region. First the book landed a seemingly permanent spot on the national bestseller lists, then Hollywood decided to turn the love story into a movie, and then before the town quite knew what was happening, Clint Eastwood and Meryl Streep were exchanging passionate kisses on Roseman Bridge. Since then Winterset has become a mecca for fans who travel from around the country and the world to see the sights immortalized in the book and movie. This formerly sleepy town may never be the same, but few in Winterset are complaining.

The covered bridges of Madison County were a tourism attraction long before the book was written (though hardly on the scale they are now). Nineteen bridges were built in Madison County between 1855 and 1885, and they were covered to help preserve their large flooring timbers, which were more expensive to replace than the lumber used to cover the bridge sides and roof. Most were named after the resident who lived closest. Six of these covered bridges remain today, all of which are listed on the National Register of Historic Places. For many years the bridges have been the focus of the **Madison County Covered Bridges Festival,** held each year on the second full weekend in October, when bus tours to all the bridges are offered and the town square comes alive with food and craft booths, a car show and parade, and other entertainment.

A visit to Winterset is enjoyable at any time of year, however—especially if you happen to be enamored of the story of Francesca and her photographer friend. Begin your tour with a visit to the **Madison County Welcome Center** (800–298–6119), which is located at 73 Jefferson Street on the town square. There you can pick up brochures on the area's attractions as well as a map that lists the locations of all the bridges in the surrounding countryside.

A few doors down from the welcome center is an establishment that played a role in the movie: the **Northside Cafe** was the setting for a scene in which Robert Kincaid learns more about the town and its attitudes. The cafe has been a Winterset institution since 1876 and has become a popular spot for *Bridges* fans (who are quick to caress the fourth seat from the door, the one that was used by Clint). The food is hearty and inexpensive, and the waitresses can tell you stories about the filming. The Northside Cafe (515–462–1523) is at 61 Jefferson Street and is open Monday through Saturday from 5:30 A.M. to 8:00 P.M. and Sunday from 6:00 A.M. to 2:00 P.M.

Another hallowed spot for fans is the **Roseman Bridge,** where Francesca left a note inviting Robert to dinner. The bridge is located about 10 miles southwest of Winterset and spans a picturesque bend in the Middle River. In the woods near the bridge is a gift shop that sells *Bridges* memorabilia. Another lovely spot is the **Cedar Bridge,** which is located a few miles northwest of Winterset and is surrounded by a park with picnic tables. In the novel, Cedar Bridge is where Francesca goes to observe Robert taking photographs.

A good place for a picnic is at the **Cutler-Donahoe Covered Bridge** located in the Winterset City Park. This little park is perfectly charming and is also the site of the Clark Tower, a three-story limestone structure that serves as a pioneer memorial and offers outstanding views of the surrounding countryside.

Roseman Bridge, Madison County

Fans will also want to tour *Francesca's House,* where most of the movie's scenes were filmed. This simple farmhouse had stood vacant for thirty years when the film's producers decided that it was the perfect spot for Francesca to live. Over the course of a few weeks the house was completely refurbished and then was "aged" to the 1960s era. Today you can tour through the home and see the rooms made famous by the movie. In the kitchen the radio plays the dreamy blues favored by Robert Kincaid, while upstairs the claw-footed bathtub recalls the lovers' intimate bath scene. The guided tour takes about twenty minutes, and includes descriptions of how Hollywood technicians re-created a 1960s-era farmhouse. Francesca's House is located about 15 miles northwest of Winterset off Road G4R. Tours are offered May through October from 10:00 A.M. to 6:00 P.M. Adult admission is $5.00; children 12 and under are $3.00. Call (515) 981–5268 for information.

Winterset has other attractions in addition to sites relating to the book and movie. Before Robert James Waller ever came to town, the *John Wayne Birthplace* put the town on the map. The famous actor was born here in a modest frame house on May 26, 1907. Back then he was called Marion Robert Morrison, son of a pharmacist who worked in a local drugstore. The Morrison family lived in the home until Marion (or John or the Duke) was three, when they moved to nearby Earlham in northern Madison County.

Restoration of the tiny four-room house began in 1981, funded by the local community and by the actor's fans and family, who have donated many items to the site. Since then it has been visited by thousands of people, including Wayne's wife, six of his seven children, and former President Reagan. Two of the rooms are furnished as they might have been in 1907, and the other two contain a collection of John Wayne memorabilia (including the eye patch he wore in *True Grit*).

The John Wayne Birthplace is located at 224 South Second Street in Winterset and is open daily from 10:00 A.M. to 5:00 P.M. Admission is $2.00 for adults, $1.00 for children. Call (515) 462–1044 for more information.

At the *Madison County Historical Complex* you can learn more about the local history of the area. This impressive eighteen-acre historical site contains a museum, 1856 restored mansion, log schoolhouse and post office, general store, 1870 train depot, blacksmith shop, stone barn, and what is probably the only outhouse in the state of Iowa to be listed on the National Register of Historic Places (made of stone, the privy was at one time wallpapered and heated for the comfort of its users). Also on the property is the Zion Federated Church, an 1881 structure that was moved to the complex in 1988 through the support of local residents.

In the complex's museum you can view exhibits on local history, including vintage clothing, quilts, farm equipment, and Indian artifacts. In the basement is another treasure, a huge collection of fossils and minerals that the Smithsonian Institution offered to buy before it was donated to the museum.

The Madison County Historical Complex is located at 815 South Second Avenue and is open from May through October. Its hours are Monday through Saturday from 11:00 A.M. to 4:00 P.M. and Sunday from 1:00 to 5:00 P.M. Call (515) 462–3263 for more information.

Don't overlook the *Winterset Art Center,* the circa 1854 brick house located at 224 South John Wayne Drive that once served as a stop on the Underground Railroad. It features a display dedicated to George Washington Carver, renowned scientist and educator. He is also honored in a

Brrr . . .

*W*hen Winterset residents were trying to come up with a name for their community they originally tried to decide between Summerset and Sommerset. Because it was a particularly cold day, someone suggested that the name Winterset would be more appropriate, and so it was called. This bit of information triggered a memory I have of a visit to a former Iowan who owned a small motel in West Yellowstone. Looking around the lobby I was mesmerized by the seemingly hundreds of photographs of family and guests frolicking in the towering drifts of snow of Montana and Wyoming. In most cases these drifts topped 10 or even 20 feet, and I felt like I was looking at pictures of the North Pole. "Why?" I asked him. "Why did you ever move out here?" Without hesitating for an instant, he replied, "Easy. To get away from the cold. There's no colder state in the nation than Iowa." I don't know if this is true or not but there are sure times when it feels like it is. All I can tell you is that if you're visiting our state in January you'll have something to brag about when you get home.

memorial park next to the fire station. This is the site of the old hotel where he once worked. The Art Center's hours vary. Call (515) 462–1196 for more information.

From Winterset travel east on Highway 92 to Indianola, home of Simpson College and the site each summer of the *National Balloon Classic.* The event is one of the most visually spectacular festivals you are likely to find any place in the country. Each August some 200 pilots are invited to bring their magnificent balloons to Indianola and compete for cash and prizes. Throughout the festival the skies of Indianola are filled with brilliant colored balloons, attracting thousands of visitors who crane their necks for hours on end to view the serene craft. Each morning and evening there are mass ascensions, and during the day special demonstrations and competitions are held. After dark there's a Nite-Glo Extravaganza, when the bursts of flames that power the balloons light up the colored fabrics above them, creating vivid patterns against the night sky.

Other events at the festival include musical performances, a town picnic, arts and crafts show, parade, classic-car show, and a carnival and amusement center. Drawings for free balloon rides are held nightly. A few tips for balloon spectators: Wear comfortable shoes and bring a lawn chair or blanket to sit on. And you'll be sorry if you don't bring your camera along—the sight of the balloons rising above the area's lush rolling hills is unforgettable (each year a photo contest is held, in fact, to recognize the best shots taken during the balloon classic).

The National Balloon Classic is held in early August, and admission for adults is $3.00 on weekends and $2.00 on weekdays, with children admitted for $1.00. Event passes, good for the entire ten-day event, are available at reduced rates. Visitors should be aware that weather conditions must be right before the balloons can fly. You may want to call ahead before you leave for the event. Phone (515) 961–8415 for more information.

If you can't make it to Indianola for the balloon classic, you can still visit its *National Balloon Museum.* The architecture of the $1 million structure is a reason to visit in itself. The motif suggests two inverted balloons, which are approached through entrance arches that accentuate the feeling of entering a balloon. The exterior is trimmed with blue and yellow ceramic tiles that recall the color, serenity, and gracefulness of balloons.

Inside you'll be able to view exhibits that chronicle more than 200 years of ballooning history. On display are balloon envelopes, inflators, gondolas, and other equipment used in both hot-air ballooning and gas ballooning. Other items include memorabilia associated with scientific, competitive, and record-setting flights, including trophies, photos, and an extensive pin collection. The gift shop is fun to browse through as well, with its displays of posters, calendars, mobiles, and mementos relating to ballooning.

The National Balloon Museum is located on Highway 65-69 on the north side of Indianola. It is open Monday through Friday from 9:00 A.M. to noon and from 1:00 to 4:00 P.M., Saturday from 10:00 A.M. to 4:00 P.M., and Sunday from 1:00 to 4:00 P.M. Admission is free. Call (515) 961–3714 for more information.

Balloons aren't the only reason to travel to Indianola during the summer. Another attraction is the

National Balloon Classic

Des Moines Metro Opera, the third largest summer opera festival in the country. Each season the Metro Opera presents three grand operas, all performed in English, at the Blank Performing Arts Theatre on the Simpson College campus in Indianola. The singers are drawn from the ranks of the country's top young performers and present both classic and contemporary operas. Since its founding in 1973, the Metro Opera has attracted national and international attention for the quality of its performances. Iowans are fortunate to have such a premier cultural resource in their midst.

The Des Moines Metro Opera presents three operas in repertory during June and July. Single or season tickets are available as well as weekend packages that include your tickets, comfortable lodging, and elegant dining. For more information call (515) 961–6221.

A wonderful place to visit or to stay while you're in Indianola is the *Summerset Inn and Winery,* billed as Iowa's newest winery. Owner Ron Mark founded the 7.5-acre Summerset Ridge vineyard in 1989. The vineyard produces 30,000 bottles of wine annually, pressed from ten varieties of French hybrid and American grapes. Pleasant walks, tours, and tastings are available April through December, Tuesday through Sunday from 11:00 A.M. to 6:00 P.M. The inn is a bed-and-breakfast with two suites and two rooms, charmingly decorated, and all have private baths. Prices range from $75 to $100. To get there, take Highway 65-69 5 miles north and turn right on Summerset Road. Go two miles to a "T" intersection and turn left. The entrance is on the left side of the road. For more information call (515) 961–3545.

Ethnic Enclaves

B egin your tour of this region of Iowa with a visit to Pella, a pristine small town that looks as if it could be the set for a Walt Disney movie. The name *Pella* means "city of refuge," for it was here that a small band of Hollanders came in 1847 to found a new city based on freedom. Today that Dutch heritage is visible throughout Pella, especially in the downtown, with its European-style architecture, a large windmill in the city square, lovely flower beds, and the Klokkenspel, a musical clock with figures that perform four times daily. The gift shops around the square stock imported Dutch treasures, and at Jaarsma's and Vander Ploeg Bakeries you can buy ethnic specialties that include the ever-popular Dutch letters, puff pastry baked in the shape of an *S* with an almond paste filling.

The best time to sample Pella's Dutch heritage is during its annual **Tulip Time** festival held on the second weekend in May. Each spring the town comes to life with hundreds of thousands of tulips, and local residents dress in colorful ethnic costumes as they host thousands of visitors from across the state. Highlights of the festival include folk dancing and crafts, parades, ethnic foods, and the crowning of the Tulip Queen. Another good time to visit is during the Christmas season, when *Sinterklaas* comes to help the town celebrate the season with traditions stretching back a hundred years.

The **Pella Historical Village** will give you the chance to learn more about the history that has shaped this town. It contains more than twenty buildings, some over a century old. Here you can see items that the early settlers brought from Holland, an outstanding collection of Delft pottery, folk costumes, Dutch dolls, Hindeloopen folk art painting, and a miniature Dutch village. The buildings include a log cabin, blacksmith shop, gristmill, potter shop, store, and church, as well as the boyhood home of gunslinger Wyatt Earp. Another historic site in town is the Scholte House on the north side of the town square, former home of Dominie H. P. Scholte, the leader of the group of immigrants who founded Pella.

The Pella Historical Village is located 1 block east of the town square on Franklin Street. It is open from April through December from 9:00 A.M. to 5:00 P.M. Monday through Saturday and January through March from 9:00 A.M. to 5:00 P.M. Monday through Friday. Admission is $5.00 for adults and $1.00 for children. Call (515) 628–2409 for more information.

Southwest of Pella lies the town of Knoxville, which calls itself the "Sprint Car Racing Capital of the World." Drivers have been racing sprint cars at the Marion County Fairgrounds for more than thirty years on a dirt track that is rated as one of the fastest in the nation. Weekly Saturday night racing programs are held from April through August each year, with the season culminating in the **National Sprint Car Championships,** an event that draws fans from around the nation and even a few foreign countries.

In honor of its racing status, Knoxville has built the **National Sprint Car Hall of Fame and Museum** at the Marion County Fairgrounds off Highway 14. The facility includes tributes to famous drivers and restored sprint cars as well as a gift shop and booths for race viewing. The museum (800–874–4488) is open daily, and the admission is $3.00 for adults and $2.00 for students.

Somehow sprint car racing and barbecue seem to go together, so once you leave Knoxville head to **Kin Folks Eatin' Place,** which is located in the tiny town of Attica, 9 miles south of Knoxville on Highway 5. This down-home restaurant offers some of the best barbecue in the state, including succulent ribs, beef brisket, ham, chicken, and turkey. For dessert try the homemade blackberry or peach cobbler with hand-cranked ice cream. Kin Folks Eatin' Place (515–943–2362) is open from 10:30 A.M. to 8:30 P.M. Sunday through Thursday and from 10:30 A.M. to 9:00 P.M. Friday and Saturday. Prices are inexpensive to moderate.

Southwest of Attica at the junction of Highways 34 and 65 lies the town of Lucas, home to the **John L. Lewis Museum of Mining and Labor.** The museum pays tribute to one of the most famous union leaders in America. Lewis was born in Lucas in 1880 and worked in the local coal mines before eventually becoming president of the United Mine Workers for forty years. The museum houses exhibits about his life, mining, and labor history.

The Lewis Museum (515–766–6831) is located 2 blocks north of Highway 34 and is open Tuesday through Saturday 8:00 A.M. to 3:00 P.M. from mid-April through mid-October. Admission is $1.00 for adults.

Just south of Lucas lies the major portion of the **Stephens State Forest,** one of the largest tracts of forest land in the state. The forest provides visitors with miles of trails that wind through deeply wooded country, as well as four stocked ponds and numerous campgrounds, three of which are set aside for equestrians.

Two other local park areas deserve mentioning. One is the **Pin Oak Marsh** (located on Highway 14 south of Chariton), a 160-acre wetland where nature lovers can spot a variety of wildlife like muskrat, mink, river otter, beaver, songbirds, shorebirds, and—during spring and fall migrations—ducks and geese. Bring your binoculars! Another favorite is the **Red Haw State Park,** known for its abundance of redbud trees. Visit this park the fourth Sunday in April for the Redbud Festival and Redbud Walk for an inspiring draught of beauty. This 420-acre park is located just one mile east of Chariton.

A visit to the town of Chariton is definitely in order while you're visiting this area. Take the time to observe the clock in the clock tower of the **Lucas County Court House**, a lovely sandstone-faced Romanesque-style building. It was purchased—the clock, that is—at the 1893 Chicago World's Fair. When the people of Lucas County go out to shop for souvenirs, they mean business! The sidewalk surrounding the court-house reinforces the time theme. In other words, look down as well as up if you want to know the time of day! Be sure to pay a visit to **Piper's Grocery Store.** Piper's is a quaint old-fashioned grocery store and a lot of fun to wander around. Don't forget to stop at the candy counter, where the store's rightfully famous homemade candy is displayed. People from across the country order boxes of these rich, delicious confections. I was told that even senators make their Christmas purchases here. Piper's is located at 901 Braden on the northeast corner of the town square. For more information call (515) 774–2131.

Wear off that toffee by taking a hike or a bike ride down the Cinder Path, the first "Rails-to-Trails" location in the state. The grade is even and the smooth cinder surface makes it easy to enjoy the 13½ miles winding from the west edge of Chariton southwest to Humeston.

Another interesting place to visit in Chariton is the **McNay Research Center** on Route 2, the largest working research farm operated by Iowa State University. Monday through Friday from 8:00 A.M. to 5:00 P.M., you can learn about the effects of various agricultural methods, as well as about sheep and cattle production.

Visit Borntreger's Quilt Shop, which sells hand-stitched quilts, located 8 miles south of town on Highway 14, or the Pine Craft Shop, 9 miles west on

County Road H50, specializing in handcrafted pine furniture and rugs. Neither shop has Sunday sales.

Southeast of Lucas lies the town of Allerton, home to the creatively named ***Inn of the Six-toed Cat.*** Housed in a turn-of-the-century structure built as a hotel, the old building served as a barber shop, feed storage building, and an apartment house before Bob Finley returned to his hometown to renovate and restore it as a first-class restaurant and inn. Since 1991 the inn has been delighting guests with gourmet dishes served amid gracious antiques and entertaining overnight visitors in its nine guest rooms, which include the Alice Roosevelt Room and an Almost Presidential Suite honoring William Jennings Bryan.

Named after a huge tomcat with six toes who wandered into the hotel during its restoration, the inn serves a menu of traditional Iowa favorites expertly prepared. Prices are moderate to expensive, and reservations are recommended.

The Inn of the Six-toed Cat is located at 220 North Central Avenue in downtown Allerton. It is open for dinner on Friday and Saturday from 5:00 to 10:00 P.M. and on Sunday from 11:30 A.M. to 4:30 P.M. For more information call (515) 873–4900.

West of Allerton you'll find the small town of Leon, site of the ***Great Cardboard Boat Regatta.*** The race is unlikely ever to rival the America's Cup, but in southern Iowa it draws several thousand people each year—no small feat for a town with only 2,000 citizens.

The rules of the regatta are simple, with all the cardboard boats divided into two categories: those propelled by canoe paddles, oars, or kayak paddles, and those propelled by all other forms of muscle-powered devices or by sails. Among the trophies awarded are the Pride of the Regatta (most creative design and best use of corrugated cardboard), Vogue Award (most attractive boat), Team Award (best-spirited and best-organized group), and the Titanic Award (most spectacular sinking). All the races are held on a 200-yard course on Little River Lake near Leon, and "instant" boat kits are available to those who lack the inspiration to create their own.

Even if you're not the nautical type, the regatta offers other activities that will keep you entertained—a flea market around the courthouse, bingo, children's games, water fights, musical entertainment, and an ice-cream social. The regatta is held during the first weekend in August each year. For more information call (515) 446–4991.

Fright Night in Tingley

Ten miles north of Mount Ayr lies the community of Tingley, a town that puts the "whee!" into Halloween. For more than fifty fears—oops! I mean years—Tingley has hosted Halloween Fun Night as a way for residents to enjoy their frights with safety. It was begun by the late Edith McIntosh, after some boys were hurt in a tractor accident on Halloween night in 1945. The festivities begin with a parade that includes floats and small mechanized vehicles as well as costumed singles, doubles, and triples, children and adults. Prizes are donated by the community. Business owners and residents get into the "spirit" of the thing, decorating their storefronts and yards with ghostly skill.

Your next stop in south central Iowa should be Lamoni, site of the *Liberty Hall Historic Center,* an eighteen-room Victorian house that was home to the Joseph Smith III family from 1881 to 1906. Joseph was the oldest son of the founder of Mormonism and the first president of the Reorganized Church of Jesus Christ of Latter Day Saints. His father, Joseph Smith Jr., was assassinated in 1844, and in the years that followed the church divided into two main groups. One group followed Brigham Young to Utah; and the other became known as the Reorganized Church and named Joseph Smith III its leader. In the 1880s they established Lamoni as their headquarters, and Smith's home became the busy center of the new church. Though the church later moved its headquarters to Independence, Missouri, Liberty Hall has been lovingly restored to its original decor and today tells the story of the Smith family and the Reorganized Church. Many of the items inside are the Smiths' original furnishings. Don't miss the fold-down bathtub! Also on the property is a schoolhouse built in 1875, plus a museum shop selling Victorian gifts.

The Liberty Hall Historic Center is located at 1300 West Main Street in Lamoni. Admission is free, and hours are Tuesday through Saturday from 10:00 A.M. to 4:00 P.M. Call (515) 784–6133 for more information.

While you're in Lamoni, take the time to browse through its thriving downtown, home to more than thirty antiques dealers. The area is also well known for its quilts. The first quilting guild in Iowa was founded in Lamoni more than one hundred years ago and is still going strong today. The guild holds a quilt show every other year at the Shaw Center on the local Graceland College campus. Another annual event is an antiques show and sale sponsored by the Lamoni Antique Association on the third weekend in April.

East of Lamoni on Highway 2 is the town of *Mount Ayr,* named after the birthplace of the Scottish poet Robert Burns. To celebrate their Scottish heritage, the residents of Mount Ayr hold "Ayr Days" every September. There are enough scones, Dundee cake, tea, and other amusements to delight everyone of all ages, Scottish or not. Make sure you sample a "bridie," a meat-and-vegetable-stuffed pastry. (And check out the corn mural in the post office!) Call the Ringgold County Tourism Board for more information at (515) 464–3704.

Continue north on Highway 169 to Highway 34 and the town of Afton (that's right—Robert Burns again). Stop in at the **Blue Highway Bakery Café,** located on the south side of the square. Owners Peggy and Rob Dietrich have done a wonderful job of renovating a 115-year-old hardware store into an appealing cafe with delicious home-cooked food. They are reputed to have the best coconut cream pie in the state, but all of their pies are great. A restored brick wall, 14-foot ceilings, prints by regional artists like Grant Wood and Marvin Cone, and huge light-gathering windows combine to make this a memorable place to stop for lunch. The Blue Highway (515–347–5669) is open for lunch Monday through Saturday and on Friday evenings for pan-fried chicken.

Mount Pisgah

*O*ddly enough, I visited the **Mount Pisgah Mormon National Monument** *in February at the same time of the year, apparently, as Mormon leader Parley Pratt led his followers here in the middle of the nineteenth century. Although the ground was thawing, it was a deeply chilling day and I must have felt as miserable as they did. And like them, I turned again and looked out over the valleys and saw what a beautiful place this must be at any other time of the year.*

The Mormon pioneers settled here, cleared thousands of acres, and dwelled in caves as well as log cabins, hoping for the best. Between 300 and 800 of them died in their struggle for adequate food and shelter. Mount Pisgah lasted as a community, however, for six years, from 1846 to 1852, and served as a stopping point for other Mormons on their westward journey to Utah. At

one point they were visited by the Potawatomi chief Pied Riche, whose people had been driven here from Michigan, and who felt sympathy for the Mormons because they had also been driven from their homes. He is reported to have said to them, "We must help one another, and the Great Spirit will help us both. Because one suffers and does not deserve it is no reason he shall suffer always. We may live to see it right yet. If we do not, our children will." Let us hope he was right.

Mount Pisgah is quite definitely off the beaten path. If you follow Highway 169 north of Highway 34, it is approximately four miles south of Lorimor. There are signs at all the right places in the road, just follow them. Right before you get there you will think you've accidentally stumbled onto private land and will be tempted to turn around. Don't, you're almost there.

The last stop to make in this region is Creston, west of Afton on Highway 34. Creston was founded in 1868 as a railroad town and is the county seat of Union County. Whatever you do, don't miss the ***C. B. & Q. Railroad Depot*** located between Union and Adams Streets. This is a real beauty, currently undergoing restoration, and it houses a small display of railroad artifacts inside. View it from the outside and be prepared to gasp for breath when you go inside—the restoration has been very simple and restrained. You can almost hear old steam engines chugging into town and whistles screeching in the distance. You might even feel that if your eyes were just quick enough you could catch a glimpse of the townsfolk and farmers of a hundred years ago. Congratulations, Creston! You've got a winner here!

Not quite as breathtaking but equally charming is the ***Frank Phillips Tourism and Information Center*** at 636 New York Avenue. Housed in a 1931 Phillips 66 gasoline station, it not only serves as a tourism center but also commemorates Frank Phillips, an erstwhile Creston resident and barber who, with his brother, founded the Phillips Petroleum Corporation in 1917. This is a great place to stop, gather your bearings, and plan your next stops.

PLACES TO STAY IN BRIDGES COUNTRY

GRINNELL
Best Western,
2210 West Street South,
(515) 236–6616,
$39–$75

ALTOONA
Settle Inn,
2101 Adventureland Drive,
(888) 222–8224,
(515) 967–7888,
$55–$125

PRAIRIE CITY
The Country Connection,
9737 West Ninety-third
Street, (515) 994–2023,
$50–$60

DES MOINES
Savery Hotel and Spa,
401 Locust Street,
(800) 798–2151,
(515) 244–2151,
$95–$125

WEST DES MOINES
Comfort Suites,
11167 Hickman Road,
(800) 395–7675,
(515) 276–1126,
$80–$200

INDIANOLA
Apple Tree Inn,
Highway 65-69 North,
(800) 961–0551,
(515) 961–0551,
$40–$60

PELLA
Dutch Mill Inn,
205 Oskaloosa Street,
(800) 647–6684,
(515) 628–1060,
$35–$75

CHARITON
Lake Vista Motel Suites,
Highway 34,
(888) 774–8421,
(515) 774–8421,
$25–$60

CRESTON
Berning Motor Inn,
301 West Adams Street,
(515) 782–7001,
$35

PLACES TO EAT IN BRIDGES COUNTRY

NEWTON
Hummingbird's,
I–80 at Highway 14,
(515) 792–7722

DES MOINES
Java Joe's,
214 Fourth Street,
(515) 288–5282

A Dong Restaurant,
1905 Cottage Grove,
(515) 284–5632

Stella's Blue Sky Diner,
400 Locust Street,
(515) 246–1953

Babe's,
417 Sixth Avenue,
(515) 244–9319

OSCEOLA
Redman's Pizza and
Steak House,
123 South Main,
(515) 342–6116

AFTON
Knotty Pine,
Highway 30,
(515) 347–5626

Fertile Plains

The rich soil of north central Iowa produces some of the nation's most bountiful harvests, on land that was once tall-grass prairie. In this region you'll find the fascinating railroad history of Boone County, the beauty of Clear Lake, and a host of other treasures that celebrate Iowa's rich past and vibrant present. From the Mesquakie Indian Pow Wow to the Surf Ballroom where the memory of Buddy Holly is celebrated, north central Iowa offers an eclectic range of attractions.

Diverse Diversions

Begin your tour of this region of Iowa with a visit to the only Indian settlement in the state. The word *settlement* (rather than *reservation*) is important, because the land here was purchased by the Mesquakie Indians, not set aside for them by the federal government. Using money from the sale of furs and ponies, the Mesquakie (also known as the Sac and Fox tribe) first bought eighty acres of land here in 1857. In the following years more land was purchased with tribal funds, and today the Mesquakie own nearly 3,500 acres of timberland and river bottom along the Iowa River in Tama County.

The best time to visit the settlement is during the **Mesquakie Indian Pow Wow,** which is held each year on the second weekend in August. This four-day celebration honors the traditional ways of the Mesquakie people, with various arts, crafts, and exhibits on display, plus old-time foods and authentic costumed dancing. The Pow Wow has its origin in the Green Corn Dance, a religious and social event that was held each year at harvest time. The fresh corn was cooked for feasting, and the bounty of the land was celebrated with dancing, games, and socializing. Around the turn of the century, more and more white visitors began attending the ceremonies, and in 1913 the festival gained its official name of the Mesquakie Indian Pow Wow.

Today the Mesquakie no longer live in wickiups, and the corn harvest is done by machine, but the traditions of the Pow Wow remain strong. The

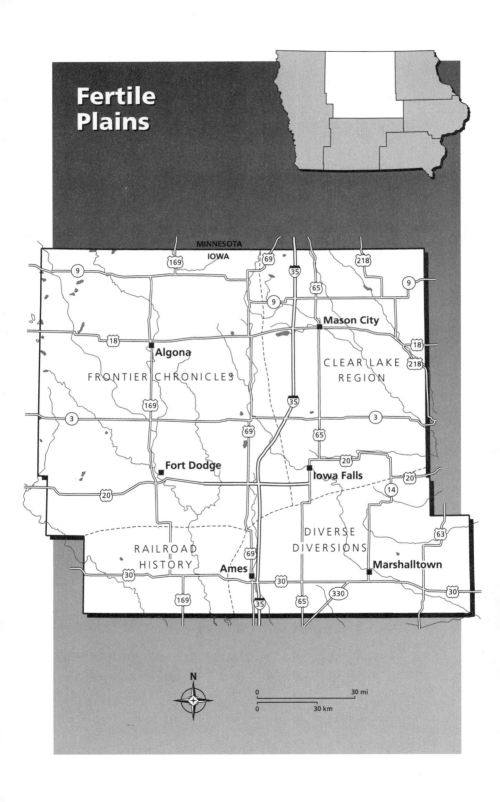

Fertile Plains

MINNESOTA

IOWA

169

69

218

9

65

9

Mason City

18

Algona

18

218

FRONTIER CHRONICLES

CLEAR LAKE REGION

169

3

35

3

69

65

Fort Dodge

20

Iowa Falls

20

20

14

63

RAILROAD HISTORY

DIVERSE DIVERSIONS

Marshalltown

30

169

Ames

30

35

65

330

30

N

0   30 mi

0   30 km

AUTHOR'S FAVORITES - FERTILE PLAINS

Big Treehouse

Watson's Grocery

Surf Ballroom

Floyd County
Historical Museum

Story City Carousel

Van Horn's Antique
Truck Museum

National Hobo Convention

Community Orchard

Union Slough
Wildlife Refuge

Mesquakie Indian
Pow Wow

center of the festival is dancing, with members from the local tribe (and often guests from other parts of the country) performing dances that have been handed down for generations. The Buffalo Head Dance, for example, honors the magnificent beast that has played a central role in Indian culture and life, and the Swan Dance mimics the beautiful, rhythmical movements of a swan in the water. For the Traditional Women's Dance, the Mesquakie women don elaborately decorated dresses. The Pipe Dance is presented to honor distinguished visitors and warriors, and the Harvest of Bean Dance is performed by young girls and boys to thank the Great Spirit for the abundance of food for the coming winter.

The Mesquakie Indian Pow Wow is held each August at the Indian settlement 3 miles west of the town of Tama. For more information call (515) 484–4678.

At any time of the year you can visit the *Mesquakie Bingo and Casino,* which operates twenty-four hours daily. Call (800) 728–4283 for information.

You can learn more about the Mesquakie Indians and the history of the area at the *Tama County Historical Museum* at 200 North Broadway in Toledo. The building was built in 1869 and served as the county jail until 1970. Today it houses pioneer tools and utensils, antique toys, musical instruments, furniture, and clothing, plus a display of Mesquakie Indian artifacts.

And while you're in the area, drive to the neighboring town of Tama to see the *Lincoln Highway Bridge* on East Fifth Street near Highway 30. The bridge was built in 1915 to promote Tama as an oasis along the new transcontinental route of the Lincoln Highway (at that time, most of the highway was dirt). The bridge has a decorative railing that spells LINCOLN HIGHWAY, and is listed on the National Register of Historic Places. The roadside park next to the bridge makes this a pleasant stop.

Next head west to Marshalltown, home of *Stone's Restaurant.* The diner is an Iowa landmark with a history that goes back to 1887, when Ebson Weed Stone, whose parents came to Iowa in a covered wagon, opened the restaurant in a former saloon that still had bullet holes in the wall. Stone's moved to its present location in 1910, a site near the railroad tracks that made it a tempting stop for travelers and train workers. Crews on the railroad used to telegraph ahead to place their orders so that their meals would be ready when they arrived.

Just as it was back then, Stone's is the place to go for homemade, stick-to-your-ribs meals. On its menu are staples like meatloaf, chicken and noodles, and beef heart with dressing. Save room for dessert, however, for Stone's is rightly famous for its feather-light, mile-high lemon chiffon pie. Visitors from across the country periodically show up on the restaurant's doorstep to sample the pie's tartness, lured by a reputation that has spread far and wide. (When a local dentist a few years ago crossed the border into Mexico, for instance, the border patrolman looked at his travel documents and inquired, "You're from Marshalltown? Isn't that where they have the restaurant with the mile-high lemon chiffon pie?")

Stone's Restaurant is located at 507 South Third Avenue (under the viaduct) in Marshalltown. It is open Monday through Saturday from 11:00 A.M. to 9:00 P.M. and on Sunday from 11:00 A.M. to 3:00 P.M. Lunches are inexpensive; dinners are moderate to expensive. For reservations or more information, call (515) 753–3626.

Another Marshalltown area attraction is the *Big Treehouse,* which is guaranteed to captivate anyone who remembers the joy of perching in a tree as a child. Few of us had access to a treehouse like this, however; this ten-level structure has electricity, running water, piped-in music, and other homey touches. You'll find the Big Treehouse at 2370-A Shady Oaks Road near Marshalltown. Call (515) 752–2946 to schedule an appointment between Memorial Day and Labor Day. A $1.00 donation per visitor is requested.

South of Marshalltown in the small town of Haverhill you'll find the *Edel Blacksmith Shop.* The shop was operated by German immigrant Matthew Edel between 1882 and 1940 and provides a vivid picture of the days before mechanized farming changed agriculture. Here Edel shoed horses, repaired tools and wagons, and manufactured implements like garden hoes and wedge makers. Edel was also an inventor who took out patents on such inventions as a perfection wedge cutter and cattle de-horner. Adjacent to the blacksmith shop is a two-story house constructed in the early 1880s, plus a summer kitchen where food was prepared during the warm months. Like the shop itself, they have been left largely unaltered and help complete the picture of what the life of a skilled craftsman was like some hundred years ago.

The Edel Blacksmith Shop (515–479–3299) is open daily from noon to 4:00 P.M. Memorial Day through Labor Day.

FERTILE PLAINS

FESTIVALS IN FERTILE PLAINS

BRR (Bike Ride to Rippey),
Perry, first Saturday in
February, (515) 465–4601

*North Iowa Blue
Grass Festival,*
Mason City, second weekend
in May

Floyd County Fair,
Charles City, third week in
July, (515) 228–1453

Lakefest,
Clear Lake, fourth weekend
in July, (515) 357–2159

Midwest Polka Fest,
Humboldt, Labor Day
Weekend, (515) 332–2539

Oktoberfest,
Hampton, first Saturday in
October, (515) 456–5668

Christmas Stroll,
Stanhope, first week of
December, (515) 626–3491

Northwest of Haverhill lies the town of State Center, which prides itself on being the Rose Capital of Iowa. During the summer the town maintains a lovely rose garden at Third Avenue SE and Third Street SE, and each year on the third weekend in June, State Center hosts a ***Rose Festival.***

After strolling through State Center's rose garden, visit ***Watson's Grocery*** on Main Street, a general store that looks as if it hasn't changed a bit since 1920. The store was built more than one hundred years ago and was operated as an old-fashioned grocery by Ralph Watson for many years until his death in 1979. At that time his widow locked its doors, and the building remained closed until she died in 1989 and her heirs put the property up for sale. Local townspeople approached the heirs with the idea of turning the store into a museum, but they refused to sell it to them. Instead they scheduled an auction to sell the store and all its contents.

But the people of State Center didn't give up so easily. A fund-raising drive was held, and more than $15,000 in pledges poured in. On the day of the auction, State Center citizens crowded into the little store and emerged successful at the end of the bidding. (When one of the other bidders said that he wanted to use the store as a movie set, the locals told him that they'd let him make his movie, but that they wanted the store.) After the auction came the hard part. Volunteers cleaned, scraped, painted, and refinished the dusty and dirty interior, decorating it with old-time advertising signs and refurbishing it with antique equipment and fixtures.

Today the grocery's solid oak counters and hardwood floors gleam once again, just as they did many years ago. Stop by the store and you can buy antique items, locally made products, old-fashioned candy, memorabilia, and reproductions of the old Watson's aprons.

Watson's Grocery in State Center is open from 1:00 to 4:00 P.M. on weekends May through Labor Day (and by appointment). For more information call (515) 483–2458.

Northwest of State Center, near I–35, lies the town of Story City, which is home to the only municipally owned carousel in the state. Built in 1913 the *Story City Carousel* first came to the town when its Iowa Falls owner agreed to let Story City use it for its Fourth of July celebrations. In 1938 the town purchased the merry-go-round, which was run each summer until 1979 when it had become too dilapidated to use.

Instead of abandoning the carousel, however, the town decided to save it, raising the $140,000 needed to refurbish and repair it. A local antiques store and refinishing business took on the laborious task, and in 1982 the gleaming, revitalized machine was once again offering rides in its new home, a pavilion located in the town's North Park.

You can sample the nostalgic joys of a ride on the Story City carousel for just $1.00. The merry-go-round is open from Memorial Day through Labor Day and is located in North Park on Broad Street. The carousel opens at noon daily; closing hours vary. For more information call (515) 733–4214.

After you ride the carousel, stop by South Park for a pleasant walk across the swinging bridge. The bridge was constructed in the early 1930s under President Franklin Roosevelt's WPA program and the park is a delightful place for a picnic lunch.

Also in Story City is the *Factory Stores of America Outlet Mall,* where you can find discounts on brand-name merchandise such as Bass shoes and Danskin sportswear. The mall is located off I–35 at exit 124.

From Story City travel south on Highway 69 until you reach Ames, home to *Iowa State University.* ISU is one of the oldest land-grant institutions in the country and is a worldwide pioneer in the establishment of agricultural studies at the college level. Some 26,000 students are enrolled here in a wide variety of undergraduate and graduate programs. The campus itself is lovely and full of green areas, with historical markers scattered throughout so that visitors can take their own self-guided tours (ask for a map at the Memorial Union on the south side of the campus). On your tour, stop by the library to see its large Grant Wood murals, and notice the sculptures by artist Christian Petersen that are located throughout the campus.

A major attraction on the Iowa State campus are the *Reiman Gardens.* The $2 million horticulture display area covers seven acres south of Cyclone Stadium on Elwood Drive and includes an herb garden, rose garden, wetlands garden, and a campanile garden, which features a 50-foot wind chime. The gardens are a beautiful place to stroll, and garden tours are also offered. Call (515) 294–2710 for information.

Two other sites should be part of your Iowa State tour. One is the **Brunnier Gallery and Museum** in the Scheman Building of the Iowa State Center, where you can view a fine collection of decorative arts as well as traveling exhibitions. Also worth a visit is the **Farmhouse Museum,** the oldest building on campus and a fully restored National Historic Landmark that has been furnished to reflect the 1860–1910 period. Located on Knoll Road, the museum is open on Tuesday, Thursday, and Sunday afternoons from noon to 4:00 P.M. For more information on Iowa State University and its attractions and events, call (515) 294–4111.

Before you leave Ames, take some time to explore the rest of the city. Several shopping areas are likely to tempt your pocketbook. Downtown Ames has more than fifty specialty shops, including the Octagon Center for the Arts, a gallery and arts and crafts shop with a wide selection of jewelry, pottery, and other works of art. It's located at Fifth and Douglas. Other unique shops can be found at Shoppes on Grand, an 1890 home filled with stores and a tearoom. Look for it at Sixth Street and Grand Avenue. Campustown, an area within walking distance of the university, also has a variety of shops and restaurants.

No visit to Ames would be complete without a stop at **Hickory Park Restaurant.** To find it, follow the crowds: On any given night it seems as though half the city is dining here. That means that you may have to wait a while to be seated, but your patience will be amply rewarded. Hickory Park serves succulent and tender barbecued meats, the kind that fall off the bone with a nudge and melt with a tang in your mouth. Its specialty is huge slabs of pork ribs, but its smoked chicken and beef ribs also have devoted followings. Each dinner comes with your choice of two side orders, which include smoked baked beans, potato, coleslaw, applesauce, and macaroni salad. For dessert try one of Hickory Park's sinfully rich ice-cream treats. Regulars agree that a chocolate mint marvel sundae is the perfect ending to a meal of barbecued ribs.

As you might expect in a college town, the atmosphere here is casual and friendly. Small wooden booths fill the restaurant's interconnected dining rooms, each with a tin-plate ceiling and vintage photographs and signs on the walls.

Hickory Park Restaurant is located at 121 South Sixteenth Street, near the Duff Avenue exit on Highway 30. Lunches are inexpensive; dinners are inexpensive to moderate. Hickory Park is open daily from 11:00 A.M. to 9:00 P.M. Call (515) 232–8940 for more information.

Another great place to go for a meal is **Ken's Cafe and Grill** at 212 Main Street. Owner Ken Dunn has gone out of his way to offer his patrons a unique dining experience. The walls of the restaurant are spatter-painted, the plates and glasses specially made. There is a wide variety of dishes to choose from, like antelope, ostrich, and quail (the ostrich and quail are raised right here in Iowa). Desserts are elegant and beautifully presented. Ken calls his menu "eclectic new American" and it changes regularly to include different dishes, as well as the freshest seasonal ingredients. Reservations for dinner are recommended. Ken's is also open for lunch, Sunday brunch, and afternoons for coffee. Call (515) 232–2225 for serving hours and to make reservations.

Overnight visitors to Ames should make reservations at the **Iowa House,** a stately 1928 home adjacent to the Iowa State campus. The bed-and-breakfast was once a fraternity house but has now been completely refurbished into an elegantly simple establishment that caters to many of Iowa State's international visitors. During your stay here you're likely to share breakfast conversation with travelers from around the world, from Russia and the Czech Republic to Nigeria and Costa Rica. Owners Susan and Ken Lassila have restored the home in the Arts and Crafts style and filled it with lovely mission-style antiques, and each morning they serve a European-style breakfast. The Iowa House (515–292–8870) is at 138 Gray Avenue, and rates for its eleven rooms range from $58 to $70 per night.

Railroad History

For more than a hundred years, scenic Boone County has been the railroad center of Iowa. At one time this was a bustling coal-mining region, with the railroads serving as a lifeline to the rest of the world. That heritage lives on today in the **Boone and Scenic Valley Railroad,** an excursion train based in the town of Boone that travels through some of the state's most spectacular scenery. The railroad is operated by the Boone Railroad Historical Society and offers a 14-mile trip through the Des Moines River Valley from Boone to Fraser, passing through densely forested bluffs and valleys.

The many train enthusiasts in Boone are especially excited about the newest addition to their railroad, a 116-ton Chinese steam locomotive. The saga of the locomotive began in 1988, when Boone resident Mel Hanson saw a picture of a Chinese steam engine in a *National Geographic* article. Society members called the Chinese Embassy to inquire about buying such an engine and eventually arranged to purchase for

$355,000 the last steam locomotive to be built by the Datong Locomotive Works, the last factory in China to build the big steam-powered engines. Then came the tricky part—figuring out how to get the huge engine from China to Boone. Political turmoil in China, a long journey by ship across the ocean, and a major accident in California when the train was unloaded all delayed the delivery of the locomotive, but it finally arrived in Boone in December 1989. Emblazoned on its front in Chinese characters was the message, "The end of a great Chinese era, the beginning of an American dream." (A Chinese crew arrived as well to explain the intricacies of the train to local engineers.)

Rides on the Boone Railroad last about two hours and are offered from Memorial Day weekend through the end of October. The train depot is located at Eleventh and Division Streets in Boone (go north on Story Street through the business district to Tenth or Eleventh Street, then west for 6 blocks). Call (800) 626–0319 for schedules and fares.

A good time to visit Boone is during its annual *Pufferbilly Days.* Held on the first weekend after Labor Day, Pufferbilly Days is a celebration of the town's railroading heritage and a community-wide festival featuring train rides, a parade, antique-car show, live entertainment, a carnival, sports events, an arts festival, and model train displays. Pufferbilly Days has become one of the largest festivals in the state, with new attractions added every year. For more information call the Boone Chamber of Commerce at (515) 432–3342.

Another piece of Boone County railroad history is preserved at the *Kate Shelley High Bridge* northwest of Boone, and the *Kate Shelley Memorial Park and Railroad Museum* in Moingona. The two sites are named in honor of a local girl who became a heroine at the tender age of fifteen. In a terrible storm the night of July 6, 1881, Kate crawled across a railroad bridge longer than the length of two football fields to warn an oncoming passenger train of a trestle washout near her home. Two crewmen had already died when a locomotive had crashed at the site, and Kate is credited with saving the lives of everyone on the oncoming passenger train. Kate's bravery did not go unrewarded: As word of her adventure spread, the young woman became a national heroine. A Chicago newspaper raised funds to pay off the mortgage on her family home, and a well-known temperance leader of the day arranged to send the girl to college.

In 1901 the North Western Railroad completed the world's longest and highest double-track railroad bridge over the Des Moines River, a marvel of nineteenth-century engineering skill (the bridge is now listed on the National Register of Historic Places). The span was christened the Kate Shelley High Bridge in honor of the local heroine, and in 1903 Kate was named the North Western station agent in Moingona. She held the position until shortly before her death in 1912. Later the Boone County Historical Society bought the depot and opened it as a museum, re-creating a typical passenger station of the late nineteenth century, complete with a period waiting-room bench, potbellied stove, ticket window, telegraph, and a wide variety of railroad memorabilia. A Rock Island Rocket passenger car parked on the tracks nearby is used as a theater in which a tape-slide presentation of the Kate Shelley story is given.

The Kate Shelley Museum is located in the small town of Moingona 5 miles southwest of Boone and is open Sunday from 1:00 to 5:00 P.M. from June through October. The Kate Shelley High Bridge is located 3 miles northwest of Boone. For information on either the museum or the bridge, call the Boone Chamber of Commerce at (515) 432–3342.

Railroads are not the only attraction in Boone County. The town of Boone is also proud of its status as the birthplace of Mamie Eisenhower, wife of the thirty-fourth president of the United States. You can learn about her life and times at the *Mamie Doud Eisenhower Birthplace,* a modest frame house where she was born in 1896. The home had been privately owned for many years before a town committee was formed in the 1970s to buy and restore it. After five years of work, the birthplace was dedicated in 1980. Though Mamie was originally against the idea of saving the house (out of modesty, it was thought), she later donated a number of items to the site. Today it is one of only a few first ladies' birthplaces that have been preserved.

Though Mamie returned to Boone a number of times as an adult, her stay here as a child was brief. Her father, John Sheldon Doud, came to Boone in the early 1890s and established a meat-packing company with his father. In 1897, one year after Mamie's birth, the family moved to Cedar Rapids and a few years later, to Colorado. Mamie met her future husband in 1915 on a vacation in San Antonio, Texas, and began living the traveling life of an Army officer's wife. Later, after eight years in the White House, Ike and Mamie retired to the farm home they had purchased in Gettysburg, Pennsylvania—the first and only home they had ever owned. After Ike's death in 1969, Mamie continued living on the farm until shortly before her death in 1979.

Visit the birthplace today and you'll gain more insight into the life of the first lady and her husband. The home has been restored to the 1890s period and contains many furnishings that were donated by Mamie's family. The master bedroom has its original furniture, including the bed in which Mamie was born, and there is also a library of Eisenhower-related materials.

The Mamie Doud Eisenhower Birthplace is located at 709 Carroll Street in Boone. Hours are from 1:00 to 5:00 P.M. Tuesday through Sunday during April

Mamie Doud Eisenhower Birthplace

and May and from 10:00 A.M. to 5:00 P.M. daily from June through October. Admission is $3.00 for adults and $1.00 for children. For more information call (515) 432–1896.

For a peaceful place to recover from all your sightseeing, visit the *Iowa Arboretum,* southeast of Boone near the town of Luther. The arboretum is a new educational facility unlike any other in Iowa. Located on 340 acres in rural Boone county, it contains hundreds of species of trees, shrubs, and flowers in a quiet, scenic setting. Its main goal is to help Iowans appreciate and better understand plant life. Here you can learn which plants are best adapted to the soils and climate of Iowa and how to use these plants properly for landscaping, gardening, conservation, and other purposes. The arboretum also serves as an outdoor laboratory for testing the hardiness and adaptability of newly introduced plants and as a center for the preservation of rare and endangered plant species.

A vital part of the arboretum is its forty-acre Library of Living Plants, where you can view varieties of cultivated trees, shrubs, and flowers. Plants with similar uses are grouped together—small shade trees are located in one area, for example, and trees useful for windbreaks in another. With this arrangement, you can quickly "look up" the best plant for your needs.

The arboretum also contains more than 300 acres of forest, prairie, and meadow, with trails that pass by scenic overlooks, deep ravines, and streams. Labels identify the native trees, shrubs, and wildflowers, and illustrated brochures will help you plan your own self-guided tour. Along the way you're likely to see some of the deer, birds, and wild turkeys that make their home here. Guided tours and educational programs are also offered.

The Iowa Arboretum is open every day of the year from sunrise to sunset; admission is $2.00 for adults. To arrange a guided tour, call (515) 795–3216. The arboretum is located about 30 miles northwest of Des Moines, 2½ miles west of the town of Luther on County Road E-57.

West of Boone lies the town of Jefferson, where you can pay a visit to the *Mahanay Bell Tower,* a 162-foot structure topped by fourteen cast bells. Take the elevator to the observation platform and you can see a view of seven counties. The tower was built with funds from the estate of William and Dora Mahanay, both residents of Jefferson. William was a sales representative for a surgical instrument company as well as the owner of a substantial amount of Green County farmland. When he died, he specified that his estate be used for the construction of a tower on the southwest corner of the courthouse square.

The bells on top of the tower were made and installed by a Chicago company. The largest, middle C, weighs 4,700 pounds and is 5 feet in diameter. The smallest is G, which weighs only 198 pounds. Concerts are played several times each day, as Mr. Mahanay wished.

Traveling the Lincoln Highway

*I*f you are traveling across the state, the route of the first transcontinental highway, the old **Lincoln Highway,** would be a grand route to take. Funded by private industry and wealthy entrepreneurs, the Lincoln Highway spanned the country from Times Square to San Francisco, crossing twelve states and leading right through the heart of Iowa, from Clinton to Council Bluffs. The original idea for this "Coast to Coast Rock Highway," as it was originally called, belonged to Carl Fisher, "an enthusiastic motorist," and the founder of the Indianapolis Speedway. Begun in 1913, the route has had many changes through the course of the years but what remains of it now roughly follows U.S. Highway 30. In this section of the state you can drive from Tama in the east to Ogden in the west. Be on the lookout for old gas stations, cafes, bridges, and buildings. The Lincoln Highway originally passed through forty-nine towns; in forty-four of them it went right down Main Street. Today you would have to make significant detours to visit all of these towns, but if you've got the time, what an adventure it would be! The Lincoln Highway's headquarters are located in Ogden. For more information on the Iowa portion of the Lincoln Highway call (515) 275–4966.

The Mahanay Tower is located on the downtown square in Jefferson (it's difficult to miss) and is open to the public from Memorial Day to Labor Day from 11:00 A.M. to 4:00 P.M. daily. In April, May, September, and October it is open on weekends, weather permitting. Admission is $1.00 for adults, 50 cents for children.

Also in Jefferson is the *Telephone Museum,* housing a collection of antique telephone equipment. It's located 1 block east of Highway 4 at 105 West Harrison Street and is open Monday through Friday from 9:00 A.M. to 5:00 P.M. On the north side of the town square, you'll find the Greene County Historical Society Museum, with displays of local history and artifacts. Call (515) 386–4141 for more information.

Mahanay Bell Tower

Frontier Chronicles

egin your tour of this region of the state in Fort Dodge. The city is the county seat of Webster County—though if a certain wrestling match in 1856 had turned out differently, Fort Dodge's destiny may have followed another path.

The story begins when John F. Duncombe, described in a newspaper of the day as "an engine in pants," arrived in Fort Dodge in 1855. At that time Fort Dodge was only a tiny settlement in contrast to the nearby thriving town of Homer. Duncombe, however, spearheaded an effort to have Fort Dodge named as the county seat. The citizens of Homer naturally objected, and an election was held to determine which town would get the coveted distinction. When the votes were counted, it was discovered that both sides had stuffed the ballot box—but the citizens of Fort Dodge were more successful in their voting fraud, as their town came out the winner. John D. Maxwell, the leader of the Homer faction, was furious. Then someone made the

Did You Know?

Prior to the twentieth century 85 percent of Iowa was prairie. An active effort is being made to restore native prairie plants to Iowa's highways and roadsides. Call (515) 239–1768 for an informative and colorful brochure of Iowa's roadside flowering plants and grasses.

Fort Dodge has been known as "Gypsum City" since 1872 and even now has four large gypsum plants.

suggestion that Maxwell and Duncombe settle the issue with a wrestling match. For an hour the two battled it out in Homer's public square in front of a large crowd. Duncombe was declared the winner and Fort Dodge was named the county seat and as a result became the leading commercial center in the area. Fort Dodge has good reason to be grateful for the athletic prowess of John F. Duncombe.

Fort Dodge's history has many more colorful episodes, and the best place to learn about them is at the city's *Fort Museum.* The site is a re-creation of Fort Williams, a garrison built in 1862 to protect local residents from Indian raids. The fort is considered one of the finest pioneer museums in the Midwest and contains a complete frontier village with stockade, blockhouse, soldiers' quarters, general store, blacksmith shop, one-room school, log chapel, and drugstore, all with period furnishings. Also on display are exhibits on military and pioneer history, plus the National Museum of Veterinary Medicine, the first of its kind in the country.

Various special events are held at the Fort Museum, including *Frontier Days* on the first weekend in June. This citywide celebration of Fort Dodge's past features a parade, Buckskinner's Rendezvous, live entertainment, historic home tours, and much more.

The Fort Museum is located ¼ mile east of the junction of Highways 169 and 20. It is open from May through October from 9:00 A.M. to 6:00 P.M. daily. Admission is $4.00 for adults, $2.00 for children. For more information call (515) 573–4231.

Also in Fort Dodge is the *Blanden Memorial Art Museum,* the first permanent art facility in the state of Iowa. You're likely to be surprised by the remarkable diversity and quality of its collection, which includes such treasures as Chagall's *The Fantastic Horsecart* (one of the painter's personal favorites), Miró's *The Cry of the Gazelle at Dawn,* and Maurice Prendergast's *Central Park,* plus bronzes by Henry Moore, a Calder mobile, and a collection of non-Western art highlighted by Asian art from the seventeenth through nineteenth centuries, pre-Columbian art, and tribal objects from North America and Africa. The museum also sponsors traveling exhibits and art classes for both adults and children.

The museum was founded in 1930, a gift to the community from former Fort Dodge mayor Charles Granger Blanden in memory of his wife. Since then other benefactors have donated money and works of art to the museum, including the well-known Philadelphia art collector Albert Barnes.

The Blanden Art Museum is located at 920 Third Avenue South in Fort Dodge. It is open on Tuesday, Wednesday, and Friday from 10:00 A.M. to 5:00 P.M., on Thursday from 10:00 A.M. to 8:30 P.M., and on Saturday and Sunday from 1:00 to 5:00 P.M. Admission is free. For more information call (515) 573–2316.

South of Fort Dodge at the intersection of Highways 169 and 175 is the **Blue Willow Tea Room** an oasis of gentility and fine food located on a farm ½ mile east of the town of Harcourt. The restaurant has become a

Fee, fi, fo, fum!

*D*id you know you were in the land of giants? One of the great American hoaxes had its origin in a great lump of Fort Dodge gypsum. Listening to a sermon in church while visiting in Ackley, George Hull, a native New Yorker, came up with the idea of staging a little resurrection of his own. Somehow he managed to ship a chunk (7,000 pounds' worth!) of Fort Dodge gypsum to Chicago. There, while Hull posed, a sculptor carved the rock into the figure of a 10-foot-tall man. Hull, his cousin, and the sculptor worked with wooden mallets and steel needles to give the giant an ancient and weathered "faux-cade." Then, using a circuitous route, the giant was shipped on to New York and given a midnight burial in a field on the cousin's farm near Cardiff. About a year later, when some men were digging a well on the farm—surprise!—a huge stone foot appeared, then a leg, then two legs, and soon they had unearthed an amazing stonelike giant! Hull and his cousin didn't let the grass grow under their feet: They put up a fence, erected a tent, charged a ten-cent admission, and went into business. Scientists, scholars, and an Indian medicine man visited the Cardiff giant; theories were advanced and some suspicions were raised. In the meantime, dimes kept rolling in. Soon they had made more than $20,000! Unfortunately (at least for the cousins) one visitor happened to be Galusha Parsons, a lawyer from Fort Dodge. And he must have known his gypsum because he recognized in the form of the giant the huge rock that had been shipped out of his hometown a year earlier. The jig was up and Hull, at last, revealed the true origins of the colossal man. But you will have to go to New York to see this sleeping giant lie. He is at rest in the Farmers' Museum in Cooperstown.

landmark for discriminating travelers, who have been known to drive 100 miles or more just for a taste of its famous chicken salad.

Owned by Connie and Rollie Gustafson, the Blue Willow serves a varying selection of three or four entrees each day and is particularly well known for its High Tea, served at 2:30 P.M. by reservation only. Don't pass up trying one of the tearoom's rich desserts, each prepared from scratch like all the menu items here. Then take a stroll through the adjacent Country Treasures Gift Shoppe, which sells an eclectic variety of merchandise.

The Blue Willow Tea Room (515–354–5295) is open from 9:00 A.M. to 4:00 P.M. Monday through Saturday, with lunch served from 11:00 A.M. to 1:00 P.M. Reservations are recommended. Entrees are moderate.

Visit Dolliver Memorial State Park, south of Fort Dodge, for a picturesque view of this part of the state. The Des Moines River and Prairie Creek flow through the park, embellished by canyons, bluffs, and even Indian mounds. Cabins, campsites, and picnic shelters are available.

East of Harcourt, about 1 mile north of Stratford, is **Hook's Point Country Inn.** Owners Marvin and Mary Jo Johnson have two rooms and one suite open for guests in their 1904 farmhouse, complete with feather beds! If you can't spend the night, try one of the wonderful home-cooked meals, either lunch or dinner (they will even pack a picnic for you). A favorite entree is the tenderloin of beef smoked over grape

An Apple a Day

*I*f an apple a day keeps the doctor away then one of the healthiest places in the state to visit is the **Community Orchard** at the northwest corner of the airport in Fort Dodge. Owned by Greg and Bev Baedke, with help from their children (son Jon just graduated from Iowa State with a degree in horticulture), the orchard is a great place to visit between August 1 and Christmas. I can't quite figure out exactly what the Baedekes won't do. There is a snack bar serving delicious desserts and lunches, a gift shop featuring hand- painted apple picking baskets, family and individual photos taken by a professional photographer (in the orchard, of course), scarecrow contests, and much, much more. And you just can't leave without taking home one of their frozen apple pies as a souvenir. I can't think of anything better than a perfect fall afternoon spent at Community Orchard. I'd start with apple pie, move on to lunch, maybe an apple dumpling next, some more apple pie. . . . You get the idea! Call (515) 573-8212 for more information.

wood and served with a horseradish cream sauce. Menus change with the availability of fresh ingredients and Mary Jo grows her own herbs. For dessert try the homemade vanilla ice cream flavored with Grand Marnier. The Johnsons emphasize the casual atmosphere and say that guests always appreciate the peace and quiet of the surroundings on this working grain farm. The inn's address is 3495 Hook's Point Drive; call (800) 383–7062 for reservations.

In the state of Iowa you'll find many small towns, but none smaller than *Country Relics Village,* which lies east of the Blue Willow Tea Room near Stanhope. Here Varlen and Fern Carlson have created a $^1/_3$ to $^2/_3$ scaled-down version of an early 1900s village. It all started in 1979 when the Carlsons bought a miniature house at an auction, thinking that their grandchildren would enjoy playing in it. Their grandsons, however, said that they'd rather have a barn, so Varlen obligingly had one built to match the house. "Things just sort of took off from there," he explains.

Visit the Carlson farm today and you'll see that the homestead has expanded to include a schoolhouse, general store, livery stable, blacksmith shop, chicken coop, and church. In the barn is a cow stanchion and horse stall, complete with a tiny milk can and miniature bales of hay in the loft. The church contains four small pews, an organ, and stained-glass windows, while the house has a small cast-iron stove and a diminutive table, cupboard, and cooking utensils. The general store is packed with hundreds of miniature supplies.

Two Fun Car Games

1. Count Ks. Iowans like to spell words that begin with Cs with Ks. You score a point for each one you find. Bonus points are awarded for double and triple Ks. For example: Kolleen's Kountry Kabinet. Look around, have fun, patronize these businesses. After all, they just might put you in the winner's circle. (Prizes should be named in advance, to avoid disagreements.)

2. License Plate Game. For the most part, Iowa license plates have three letters of the alphabet in them. Following the order they come in make words out of them. For example, BND could be bind, bend, bandanna, abundant, abandon, etc. In some counties this will be more difficult than others and you may have to make adjustments to the rules like making phrases, proper names, or even sentences out of the letters. For example: SRO could be "standing room only" or "Sally Roberta Olson" or, if you're paying attention to the road, "see rigid opossum."

Country Relics is located 1½ miles north of Stanhope on Highway 17. It's open from May through October from 9:00 A.M. to 5:00 P.M. daily. For more information call (515) 826–3491.

North of Country Relics off I–35 on County Road C47 is the community of Dows. Visit the Depot Welcome Center, an 1896 building that formerly housed the depot serving the "Slippery Elm Railroad," the tracks connecting Cedar Rapids and Sioux City. It is decorated with railroad memorabilia and serves as a handy place to gather information on the area. While you're in Dows, stop by the ***Dows Mercantile Store & Fillmore Building*** on Main Street. Built in 1894, after a disastrous fire had all but destroyed Main Street, it is now run by the Dows Historical Society and features changing art displays as well as selling Iowa handcrafts and products. The store is open from 9:00 A.M. to 5:00 P.M. Monday through Saturday and from noon to 5:00 P.M. on Sundays. If you're interested in old machines you might want to step into the ***Quasdorf Museum*** which

What Is the Proper Way to Eat Sweet Corn?

*T*here are, as far as I know, only three alternatives:

1) Hold the large end in your left hand (in your right, if you're left-handed), the small end in your right. Pick the best spot at the left end and start to chew to the right in an orderly fashion, remembering to surface occasionally for air. When you get to the extreme right end, stop! Do not bite your fingers! Return calmly to the left end just under the place where you started the first row. Proceed in this manner, being orderly and neat. (This, of course, is the right way!)

2) Begin as in 1 but eat vertically, i.e., the small way around instead of the long way down, making wasteful circular motions with your wrists.

3) Eat at random, taking a bite here, a bite there, using no method whatsoever. (I have actually seen people eat

sweet corn this way! I am happy to say I didn't know them very well.)

Once, when I was in high school, a friend of mine had an exchange student from France staying with her family for the summer. I was invited there for dinner one evening and, as we all crowded around the large dining table, I was happy to see sweet corn was on the menu. We all sat down to eat and as we "dug in" as the saying goes, I saw Pierette's face fill with shock, then amazement, followed quickly by horror. "Why, Pierette, whatever is the matter?" someone asked. She replied, barely able to get out the words, "You eat za corn like . . . like zee peegs!" We all shifted uneasily in our chairs for a few seconds, looked furtively at one another (wondering to whom she could possibly be referring), and then simply resumed eating our corn like "zee peegs."

has displays of blacksmith, wagon, and machine shops. It is located across from the depot and no admission is charged. A good time to visit Dows is during Corn Days held the first weekend in August.

From Dows head north to the town of Clarion, home to the *4-H Schoolhouse Museum.* The museum, located in the town's Gazebo Park, is housed in the turn-of-the-century schoolhouse where O. H. Benson, superintendent of schools for Wright County, originated the idea for the emblem of the 4-H Clubs in 1907. The four-leaf clover of the youth organization is a familiar sight to most Iowans, and Clarion takes great pride in its status as the emblem's birthplace.

Inside the museum you'll see various displays on 4-H memorabilia and history, including 4-H uniform style changes through the years. Other displays take you back in time to the days of the one-room country schoolhouse. The museum is open Tuesday and Thursday 1:00 to 4:00 P.M. and Saturday 9:00 A.M. to noon, June through August. Admission is free. For more information call (515) 532–2256.

North of Clarion lies the town of Britt, which each August plays host to one of the state's most unusual events, the *National Hobo Convention.* Hoboes have been traveling to the convention since 1900, though their numbers have dwindled, and by now most of them are well past middle age. Each year they return to Britt to swap stories, meet old friends, and enjoy the hospitality of the town.

Britt hosted its first hobo convention in 1900, eager to gain some publicity for the town and show the rest of the world that "Britt was a lively little town capable of doing anything larger cities could do." The national media did indeed report on the convention, not realizing that the town was serious in its intentions until hundreds of hoboes began arriving for the event. The travelers were treated to games and sports competitions, musical performances, and a clean place to stay, and the newspapers around the state gave Britt the publicity it had hoped for.

Though the 1900 convention was declared a rousing success, it wasn't until 1933 that Britt once again hosted the convention. Some townspeople were reluctant to sponsor the event again, but they were won over by those who pointed out that the convention was for hoboes, not tramps or bums. A hobo is defined as a migratory worker who is willing to work to pay his way; a tramp is a traveler who begs for food rather than works for it; and a bum is too lazy either to work or to roam around. At a time when many people were out of work and homeless, a hobo was seen as an honorable—even romantic—character.

The town agreed to host the convention again and renewed a tradition that continues to this day. Through the years the event has grown to include more activities, from the crowning of a hobo king and queen to the serving of free mulligan stew. Hoboes like Mountain Dew, Hardrock Kid, and Fry Pan Jack have become legendary in Britt, though today fewer and fewer of their brethren come to the event each year. A new breed is taking their place, however: "weekend hoboes" who love the open road but still have stable jobs. Both groups gather in Britt once a year to renew their ties to each other and the traveling life.

You don't have to be a hobo to attend the convention, however. Visitors are welcomed, and the town offers a full slate of activities for their amusement: a flea market, parade, antique and classic car show, musical entertainment, art show, carnival, and fireworks display. Visitors are welcome to stop by the "hobo jungle" (the area where the hoboes camp) to listen to storytelling and singing and learn more about life on the

The Remarkable Gift of the Prison on the Prairie

*D*uring World War II a German prisoner of war camp was established just outside the town of Algona. One of the 3,200 prisoners, an architect and noncommissioned officer named Eduard Kaib, enlisted the help of some of his fellow prisoners, and together they went to work to fashion a nativity scene. It was a way, Kaib thought, for them to fight their loneliness and their longing for their families and the festivities of Christmas in their native land. They pooled their money in order to purchase the materials they needed and built the figures to a one-half life-size scale, using concrete over wire frames. They finished the detailing with hand carving in plaster. The project took more than a year to complete, and it was displayed at the edge of the camp for the first time in December 1945. When the camp was being dismantled after the war, the citizens of Algona asked that the nativity scene be left behind for the community to enjoy. Kaib and his helpers agreed, with the stipulation that no admission fee ever be charged. They helped the townspeople assemble the display in a newly repaired building. It remains open to the public during the Christmas season, and several of the prisoners have returned here to visit. One of them, freelance photographer Werner Meinel, stopped in Algona in 1963 while returning to his home in Massachusetts from a shoot in Alaska. Surprised that the nativity scene was still being displayed and touched by the friendliness of the Algona residents, he sent one of his prize-winning photographs—a pair of white swans flying side by side titled Correlation— to be hung in the nativity building as a symbol of peace.

Did You Know?

The first Kossuth County law (1856) was known as the "hog law" because it prohibited hogs and cattle from running around at large. Watch out for escapees!

road. The National Hobo Convention is held each year on the second weekend in August. For more information call (515) 843–3867.

If you can't make it to Britt for the convention, from May through September you can still learn more about the hobo life at the town's *Hobo Museum.* Located in the former Chief Theatre in downtown Britt, the museum celebrates hobo history through photographs, printed materials, musical instruments, and other artifacts. For information call (515) 843–3867.

Plan a visit—especially during spring and fall migration seasons—to the *Union Slough Wildlife Refuge.* Take County Road B35 north from Britt to County Road A42 and head east to Bancroft. This area was established in 1938 by the Department of the Interior to help maintain the waterfowl population of the Midwest Flyway, including ducks, geese, whistling swans, and a wide variety of shorebirds. The slough is all that remains of a pre-glacial riverbed. Now 2,200 acres, it once covered more than 8,000. It marks the confluence, or union, of two watersheds: the Blue Earth River and the East Fork of the Des Moines. There is a picnic area and nature trail at the southern end of the refuge. More information is available from the Refuge Manager at (515) 928–2523. The refuge office is located off County Road A42 6 miles east of Bancroft, and is open from 7:30 A.M. to 4:00 P.M. Monday through Friday.

Drive west to the town of West Bend, the site of the *Grotto of the Redemption.* Each year more than 100,000 visitors travel to see the grotto, which is believed to be the largest collection of minerals and semiprecious stones concentrated in any one spot in the world (the shrine's estimated geological value is more than $2.5 million).

The grotto was the lifetime work of Father Paul Dobberstein, who started its construction in 1912. As a young seminary student he suffered a serious illness and vowed that if he recovered, he would erect a shrine to the Virgin Mary. For forty-two years he labored to build the grotto in West Bend, setting into concrete ornamental rocks and gems from around the world. Since his death in 1954, his work has been continued by Father Louis Greving.

Today the Grotto of the Redemption covers an area the size of a city block. Contained within its twisting walls and encrusted caverns are nine separate grottoes, each portraying some scene from the life of Christ. Highlights include a replica of Michelangelo's *Pietà* and a life-size statue of Carrara marble portraying Joseph of Arimathea and

Nicodemus laying Jesus into the tomb. Adjacent to the grotto is St. Peter and Paul's Church, which includes a Christmas Chapel that is considered to be Father Dobberstein's finest work. It contains a Brazilian amethyst that weighs more than 300 pounds. The church's main altar (a first-place winner at the Chicago World's Fair in 1893) is of hand-carved bird's-eye maple.

The grotto is financed by the freewill donations of visitors, and hourly tours are given from 10:00 A.M. to 5:00 P.M. daily from June to October 15 (though the grotto is open for viewing year-round). The Grotto Restaurant serves inexpensive home-cooked meals from 8:00 A.M. to 4:00 P.M. in season. Camping and motel facilities are also available. The grotto is located 2 blocks off Highway 15 at the north end of West Bend. For more information call (515) 887–2371.

Also of interest in West Bend is the *Sod House*, a home built of earth and managed by the West Bend Historical Society to help preserve part of the pioneer heritage of the area. At one time sod houses could be found throughout the prairie states, for in a land of few trees they were a quick and inexpensive answer to the housing needs of new settlers. A sod home cost between $15 and $30 to construct, and its thick walls and roof were good insulation against the heat of summer and cold of winter. The sod house era in Iowa lasted only thirty years, from the 1850s to the 1880s. It ended when the expansion of the railroad made lumber cheap enough to be used as a common building material.

The Sod House in West Bend will give you the chance to experience what life was like for most of the early pioneer settlers on the plains. It is located on Highway 15, 1 block east of the business district in West Bend and is open every Saturday and Sunday from 2:30 to 4:00 P.M. from Memorial Day through Labor Day. The historical society also operates a country schoolhouse and a historical museum, both of which have the same hours as the Sod House. Admission for all three attractions is $1.00. For more information call (515) 887–2371.

The town of *Emmetsburg*, which lies northwest of West Bend, is also worth a visit, particularly if you have a bit of Irish in your background. The town was settled by Irish immigrants and named in honor of Robert Emmet, the Irish patriot who was executed by the English in 1803. The customs and heritage of the old country remain strong in Emmetsburg, especially during its annual St. Patrick's Day celebration. This three-day festival includes a Miss Shamrock Pageant, marathon run, banquet, dances, luncheons, and various entertainment.

Clear Lake Region

The region that surrounds beautiful Clear Lake is dominated by two towns, Mason City and Clear Lake. Mason City is perhaps best known as the birthplace of Meredith Wilson, who wrote the book, lyrics, and music for the award-winning musical *The Music Man.* Mason City has another claim to fame as well: Architecture buffs regard Mason City as a mecca for Prairie School architecture. The city is credited with having one of the finest collections of Frank Lloyd Wright–inspired architecture to be found anywhere, a style known for its open, flowing designs, low roofs, and skillful use of natural materials. The **Rock Glenn-Rock Crest National Historic District** includes eight houses that were designed by Walter Burley Griffin and Barry Byrne of the Chicago office of Frank Lloyd Wright and built between 1912 and 1917.

Adjacent to the district is the **Frank Lloyd Wright Stockman House,** a Prairie School house designed by the famous architect himself. Constructed in 1908, the home was one of very few houses built by Wright in this period to address middle-class housing needs. It features such details as an open floor plan, ribbon windows, overhanging eaves, and exterior wood banding that emphasizes its horizontal lines. The Stockman House (515–423–1923) is located at 530 First Street NE and is open Thursday through Sunday from Memorial Day through Labor Day and on weekends only in May, September, and October. Admission is $3.00 for adults and $1.00 for children.

A good way to see all of these architectural treasures is on a **Mason City Walking Tour.** The Mason City Convention and Visitors Bureau puts out a detailed booklet that will guide you on your walk, with photographs of the significant landmarks and explanations of their architecture. Thirty-seven buildings are described, as well as the Music Man Footbridge over Willow Creek. Copies of the guide are available for $4.00 at the Convention and Visitors Bureau at 15 West State Street. For more information call (800) 423–5724.

On your tour of the city, you should also plan a visit to the **Charles H. MacNider Museum.** Housed in a handsome Tudor-style building, the museum has a permanent collection focusing on American art and boasts works by such well-known artists as Thomas Hart Benton, Grant Wood, Alexander Calder, Moses Soyer, and Adolph Gottlieb. Another highlight of the museum is its collection of Bil Baird puppets and memorabilia. Baird was a native of Mason City and famous puppeteer whose creations appeared in the theater, in films, and on

Frank Lloyd Wright Stockman House

television for more than fifty years. His puppets starred in the Ziegfeld Follies, appeared in the movie *The Sound of Music,* and performed on television for Ed Sullivan, Jack Paar, and Sid Caesar. In 1980 Baird donated a major collection of his work to the MacNider Museum, including some 400 puppets and marionettes.

The Charles H. MacNider Museum is located at 303 Second Street SE in Mason City. Its hours are from 10:00 A.M. to 9:00 P.M. on Tuesday and Thursday; from 10:00 A.M. to 5:00 P.M. on Wednesday, Friday, and Saturday; and from 1:00 to 5:00 P.M. on Sunday. Admission is free. For more information call (515) 421–3666.

Two other Mason City museums provide glimpses into the region's past. The ***Kinney Pioneer Museum*** off Highway 18 West includes a pioneer village with a one-room schoolhouse, log cabin, and blacksmith shop and on weekends features demonstrations of old-time crafts and trades. The museum (515–423–1258) is open Wednesday through Sunday from May through September. Admission is $2.50 for adults.

Don't miss ***Van Horn's Antique Truck Museum*** and Circus Room Display. This is a great and interesting collection of trucks—one of the nation's oldest and rarest—built between 1909 and the 1930s. They are displayed in a turn-of-the-century setting that includes a storefront street. Recently added is the "Gasoline Alley" featuring delivery trucks, old gas pumps, oil cans, advertising signs, and other gasoline memorabilia. The circus room, enclosed in a 30-foot glass showcase, is a large scale model circus, the cumulative thirty-four-year effort of one man who designed and built it. On Highway 65, just north of Mason City, Van Horn's is open May 25 through September 22, seven days a week. Admission charge is $5.00 for adults and $1.50 for children. Call (515) 423–0550 during the season and (515) 423–9066 the rest of the year for hours and more information.

Another Mason City institution is the ***Northwestern Steakhouse,*** purveyor of tender steaks and various Greek specialties. Its founder, Tony

Papouchis, the son of a Greek Orthodox priest, came to the United States in 1912. In 1920 he opened the Evia Cafe, named after his home island in Greece, a business he later sold so that he could open the Northwestern Steakhouse. In the Depression era he sold more chicken and ribs than the more expensive steaks, but in the years since steaks have become the menu's staple. Greek specialties are also served here on Sunday nights, from *dolmathes* (stuffed grape leaves) to Greek chicken roasted with lemon and herbs.

Tony's sons John, George, and Bill have taken over ownership of the business and have opened two additional restaurants in Des Moines and Ames. The secret to their success: "Keep people happy and they'll keep coming back," says John.

Northwestern Steakhouse is located at 304 Sixteenth Street NW in Mason City. Hours are from 5:00 to 10:00 P.M. daily, and prices are moderate. Call (515) 423–5075 for more information.

Just west of Mason City on Highway 18 is *Clear Lake,* one of the state's most popular recreation areas. The lake itself is one of the few spring-fed lakes in Iowa, a lovely 3,600-acre expanse of water that draws boating and fishing enthusiasts, water-skiers, swimmers, and confirmed beach bums all summer. Even in winter the area is a popular tourist spot, with cross-country skiing, snowmobiling, and ice fishing for those who don't mind the cold.

The water is not the only attraction in Clear Lake. In the downtown area you'll find a number of antiques stores and specialty shops, and during the summer months many special events are scheduled, from fishing tournaments to band concerts in the park.

Clear Lake offers a couple of unusual ways to see its attractions. Visit the *Iowa Trolley Park* to book a ride on board a historic trolley car. The trolley was once a major form of transportation between Clear Lake and nearby Mason City, and the popular attraction has been revived during the summer months. In Clear Lake passengers board at the Iowa Trolley Park on East Main Avenue. The trolley operates on weekends and holidays from 12:30 to 4:30 P.M. Memorial Day through Labor Day. Call (515) 357–7433 for information.

Another way to see the area is on board the *Lady of the Lake,* a sternwheeler ferryboat that takes passengers on a scenic cruise around Clear Lake. Cruises are offered daily from May through September. Tickets are $10.00 for adults and $5.00 for children. Call (515) 357–2243 for information.

Don't miss the **Surf Ballroom** on your tour of Clear Lake. The ballroom is best known as the site of the last performances given by rock 'n' roll legends Buddy Holly, Ritchie Valens, and J. P. "The Big Bopper" Richardson. Following their concert, the three were killed nearby in the crash of their small plane in the early morning hours of February 3, 1959—an event that became the basis for Don McLean's hit song "American Pie." In 1988 a monument was erected in their memory outside the Surf, and their music lives on in an annual memorial concert. For devoted rock 'n' roll fans, the Surf has become a landmark on the same order as The Cavern in Liverpool where the Beatles got their start. People from around the country make pilgrimages here to relive the memories.

Even without the Buddy Holly connection, the Surf is worth a visit on its own. At a time when most ballrooms have gone the way of the horse and buggy, the Surf is a living reminder of the Big Band era, when swing was king. Today it books a variety of music and dance bands, from country to big band to fifties and sixties classics. The Surf Ballroom is located at 460 North Shore Drive in Clear Lake. For more information call (515) 357–6151.

Clear Lake is also home to the **Clear Lake Fire Museum.** The facility opened in 1986 and depicts a fire station from the early 1900s. Inside you can see some of Clear Lake's earliest fire-fighting equipment, along with other antique fire-fighting memorabilia. Highlights of the museum include the town's 1924 Ahrens-Fox fire truck, an 1883 hand-pulled hose cart, a fire bell, antique fire extinguishers, photographs, and brass poles.

The Clear Lake Fire Museum is located at 112 North Sixth Street, ½ block north of the fire station. It is open from Memorial Day through Labor Day on Saturday and Sunday from 1:00 to 5:00 P.M. Admission is free. Donations are welcomed. For more information call (515) 357–2159.

Clear Lake boasts several fine bed-and-breakfasts where you can stay as you explore the area. One of my favorites is the **North Shore House,** a cottage on the north side of the lake owned by Jay and Ruby Black. The Blacks used to live in Des Moines and traveled north to Clear Lake just for the summer months, but they loved the area so much that they made it their permanent home in 1988. Their home is a 1920s-vintage rustic cottage that had fallen into disrepair, and Jay and Ruby spent years fixing it up before it was livable year-round. Today you'd never suspect its dilapidated past. Light, airy, and comfortable, the house is furnished in a modern style, with antique boat parts decorating the walls. The patio has a lovely view of the lake and is the perfect place to enjoy a delicious breakfast. You'll find the Blacks to be friendly hosts, people who obviously enjoy their part-time business.

The North Shore House is located at 1519 North Shore Drive in Clear Lake and has two rooms open to visitors, each with a private bath. Rates range from $75 to $90 per night and include a full breakfast. For reservations call (515) 357–4443. You can visit the North Shore House Web site at *http://members.aol.com/jcblacknsh,* or e-mail them at jay-black@netins.net.

Continue your tour of north central Iowa with a visit to Charles City, which lies east of Mason City. In 1968 the town was devastated by a tornado that destroyed nearly one-third of the community's buildings. Instead of giving up, the people of Charles City chose to rebuild their town, so that today it is one of the most modern small cities in the country. The town has hundreds of new buildings, including a new fire station, city hall, and library, plus a new mall in the middle of the downtown business district.

Not all of Charles City's historic structures were destroyed, however. One of its landmarks is the downtown Charles Theater, built in 1935 in

Who Was Carrie Lane Chapman Catt?

*B*orn in 1859 in Wisconsin, Carrie Lane moved with her family to Charles City, Iowa, in 1866 and graduated from Iowa State University in 1880 as valedictorian and the only woman in her graduating class. Because her father opposed her ambition to receive a higher education, she worked for a year at a country school and then as a dishwasher and library aide for nine cents an hour to pay her way through college. During her college years she fought for the right of women to participate on the university debating team and in military exercise. Nationally, she led the women's suffrage movement until the ratification of the nineteenth amendment in 1920.

(When she married her second husband, George Catt, in 1890, they both signed a contract allowing her four months a year to work on suffrage issues.) She founded the League of Women Voters, worked ardently for international peace, and remained a powerful and well-respected advocate for women's rights issues until her death at the age of 88 in 1947.

When visiting the Charles City area, plan a visit to the **Carrie Lane Chapman Catt Childhood Home.** Go south on 218, turn right on 220th Street, then left on Timber Avenue and it will be about 2 miles down the road on the right side.

an art deco design with a facade of glittering gold lead and terra-cotta. At one time hundreds of such theaters dotted the small towns of Iowa, but today only a handful remain intact. The town's suspension bridge is also a historic landmark, built in 1906 to connect the main part of the city with the county fairgrounds and the Chautauqua festivals held there. The single-span structure is more than 200 feet in length, with a 4-foot-wide pedestrian walkway.

Charles City also boasts one of the largest county museums in Iowa, the *Floyd County Historical Museum.* The museum is housed in the former Salsbury Laboratory Building, constructed in 1933, and contains more than forty rooms of exhibits. Its best-known display is a complete original drugstore that operated on Charles City's main street from 1873 to 1961. The store was founded by German immigrant Edward Berg and was later owned by John Legel Jr., who donated it to the historical society in 1961. Tour the store today and it's like stepping back a generation or more. The shelves are filled with patent medicines designed to cure every ailment known, plus items like cigar molds, chimneys for kerosene lamps, ink bottles, and cosmetics like 7 Sutherland Sisters Hair & Scalp Cleaner.

Elsewhere in the museum you can see a restored 1853 log cabin, displays of old-time vehicles and tools, and materials relating to the history of the county. The museum also contains the nation's most complete collection of information relating to the founders of the gasoline tractor industry, the Hart-Parr Company. The business was founded in Charles City and produced the first successful gasoline tractor in 1901. Another display contains information about Carrie Chapman Catt, a Charles City native and early leader in the women's suffrage movement.

The Floyd County Historical Museum is located at 500 Gilbert Street and is open year-round Monday through Friday from 9:00 A.M. to 4:30 P.M. During the months of May through September, the museum is also open on Saturday from 1:00 to 4:00 P.M. Admission is $2.00 for adults, $1.00 for ages 12 to 18, and 25 cents for ages 5 to 12. For more information call (515) 228–1099.

If you've brought your fly rod along, you may want to take a trip up to Otronto just south of the Minnesota border to the catch-and-release zone of the *Big Red Cedar.* The "no kill" zone, established in 1993, runs from there to Halverson Park south of St. Ansgar. This is a beautiful spot to fish for smallmouth bass, but please remember the first rule of anglers' etiquette: DO NOT encroach on another angler's spot! Usually this is not a problem at this particular location, but you should always be on the lookout for other established anglers and avoid them. Remember, this is not a group activity. Look for large rocks that break the current or fallen trees or logs where there is shade and you may be rewarded.

Try the **Rockford Fossil and Prairie Park** on B47, 1 mile west of the town of Rockford. There are several miles of trails to hike as well as fossils from the Devonian era. This area has been studied for well over a hundred years and yes, collecting is allowed, but use restraint—all of our resources are finite!

Just north of Charles City, in the town of Floyd on Highway 218, visit the **Greenman Carriage Company** and take a look at the remarkable craftsmanship of old carriages and wagons. If you have a buggy, a sleigh, or a surrey that needs to be repaired or restored, this is the place to bring it. Old wooden wheels are also repaired and new ones can be built to your order. All work is handcrafted. One of their restorations, an 1871 "Boston Booby" Hut Sleigh is on display at the Smithsonian Institute. This is truly a fascinating stop and well worth the trip. The Greenman Carriage Company (515–398–2299) is closed Christmas through New Year's. Who knows whose sleigh they may be working on?

PLACES TO STAY IN FERTILE PLAINS

TAMA
Foley's Motel,
Highway 30 East,
(515) 484–3148,
$30–$36

MARSHALLTOWN
Best Western Regency Inn,
Highways 30 & 14,
(800) 241–2974,
(515) 752–6321,
$54–$95

CONRAD
Makarios Mansion,
31121 Hawk Avenue,
(515) 366–2484,
$150–$225

AMES
Ames Budgetel Inn,
2500 Elwood Drive,
(800) 428–3438,
(515) 296–2500,
$50–$105

BONDURANT
Goddard's Country Breeze,
7783 NE 102nd Avenue,
(515) 967–3176,
$60–$75

IOWA FALLS
Rivers Bend Bed
and Breakfast,
635 Park Avenue,
(515) 648–2828,
dhkrieger@aol.com,
$75–$105

HAMPTON
Spring Valley Bed
and Breakfast,
2038 B Highway 3,
(515) 456–4437,
$30–$45

FORT DODGE
Best Western
Starlite Village,
Highways 169 and 7,
(800) 903–0009,
(515) 573–7177,
$50–$65

MASON CITY
Hanford Inn,
Highway 18W,
(800) 424–9491,
(515) 424–9494,
$48 and up

CLEAR LAKE
North Shore House,
1519 North Shore Drive,
(515) 357–4443,
members.aol.com/
jcblacknsh,
$75

ST. ANSGAR
The Blue Belle Inn,
513 West Fourth Street,
(515) 736–2225,
bluebell@deskmedia.com,
$60–$130

CHARLES CITY
Heartwood Inn,
1312 Gilbert Street,
(800) 972–2335,
(515) 228–4352,
$34–$50

**PLACES TO EAT IN
FERTILE PLAINS**

MONTOUR
Rube's,
118 Elm Street,
(515) 492–6222

STORY CITY
Carousel Tea Room
& Bakery,
619 Elm Avenue,
(515) 733–2388

FORT DODGE
Colonial Inn,
1306 A Street,
(515) 576–5757

FORT DODGE
Marvin Gardens,
809 Central Avenue,
(515) 955–5333

MASON CITY
Martin Bros.,
711 South Federal,
(515) 423–2325,
www.martinsnet.com

CLEAR LAKE
Sand Bar Restaurant
and Lounge,
211 North Fourth Street,
(515) 357–3733

Martha's,
305 Main Avenue,
(515)357–8720

Prairie Borderland

Western Iowa has a rich array of attractions to tempt travelers, including the Loess Hills, a rare and beautiful geological formation that borders the Missouri River between Sioux City and Council Bluffs. Here you'll also find the scenic beauties of Iowa's Great Lakes Region, plus the cultural treasures of the Council Bluffs area.

Spirit Lake Region

Tucked into the far northwestern corner of the state you will be delighted to discover the **Gitchie Manitou State Preserve.** Located about 10 miles northwest of the town of Larchwood (follow County Road A18), this is a beautifully preserved and fascinating geological area of the state. It contains the oldest rock bed (Precambrian) left exposed in Iowa. The outcroppings of Sioux quartzite that you see here, battered and polished by the winds for more than a billion years, are composed of sand compacted by silica. Earlier, because this rock was so beautiful, it was quarried. The resulting quarry, filled now with water, is called Jasper's Pool. The surrounding prairie and woodlands are definitely worthy of notice and have been attracting Iowa botanists for decades.

Continue your tour of western Iowa by exploring the Iowa Great Lakes, which have been one of the state's most popular recreation areas ever since the railroad first came here in the early 1880s. Thirteen lakes are located here, the largest being Big Spirit Lake and West Lake Okoboji. Here you'll find some of the best swimming, boating, fishing, camping, and golfing in the state, in a beautiful setting surrounded by sparkling water. Once you visit you'll realize why midwesterners have been flocking to the area for more than a hundred years.

Many of the charms of Dickinson County are best discovered on your own—antiques stores, lovely parks and nature areas, fine restaurants, and quiet walks by the water. On your tour be sure to schedule time for a visit to *Arnolds Park,* an amusement park that has been attracting

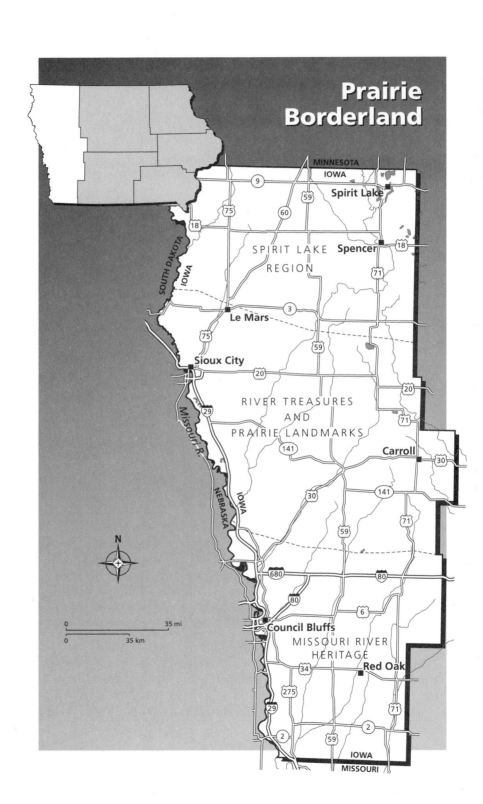

Prairie Borderland

MINNESOTA
IOWA

Spirit Lake

SPIRIT LAKE REGION

Spencer

Le Mars

Sioux City

RIVER TREASURES AND PRAIRIE LANDMARKS

Carroll

SOUTH DAKOTA

IOWA

Missouri R.

NEBRASKA

IOWA

N

0   35 mi
0   35 km

Council Bluffs

MISSOURI RIVER HERITAGE

Red Oak

IOWA
MISSOURI

PRAIRIE BORDERLAND

**AUTHOR'S FAVORITES -
PRAIRIE BORDERLAND**

Arnolds Park

*Gitchie Manitou
State Preserve*

Storm Lake

Loess Hills Scenic Byway

Orange City Tulip Festival

Stanton

LaJuice's Bar-B-Q

Woodbine

*DeSoto National
Wildlife Refuge*

Hitchcock House

visitors to the area since 1915. It has undergone $2 million in improvements, a renovation designed to update the park without destroying its old-fashioned flavor.

A highlight of any visit to Arnolds Park is a ride on one of the country's few remaining wooden roller coasters, the Coaster. The ride made its debut in the park in 1929 and has thrilled thousands of children (and adults) with its clackety-clack ride and stomach-churning maneuvers. When Arnolds Park was being restored, a top priority was saving the local landmark. The Coaster was completely dismantled, cleaned, repainted, and refurbished, and new side rails, bearings, cars, and brakes were installed. Today it is once again the park's featured attraction, drawing roller-coaster connoisseurs from across the country.

The Coaster isn't the park's only asset. Twenty-five rides and attractions, gift shops, restaurants, picnic areas, and sandy beaches will tempt you into relaxing. The park's Majestic Pavilion revives another lake tradition, that of dancing and fine musical performances by local and touring artists.

Arnolds Park is located on the south side of West Lake Okoboji off Highway 71. A full day pass is $13.95 for people taller than 48 inches and $9.95 for those 36 to 48 inches tall; if you come in under 36 inches you get into the park for free. The park is open daily (with some exceptions made for the local school year) from Memorial Day through Labor Day. For more information call (712) 332–2183.

Another attraction in the area with a long history is the **Queen II,** a faithful reproduction of the 1884 *Queen* that plied the waters of the Iowa Great Lakes for eighty-nine years. Local volunteers are responsible for her existence, working both to help raise money for the boat and to help with her construction. More than half of the boat's $350,000 cost was raised through auctions, bake sales, and door-to-door solicitations. In 1986 the *Queen II* was officially launched, with Iowa Governor Terry Branstad commissioning her as the "Flagship of the Iowa Navy."

Today the *Queen II* offers five daily excursions from Memorial Day through Labor Day on West Lake Okoboji (board near Arnolds Park). The cruises last for seventy-five minutes, with the captain providing a narrative of the history and attractions of the region. The fare is $7.50 for adults. Call (712) 332–5159 for more information.

The Coaster, Arnolds Park

After your cruise, don't miss paying a visit to the nearby **Maritime Museum.** There you can see nautical exhibits, old wooden boats, and historical photos and artifacts and also view a video of Iowa Great Lakes history. Admission to the museum is free.

History buffs will want to further explore the area's colorful past. Indians first settled near the lakes after being pushed westward by settlers, but by the mid-1800s the area was attracting more and more white people. The tension between the two groups eventually led in 1857 to the infamous Spirit Lake Massacre, in which forty settlers were killed by a band of warriors led by the Dakotah Sioux chief Inkpaduta. The murders sparked an Indian uprising that echoed through Minnesota and the Dakota Territory.

You can learn more about the history of the area at several sites in Dickinson County. The **Gardner Cabin** in the town of Arnolds Park was the only dwelling left standing after the massacre and is now a museum as well as the last resting place for the victims of the tragedy. The cabin is also the site of the **Spirit Lake Massacre Monument,** erected by the state in 1895 in memory of those who had lost their lives. The cabin is open Memorial Day through Labor Day from noon to 4:00 P.M. on weekdays and from 9:00 A.M. to 4:00 P.M. on weekends and admission is free. It is located on Monument Drive, 1 block west of the amusement park. The **Dickinson County Museum** in Spirit Lake contains additional information on the massacre, plus displays on the steamboat and railroad eras and other historical items from the Iowa Great Lakes area.

No description of the Iowa Great Lakes region would be complete without mention of the **University of Okoboji.** Its campus is one of the largest in the world, stretching from the northern tip of Big Spirit Lake to south of Milford. As you walk through its campus you'll see many

PRAIRIE BORDERLAND

signs of a strong school spirit: thousands of bumper stickers, sweatshirts, and pennants proudly bearing the university's name and hundreds of trash barrels that read HELP KEEP YOUR CAMPUS CLEAN. Prospective students will be relieved to learn, however, that the administration of the University of Okoboji believes that standard academic pursuits like books and lectures are unnecessary to true learning. Instead, its students major in roller-coaster engineering at Arnolds Park, culinary arts at local restaurants, and human anatomy at local beaches.

The school was founded more than twenty years ago, when Herman Richter (director of student affairs), his brother Emil (administrative dean), and Roger Stolley (director of admissions) ordered T-shirts emblazoned with the university's logo to wear at local sporting events. Before long, the joke had spawned a local—and then a national—phenomenon. Today there are U of O alumni chapters all over the country, made up of former visitors to the Great Lakes region. The school has its own radio station, KUOO, and even established an endowment fund that is used to support community projects. Each year many local events are sponsored by the school, including a homecoming weekend, rugby tournament, and world tennis classic. Its football team, the Phantoms, is undefeated despite one of the most grueling schedules in college football. It's not unusual for the Phantoms to play the University of Iowa at 1:00 P.M., Nebraska at 4:00, and Notre Dame at 8:00. At each game, all the tickets sold are for Row A, Seats 1 and 2 on the 50-yard line, with proceeds going for a dome over West Lake Okoboji. University officials concede that the school's amazing record is helped by the fact that no other teams ever show up to play but contend that their team's excellence is so intimidating that other schools know they could never win.

Even if you can't get tickets for the U of O football games, you'll still enjoy your time as a student at the University of Okoboji. The tuition is low, the classes easy, and each year everyone graduates at the top of the class.

FESTIVALS IN PRAIRIE BORDERLAND

Winter Fun Fest, Storm Lake, last weekend in January, (712) 732–3780

St. Patrick's Celebration, Emmetsburg, weekend before March 17, (712) 852–4326

Annual Tulip Festival, Orange City, third weekend in May, (712) 737–4510

Loess Hills Indian Market & Fine Arts Festival, Council Bluffs, last weekend in May, (712) 678–3776

Waterfest Weekend, Sioux City, third weekend in June, (712) 279–4800

Clay County Fair, Spencer, begins second week in September, (712) 262–4740

Clarinda Ghost Walk, Clarinda, October 31, (712) 542–2166

Winter Wonderland and Walk, Anita, second Sunday in December, (712) 762–3947

147

Another Great Lakes region attraction is **Cayler Prairie,** a 160-acre tract of virgin prairie located west of Big Spirit Lake. The site is one of the largest remaining areas of prairie in the state. It is both a State Botanical Preserve and a National Historic Landmark, and it will give you a chance to see a little of Iowa's once-vast grasslands as they appeared more than a century ago. As you walk through its waist-high grasses, it's easy to imagine how it must have seemed to the early pioneers. Here you will find more than 250 types of grasses and wildflowers. Blooming begins in April with delicate pasqueflowers and ends in October with brilliant blue gentians. Other wildflowers can be found in bloom throughout the summer, with the height of color to be seen in early August. The prairie is also home to badgers, foxes, jackrabbits, meadowlarks, partridge, and the rare upland sandpiper.

Cayler Prairie is located 6 miles west of Big Spirit Lake off Highway 9. A parking lot is provided along the country road on the southwest side of the prairie. Visitors are welcome during daylight hours but are urged to read the regulation signs before entering the prairie. The picking or digging of plants is forbidden because of the rarity of many of the prairie's species.

From the Great Lakes region head south to **Hannah Marie Country Inn** near Spencer, a "country Victorian" farmhouse that offers overnight accommodations for visitors as well as elegant afternoon teas and luncheons. Mary Nichols operates the inn with her husband and son. Mary is a retired home-economics teacher who named their place *Hannah Marie* after her mother. Mary's warm touch is evident throughout the house, as well as in the individually themed rooms. "People feel at home here, but still pampered," says Mary.

The two-story frame farmhouse offers a comfortable place to relax and unwind. In the morning you'll be served a hearty breakfast or you can have a basket delivered to your room. There are six guest rooms, all with queen-size feather beds and down comforters.

In 1990 the Nicholses expanded their operation by moving another vintage farmhouse to a site next to the inn. The Carl Gustav House accommodates overnight visitors and is also the site of afternoon teas and luncheons. The Hannah Marie Country Inn is located 4 miles south of Spencer on Highway 71. It is open year round and room rates are $77 to $110. For reservations and a schedule of their special events call (712) 262–1286.

Another attraction that begins in Spencer is the **Inkpaduta Canoe Trail** on the Little Sioux River. The trail winds for 134 miles from

Spencer south to the town of Smithland in Woodbury County. The Little Sioux is the largest interior stream of the Missouri River watershed in Iowa and has a sand, mud, and gravel bottom and high banks along most of its scenic course. The river current is quite slow, which makes for excellent fishing as well as canoeing.

The trail is named for the Sioux Indian who led the Spirit Lake Massacre. Inkpaduta and his followers were never caught after the raids, which ignited anti-Indian sentiments and raised fears throughout the Midwest.

As you travel the canoe trail, you can focus on a happier topic by keeping your eyes on the lookout for river otters. Once the most prevalent mammal in North America, unregulated hunting and trapping and habitat destruction decreased its numbers to the point of extinction in Iowa. In 1985 a program was started to reintroduce the river otter to the state. Iowa's native wild turkeys were trapped and traded for Louisiana otters. To date more than 170 otters have been released at the Little Sioux River near Peterson. If you're lucky enough to see one of these graceful creatures, you're asked to report the information to the office of a county office of a county conservation board along the trail. Many other animals can be seen along the river as well, including great blue herons, raccoons, beavers, muskrats, turtles, and white-tailed deer.

The Inkpaduta Canoe Trail can be entered at various sites. For a brochure and map, write to the Clay County Conservation Board, 420 Tenth Avenue SE, Spencer 51301; or call (712) 262–2187. (Don't plan on using the trail in winter.)

West of Spencer lies the town of ***Orange City,*** which takes great pride in its ethnic heritage and offers a number of attractions. Here you can see a variety of Dutch architecture (including a drive-in bank housed in a windmill), hundreds of beautiful flower beds full of tulips in season, and stores selling traditional Dutch dolls, pottery, lace, baked goods, wooden shoes, and meats.

Each spring during the third weekend in May, Orange City becomes even more of a Little Holland during its annual ***Tulip Festival.*** One of its most popular attractions is the Volksparade, when hundreds of people take to the streets with their buckets and scrub brushes to make the way clean for the festival's queen. Then board the *Wilhelmina* or the *Juliana,* the town's two horse-drawn streetcars, to see the rest of the sights in town. The Dutch Street Organ will likely catch your attention—one of only two in the United States, the organ was built in Holland and plays melodies for the enjoyment of passersby. The Dutch Dozen is a musical and dance group that will also entertain you, and in the evening you can kick up your own heels in a street dance or attend a theater performance.

At any time of year you can visit the **Century Home,** a house built in 1900 by Orange City's first mayor and decorated with furnishings that might have belonged to a typical Orange City family at the turn of the century. Included within are a pump organ handmade in 1903, a silver tea service that belonged to the home's original owner, and a clock brought from the Netherlands by the founder of Orange City. One of the upstairs rooms is filled with memorabilia from former tulip queens. The home is located at Albany Avenue and Fourth Street NE and is open during the Tulip Festival and by appointment.

At the **Old Mill** at the entrance to the Vogel Paint and Wax Company you can learn more about the Dutch influence in Orange City. The site contains three different types of windmills and an office building designed after a Dutch *stadshuis* (city hall). The Old Mill itself has displays on how wind power can be used for a variety of purposes, and the living quarters show life as it was generations ago. Some of the furnishings were brought from Holland and others came from local pioneers. The Old Mill is open Monday through Friday from 9:00 A.M. to 5:00 P.M. May through October.

And before you leave Orange City, stop by the Dutch Bakery at 221 Central Avenue NE. There you can buy such treats as almond patties, St. Nick cookies, Dutch rusks, apple rolls, and Wilhelmina Peppermints imported from Holland.

For more information on attractions in the Orange City area, call the town's chamber of commerce at (712) 737–4510.

Southeast of Orange City lies the town of Cherokee. There you'll find the **Sanford Museum and Planetarium,** the first museum in the state to be accredited by the American Association of Museums. The facility was donated to the town by a local couple in memory of their son, Tiel Sanford, and was officially opened to the public in 1951. Since then, more than three-quarters of a million people have viewed its displays.

Permanent exhibits at the Sanford deal with a variety of subjects relating to this region of the country and its past. Rocks, minerals, and fossil and animal specimens help explain the natural environment of the region, and there are also displays on the Native American tribes who once lived in the area.

The planetarium itself was built in 1950 and was the first such facility in Iowa. Planetarium shows are given on the last Sunday of each month at 2:00 P.M.

The Sanford Museum and Planetarium is located at 117 East Willow Street in Cherokee. Its hours are from 9:00 A.M. to 5:00 P.M. Monday through Friday and from noon to 5:00 p.m. on Saturday and Sunday. Admission is free. For more information call (712) 225–3922.

Before you leave the area, you might want to pay a visit to a natural landmark located about 2 miles south of Cherokee on Highway 59. Pilot Rock is an enormous boulder of red Sioux quartzite about 160 feet in circumference and 20 feet high. It was left behind when the last continental glacier receded and offers a panoramic view of the surrounding landscape. During pioneer days, Pilot Rock served as an important landmark for travelers.

Southeast of Cherokee lies *Storm Lake,* a lovely town of about 10,000 people on the shore of the 3,200-acre natural lake of the same name. Home to Buena Vista University, the town also boasts a beautiful network of parks that follows the shoreline, each park connected by a biking and walking trail that winds for about 5 miles.

In Sunset Park on West Lakeshore Drive, visit the *Living Heritage Tree Museum,* where you can see a unique collection of trees with illustrious histories. The "Village Blacksmith Chestnut," for example, is a descendant of the tree that inspired the poet Longfellow to write "Under the Spreading Chestnut Tree." Another tree nearby was grown from a seed carried to the moon and back. Also in the museum is a tulip poplar descended from a tree planted by George Washington at Mount Vernon, as well as an apple tree traced back to the famed Johnny Appleseed. Dozens of historically significant trees are interspersed amid serene landscaping near the lake. The park is open to the public at no charge, twenty-four hours a day.

A couple of historical attractions in Storm Lake are worth a visit. One is the Victorian-era *Harker House* at 328 Lake Avenue, built in 1875 by a local banker in the French Mansard Cottage style. The home, which contains many of the original furnishings, is open for afternoon tours from May through October on Thursday, Saturday, and Sunday. Call (712) 732–4868 for information. The Storm Lake Historical Society also operates a museum at 214 West Fifth Street that is open Monday through Saturday, Memorial Day through Labor Day. Call (712) 732–4955 for more information.

Santa's Castle is a fascinating place to visit if you're in Storm Lake between Thanksgiving and Christmas (or any other time of the year if you make an appointment). Begun in 1962 with the purchase of some animated elves, the castle now houses what may be the largest operating collection of mechanical Christmas figures in the Midwest. These are real classics from old department store displays. They make their home in an original Carnegie Library building. For more information or to arrange a tour call (712) 732–3780.

For a Middle-Eastern treat in the Midwest, drive east of Storm Lake to Newell and *Keith's Arab Heritage House.* Keith Carter, a Newell native, has amassed a wonderful collection of artwork, rugs, weavings, coffee pots, and needlework from his extensive travels as an educator in various countries of the Middle East. To arrange a tour of this collection housed in a large Victorian house call (712) 272–3527. Arabic coffee and tea are served as refreshments.

North of Newell lies the town of *Albert City* and a rather unique historical museum. Don't miss the depot where a shoot-out following a bank robbery claimed the lives of three. You can still see the bullet holes in the walls and look at the gun used by one of the robbers. There are many vintage cars as well. Check out the funeral parlor where you can view old memorial wreaths and candlesticks as well as a picture of the first motorized hearse.

River Treasures and Prairie Landmarks

From Storm Lake head west to Iowa's western border. At the junction of Iowa, South Dakota, and Nebraska lies Sioux City. Ever since the Lewis and Clark expedition passed through here in 1804, Sioux City has been a focal point for travelers and settlers heading west. Located on the bank of the Missouri River, the city became a major nineteenth-century river port and the center of a booming stockyard and meatpacking industry. The Missouri River is still important to the city, though today it's prized primarily for its recreational attractions. Sioux City has developed its riverfront into an extensive park and trail system, with a number of historical points of interest along the way.

Several of these attractions focus on Sergeant Charles Floyd, a member of the Lewis and Clark expedition who died here on August 20, 1804—the only casualty of the entire two-year expedition. His death is memorialized at the *Sergeant Floyd Monument,* a 100-foot-high white stone obelisk that is located on a high bluff overlooking the Missouri River.

The monument became the country's first National Historic Landmark in 1960 and is located on Highway 75 near Glenn Avenue.

The young soldier is also remembered at the **Sergeant Floyd Welcome Center and Museum.** The center is housed aboard an original 1932 Army Corps of Engineers vessel, named in honor of Sergeant Floyd. From 1933 to 1975 the boat did towing, survey, and inspection work on the Missouri River, and in 1983 it was permanently dry-docked to serve as a combined welcome center and river museum. On the main deck you'll find tourist information and on the second deck an Upper Missouri River history museum. The displays include the largest collection of scale-model Missouri River steamboats in the Midwest.

The Sergeant Floyd Welcome Center and Museum is located off I–29 at exit 149. It is open daily and admission is free. Call (712) 279–4840 for information.

Another riverfront site recalls a more recent part of Sioux City history. The **Flight 232 Memorial** commemorates the heroic rescue efforts made by the Sioux City community after the crash of United Flight 232 in 1989. The monument includes a statue of Colonel Dennis Nielsen carrying a young child to safety. Nearby is the **Anderson Dance Pavilion,** a lovely public space that is used for festivals that include Labor Day Weekend's ARTSPLASH. You'll find the memorial and pavilion on the riverfront in Gateway Park.

"A small river without a name . . ."

*R*egarding the death of Sergeant Floyd, the journals of Lewis and Clark read thus:

"20th August, 1804—I am Dull & heavy been up the greater Part of last night with Sgt. Floyd who is as bad as he can be to live. . . We set out under a jentle Breeze from the south-east. . .We came to make a bath for Sgt. Floyd hoping it would brace him a little, before we get him into his bath he expired with a great deal of composure . . . having Said to me before his death that he was going away and wished me to write a letter . . . . We buried him to the top of a high round hill overlooking the river & Country for a great distance situated just below a small river without a name to which we name & call Floyd's river, the Bluffs, Sergt. Floyd's Bluff. . . we buried him with all the honors of War, and fixed a Ceeder post at his head with his name title and day of the month & year . . . we returned to the Boat & proceeded to the Mouth of the little river 30 yd wide & camped a butiful evening . . ."

One more spot worth a visit is the **Sioux City Public Museum,** housed in one of the most spectacular homes ever built in the city. Its original owner was John Pierce, an early Sioux City realtor and developer who lost his fortune soon after building the house in the early 1890s. The house is a Romanesque mansion of Sioux quartzite with twenty-three rooms filled with stylish paneling and ornately carved woodwork.

On the first floor of the museum you'll find exhibits on Sioux City history, the Civil War, and life on the frontier. The second floor has displays on natural history, fossils, and minerals, while the third floor is devoted to an extensive Native American collection. On display are various Indian artifacts, including articles of clothing and beautiful quill and bead work. Most items are from the Plains and Woodland tribes that once inhabited this area.

The Sioux City Public Museum is located at 2901 Jackson Street. Its hours are Monday through Saturday from 9:00 A.M. to 5:00 P.M. and Sunday from 2:00 to 5:00 P.M. Admission is free. For more information call (712) 279–6174.

A fun and interesting place to visit while you're in Sioux City is the **Historic Fourth Street** area downtown. This area's turn-of-the-century architecture now houses numerous pubs, restaurants, and antiques and specialty shops. The buildings along this street, noted for their Richardsonian Romanesque style popular in the late 1800s, line a 2-block-long area from Virginia Street to Iowa Street. Two of the buildings, the Evan's Block and the Boston Block are included on the National Register of Historic Places.

There are several places to eat along Fourth Street. You may want to try the recently opened **Bluestem Restaurant,** located at 1012 Fourth Street, which specializes in contemporary American cuisine with a focus on fresh fish dishes like rosemary grilled scallops served on a bed of Parmesan mashed potatoes. Enjoy what owner Adam Feiges calls the "techno-barnyard" decor featuring corrugated sheet metal. In the summer months, you can eat al fresco at one of the outdoor tables lining the front of the Major Block building in which the restaurant is housed. Reservations are accepted during the week, and for parties of six or more on Fridays and Saturdays. The restaurant is closed on Sundays. Prices for lunch are moderate to expensive and dinner prices are expensive. Call (712) 279–8060 for more information.

If you're an aeronautics buff make sure you include a trip to the **Mid America Air Museum** at the Sioux Gateway Airport (6715 Harbor Drive). This museum houses a number of full-size aircraft, including helicopters, gliders, a spray plane, several "homebuilts," and something called the "Orthencopter designed by Leonardo Deviancy." Check it out for yourself! The museum is open on Saturdays from 9:00 A.M. to 5:00 P.M. and Sundays from 1:00 to 5:00 P.M.

Other attractions in the Sioux City area include the *Belle of Sioux City Riverboat Casino* and the new *Sioux City Art Center,* which features both traditional and contemporary works of art in a dramatic three-story building with glass atrium. For more information about Sioux City attractions, call its convention and visitors bureau at (800) 593–2228.

No description of western Iowa would be complete without mention of the *Loess Hills.* The hills begin just north of Sioux City and stretch in a narrow band south to the Missouri state line and are formed from deposits of windblown silt—a unique geological phenomenon found only in Iowa and in the Kansu Province of northern China. In places they look like a miniature mountain range rising out of the Iowa plains, soft hills covered with a mixture of prairie and woodland plants. They were formed after the retreat of the last glaciers and since then have been eroded by wind and rain into the beautiful ridges and valleys visible today.

An excellent place to learn more about this unique and diverse ecosystem is at the *Dorothy Pecaut Nature Center,* which is located by Stone State Park on the northeast edge of Sioux City. The $1.4 million nature center includes a variety of interactive exhibits, including a model of the underground life of the Loess Hills, displays on the wildlilfe and plants of the region, and exhibits on the geologic forces that formed the hills. A network of hiking trails outside the center lets visitors explore the hills on their own. The Dorothy Pecaut Nature Center (712–258–0838) is open from 9:00 A.M. to 4:00 P.M. Tuesday through Friday and from 1:00 to 4:00 P.M. on weekends, closed holidays.

As part of your tour of western Iowa you may want to explore part or all of the *Loess Hills Scenic Byway,* which flanks Iowa's western border. This route stretches from Plymouth County in the north to Fremont County in the south and roughly parallels I–29. It is anchored by the town of Akron in the north and Hamburg in the south. Make sure you take advantage of the numerous "loops" off the main byway; they offer a unique opportunity to experience the Loess Hills more intimately. Some of these roads are gravel, however, so drive carefully. Some particularly nice loops are the Ridge Road Loop near Westfield, the Preparation Loop just south of Turin (home of the Turin Man, an assemblage of human bones 5,500 years old, discovered here in 1955 by a young girl), and the Spring Valley Loop near Sidney. An informative and detailed guide to the byway is made available by the Loess Hills Hospitality Association. Call (712) 886–5441.

Another good resource is Cornelia F. Mutel's book *Fragile Giants,* which explores the Loess Hills and their delicate ecology. The book is available from the University of Iowa Press, University of Iowa, Iowa City 52242.

From Sioux City travel east on Highway 20 for 60 miles and then head south on County Road M43 to the **Prairie Pedlar** in Odebolt. Here you

The Great Morel Hunt

*I*f you spend much time with Iowans you may, if you're wily enough, discover one of their private passions that amounts almost to an addiction: morel mushrooms. I don't know if it's their general elusiveness (I mean the mushrooms, not Iowans!), their wonderful woodsy flavor, or just the thrill of the chase that makes people go to such lengths to keep their private morel locations to themselves. These secret places are guarded possessively and guarded well. The best places to find morels are often passed along only within families. If someone sidles up to you with a confidential wink and a knowing smile and promises that they'll head you in the right direction you should be immediately on your guard. You have been taken for a greenhorn.

I notice with interest that the DeSoto Wildlife Refuge lets people wander into "usually closed" areas of the park from April 15 through May 31 during daylight hours. This is the time when, as their brochure hints, "a profusion of morels usually *emerges*" (roman mine). I have a sneaking suspicion that the profusion is probably somewhere else,

unmarked and unknown, except by a few initiates. But maybe the guidelines for a national refuge are more stringent and misdirection is not permitted. My father assures me (and he is a champion morel hunter) that the best place to look is on the north side of dead elm trees, but I have noticed through the years that he always, always, finds more than I do. Would a father mislead his own daughter? Nothing, I've found, is impossible when morels are involved. Here's what you do when (or if) you find them:

Soak the morels overnight in saltwater. Like leeks or spinach they harbor a lot of grit. This bath removes the grit and any lingering wildlife. Take a frying pan, get it hot, and melt a lot of butter in it. (If you're conscientious you may substitute olive oil, but there are some instances when I think a lot of butter is, if not okay, at least good.) Slice the mushrooms—or the mushroom if, like me, you've only found one—and fry them (sauté, if you prefer). Purists eat them straight out of the pan; martyrs fold them into crepes, omelettes, or quiches because they like to wait for the good things to come. Enjoy!

can stroll through an acre of perennial and annual theme gardens filled with hundreds of varieties of flowers and herbs. This family-owned business sells dried flowers and Early American folk art in a small barn near the edge of the fragrant gardens, and visitors are welcome to wander among

The Prairie Pedlar

the plants and gather ideas for their own gardens at home.

Owner Jane Hogue began the business more than ten years ago and since then has seen her hard work blossom into an enterprise that draws visitors from across the state. Assisted by her husband, Jack, their three children, and both sets of parents, Jane raises the flowers in the gardens and harvests, dries, and arranges them in delightful combinations.

The Prairie Pedlar gardens and gift shop are open April through October Monday through Saturday from 11:00 A.M. to 4:00 P.M. and Sunday from 1:00 to 4:00 P.M. Free garden walks convene at 2:00 P.M. each Sunday afternoon in July and August, weather permitting. Call (712) 668–4840 for more information.

Next head south to Denison, site of the **W. A. McHenry House.** This beautiful Victorian home was built in 1885 by Denison pioneer William A. McHenry. With six fireplaces and fourteen rooms (including a ballroom), the home was for many years a showplace for the area. Today it has been restored and contains a variety of historical artifacts.

The W. A. McHenry House is located at 1428 First Avenue North in Denison. It is open Wednesday, Thursday, and Sunday from 1:00 to 4:00 P.M. Memorial Day through Labor Day. Admission is $2.00 for adults and 50 cents for children. For more information call (712) 263–5057.

The town of Denison also takes pride in its status as the birthplace of everyone's favorite mom, actress Donna Reed. Reed was raised on a farm near Denison and completed her schooling here. After graduation she left Iowa to become an actress, starring in *The Donna Reed Show* and more than thirty movies, including *From Here to Eternity,* for which she won an Oscar for best supporting actress (the Oscar is now on display at the W. A. McHenry House). Reed returned often to Denison, remaining in contact with her family and friends in the area until her death in 1986.

In honor of the famous actress, each June Denison hosts the **Donna Reed Festival for the Performing Arts.** The festival draws an impressive list of professionals. In years past participants have included Debbie Reynolds, Shelley Fabares, Nanette Fabray, and Bonnie Franklin, plus nationally known writers, directors, and producers. Workshops are held on various topics relating to musical theater, television, writing, acting, and directing, and large assemblies and small group discussions are also offered.

The Donna Reed Festival for the Performing Arts is held each year in Denison on the third weekend in June. For more information call (800) 336–4692.

Southwest of Denison lies Dow City, site of the **Simon E. Dow House.** The historic home sits high on a hill with a commanding view of the surrounding countryside. Its builder, Simon Dow, was traveling through Iowa on his way west in 1855 when he decided to cut his journey short and remain here because he liked the area so much. Later he became a prominent cattleman, and in 1874 he built a substantial redbrick house that became the nucleus of a settlement called Dow City. At a time when the average home cost $2,000, Dow spent a princely $11,000 for his home.

The Dow House is unusual in that its floor plan is the same on all three floors. All the walls are three bricks wide to keep the home warm in the winter and cool in the summer, and ornamented keystones and carved roses are centered over the first- and second-floor doors. Today the home has been restored to its original appearance and will give you an interesting introduction to the lifestyle of a prominent, upper-middle-class citizen of the nineteenth century.

The Simon E. Dow House (712–674–3734) is located south of Highway 30 at the end of Prince Street in Dow City. It is open May through October from 1:00 to 5:00 p.m. Tuesday through Sunday.

A lovely place to stop in this area of the state is the community of **Woodbine.** It really is as romantic as it sounds. Once a stop on the old Lincoln Highway, the town has relaid all of its downtown sidewalks with brick to match the oldest remaining brick segment of the first highway to span the country. Several stately Victorian houses still overlook this section of the road. Don't miss the old Lincoln

Highway marker near the Harrison County Genealogical Center. You may also want to visit Eby's Drug Store (423 Walker Street), in business since 1916, with its old-fashioned soda fountain, or the DeBeck Bavarian Bakery (511 Walker Street), which offers fresh and authentic Bavarian bread and pastries. Or if you're still hungry, check out Rex's Meat Market (510 Walker Street) with its old-fashioned meat counter. If you feel the need to walk this all off, take a stroll through the White Floral Gardens at Eleventh and Park Streets, a lovely park filled with peonies, shrubs, and trees.

Plan a visit to the community of Gray at the end of May or June. Gray may be its name but gray is not its nature, especially during the summer months when the *Heritage Rose Garden,* located on the first block of Main Street, comes alive with the fragrance and color of roses. This particular garden has been planted with old garden roses known for their hardiness, durability, fragrance, and beauty. Here you'll find rugosas, climbers, gallicas, albas, and lovely big-headed cabbage roses. Don't miss the angel garden and the other old-fashioned flowers.

Traveling south on Highway 71 you may think your eyes are deceiving you but look again—it's *Albert the Bull* of Audubon. The world's largest anatomically correct bull stands as a monument to the beef industry and weighs in at forty-five tons. Erected in 1963 and made of concrete and steel, he is a mere 30 feet tall with a horn span of 15 feet.

While you're in Audubon don't miss the wonderful mural of John James Audubon, artist and naturalist, for whom the town and county were named, located in the post office. Commissioned by the WPA in the 1930s, it was painted by Virginia Snedecher of Brooklyn, New York. Also in Audubon are fifty-six bird banners along the highway and in the business district, commemorating every state's birds and flowers.

Traveling farther south toward Hamlin and easily seen from Highway 71 are the eighteen antique windmills that were donated by local farmers and are used now to show the way to *Nathaniel Hamlin Park.* This park, part of the old Audubon County Home, includes a bluebird house trail, a preserved prairie, and an elk couple.

Southeast of Dow City you'll find the charming villages of Elk Horn and Kimballton, home to the largest rural Danish settlement in the United States. In these communities you can still hear Danish spoken on the street, and the telephone book is filled with good Danish names like Christensen, Overgaard, Johansen, Madsen, and Andersen. Danish immigrants settled the area in the late nineteenth century, and their descendants have worked hard to preserve their unique heritage.

Two Tall Tales

Two famous trees are located not far from each other in Audubon County between Exira and the Cass county line. The "Plow-in-the-Oak" is located one mile south of Exira on Highway 71. Legend has it that a farmer left his plow leaning against a sapling when he went off to the Civil War and that the tree has been growing around it ever since. Set in a five-acre park, you'd better hurry to see the plow, for less and less of it is visible every year.

The "landmark tree," a cottonwood that separates Audubon County from Cass County, is said to have taken root when a surveyor stuck a stick into the ground to mark the county line. Local legend has it that the stick grew into the tall tree you see today. Sorry, you have to ask for directions—that's half the fun of getting there!

Your first stop on a visit to the area should be the ***Danish Immigrant Museum,*** which tells the story of the Danish settlement of North America and the Danish-American ethnic heritage that lives on today. Located in Elk Horn, the three-story structure has a pitched roof and a half-timber, half-stucco finish that suggests a Danish farmhouse. Inside are exhibits that describe the immigrant experience both in the Old Country and the New World. Elkhorn was chosen as the site of the $3.5 million museum after a nationwide search because of its strong town spirit and commitment to the project. One indication of the museum's success is its designation as the 1994 Iowa Tourism Attraction of the Year. The Danish Immigrant Museum (800–759–9192) is located at 2212 Washington Street and is open daily. Admission is $3.00 for adults and $1.50 for children.

Next pay a visit to Elk Horn's ***Danish Windmill.*** The landmark brings to mind the bumper sticker that says, YOU CAN TELL A DANE, BUT YOU CAN'T TELL HIM MUCH. If that weren't the case, it's doubtful the historic mill would ever have left its home in Norre Snede, in the Danish province of Jutland. It was during the worst days of the farm crisis in the mid-1970s that local resident Harvey Sornson came up with the idea of finding a Danish windmill to bring to the area. Many people thought the idea was crazy, but their skepticism gradually gave way to Sornson's persistence. A mill was located in Denmark, and an emergency town meeting in Elk Horn resulted in $30,000 being pledged to the project in just a few days. The 1848 structure was then laboriously dismantled and brought over piece by piece to Iowa. When it arrived it still had ocean salt on its timbers, and eighty-seven-year-old Peder K. Pedersen, who had left Denmark at the age of twenty-one and never returned, tasted the salt of a distant sea and cried.

Many townspeople worked together to reassemble the jigsaw puzzle of the dismantled mill, which was rebuilt in 1976. The total cost of the project eventually came to $100,000, an amount raised through fund-raising projects and contributions from all over the country. Today the windmill stands some 60 feet high, with four 30-foot wings that catch the wind, turn the gears, and grind locally grown grain. The base of the mill houses a welcome center with extensive tourist information, and the adjacent Danish Mill Gift Shop offers stoneground flour and a wide selection of Scandinavian gifts and foods.

The Danish Windmill is located on the main street in Elk Horn and is open daily. Tours of the mill are available for $2.00 for adults and $1.00 for children. For more information call (712) 764–7472.

Danish Windmill

Another Elk Horn attraction that owes its existence to the town's volunteer spirit is **Bedstemor's House,** meaning "grandmother's house." More than a hundred volunteers have donated time, materials, and furnishings to restore the 1908 home. Inside you'll find a glimpse of the life of a Danish immigrant family at the turn of the century. (To furnish the home, volunteers used a 1908 Sears Roebuck catalog as their guide.)

Bedstemor's House is located 3 blocks north and 1 block west of the Danish Windmill in Elk Horn, at 2015 College Street. It is open daily (call for hours), and admission is $1.50 for adults and 75 cents for children. For more information call (712) 764–7001.

At the **Danish Bakery** at 4234 Main Street, you can sample such ethnic treats as *smorrebrod, rullepolse, kringle,* and *kransakage* (the bakery's fame is so widespread that it even offers a shipping service for homesick Danes across the country). Another popular stop for overnight visitors is *The Traveling Companion,* a bed-and-breakfast in a 1909 home owned by Karolyn and Duane Ortgies. Each guest room is named after a fairy tale by Hans Christian Andersen, and afternoon teas and luncheons are offered by appointment. Call (712) 764–8932 for more information.

Two miles north of Elk Horn you'll find its sister village of Kimballton, also an enclave of Danish-American culture. The town's pride and joy is the *Little Mermaid,* a statue modeled after the famous landmark in Copenhagen's harbor (the Little Mermaid, of course, is the immortal character from the fairy tale by Hans Christian Andersen). Kimballton's little mermaid is the focal point of the town's Little Mermaid Park on Main Street. Nearby is the Mermaid Gift Shop featuring many imported gift items.

While touring Kimballton you may also want to visit the *General Store Museum,* where you can see antique toys, vintage machinery, and examples of the skill of the Danish immigrant mason Nels Bennedsen. The building was constructed in 1910 and was used as a barbershop until 1940. Its hours are from 1:00 to 5:00 P.M. Monday through Saturday from May through October.

On the second weekend in October Kimballton hosts the *State Hand Cornhusking Contest.* This is a time when cornhuskers of all ages gather to pick, husk, and toss ears of corn into horse-drawn wagons. Deductions are made for husks remaining on the corn and for corn left in the field. The weekend event includes an *aebleskiver* breakfast (a Danish combination of pancake and waffle), a parade of huskers, and a harvest stew supper. For more information call (712) 773–2112.

Another good time to visit this area is during its two annual *Danish festivals.* Tivoli Fest is held each year on Memorial Day weekend. Julefest (the town's Christmas festival) is held the weekend after Thanksgiving and celebrates the season in true Danish style. Whenever you visit you're likely to leave these friendly communities with an appreciation for their Danish heritage and with plans to return again. For more information on attractions in Elk Horn and Kimballton, call the Danish Windmill Corporation at (712) 764–7472.

From the Danish villages head south to the small town of Walnut, which is known as *Iowa's Antique City.* More than a dozen antiques stores make Walnut one of the best havens for nostalgia buffs in the state. Between the independently owned shops in town and six large antiques malls, several hundred dealers sell their wares here. From antique brass beds to ice-cream parlor stools and vintage dollhouses, you're likely to find an eclectic mixture of treasures on a visit to Walnut.

The town's old-fashioned downtown provides a picturesque setting for all of the commerce. Another attraction is the recently restored *Walnut Country Opera House.* Built in 1899, the opera house now hosts performances of traditional country music and contains an Old-Time Country Music Hall of Fame and a collection of antique instruments. For more information on the opera house and other attractions in the area, call (712) 784–2100.

Missouri River Heritage

From Walnut head west to Harrison County, which borders the Missouri River and contains some of the most varied and beautiful scenery in the state of Iowa: lush farmland, gently rolling foothills, and the fragile loveliness of the Loess Hills. The county is also known as an apple-producing area. The fruit was first planted here before 1880, and today Harrison County has more acreage in apples than any other county in Iowa. The orchards, many of which line the county roads, are located near the towns of Missouri Valley, Mondamin, Pisgah, and Woodbine. Several orchards have facilities for picking your own apples, and orchard tours are also available. Apples are available for sale from mid-August to the end of the season. For more information call the Harrison County Development Corporation at (712) 644–3081.

Near the town of Missouri Valley in Harrison County you'll find one of the state's major wildlife areas, the *DeSoto National Wildlife Refuge,* located 5 miles west of I–29. The refuge lies on the wide plain formed by prehistoric flooding and shifting of the Missouri River. Each spring and fall since the end of the last ice age, spectacular flights of ducks and geese have marked the changing seasons along this traditional waterfowl flyway. During a typical year some 200,000 snow and blue geese use the refuge as a resting and feeding area during their fall migration between their arctic nesting grounds and their Gulf Coast wintering areas. Peak populations of 125,000 or more ducks, mostly mallards, are common in the refuge during the fall migration. Other birds commonly seen in the area include bald eagles, warblers, gulls, pheasants, and various shorebirds.

Bird life is not the only attraction at the refuge. Deer, raccoon, coyote, opossum, beaver, muskrat, and mink make their home here and can often be seen by patient observers. During the spring and summer, the refuge is open for fishing, picnicking, mushroom and berry picking, hiking, and boating. Twelve miles of all-weather roads meander through the refuge, and during the fall a special interpretive brochure is available to guide visitors and explain the annual migration.

The visitor center at the refuge should definitely be part of your visit to Harrison County. In addition to natural-history displays, viewing galleries, wildlife films, and special programs, the center is also the site of the *Bertrand Museum,* a facility housing some 200,000 artifacts recovered from the steamboat *Bertrand,* a vessel that sank with all its cargo in the treacherous Missouri River in 1865.

The wreck of the *Bertrand* mirrors that of many steamers, 400 of which sank in the Missouri during the nineteenth century. The boat was a mountain packet stern-wheeler designed for the shallow, narrow rivers of the West. She was built to carry supplies that would eventually find their way to the gold miners of the Montana Territory and was said to be loaded with 35,000 pounds of mercury, $4,000 in gold, and 5,000 gallons of whiskey—a fortune worth $300,000 or more. Luck was not with the steamer, however, for on her first trip upriver she hit a snag and sank in 12 feet of water. The passengers and crew escaped unharmed, but the bulk of the cargo had to be abandoned. By the time a full-scale salvage operation could be mounted, the boat was irretrievable.

Over the years many treasure hunters searched unsuccessfully for the *Bertrand* and her costly cargo. With time, the Missouri changed its course, leaving the boat in a low-lying field under 25 to 30 feet of silt and clay. It wasn't until 1967 that the wreck was located after an extensive search by treasure hunters Sam Corbino and Jesse Pursell. Unfortunately for them, the cargo didn't contain the rumored riches, though it did contain bounty of another sort: some 10,000 cubic feet of hand tools, clothes, foodstuffs, furnishings, munitions, and personal effects, a virtual time capsule of nineteenth-century life. What was even more remarkable was that most of the cargo was in an excellent state of preservation, though the boat itself had to be returned to its resting spot once the artifacts were removed.

Visit the *Bertrand* Museum today and you can view many of those items, a collection that provides a fascinating look at a vanished time. More than the story of the *Bertrand* is revealed here: The saga of the western expansion unfolds through the boat's artifacts and other exhibits depicting the history and wildlife of the Missouri River basin.

The *Bertrand* Museum, located in the DeSoto National Wildlife Refuge Visitor Center, is open from 9:00 A.M. to 4:30 P.M. daily, except for New Year's Day, Easter, Thanksgiving, and Christmas. Additional interpretive displays can be seen at the *Bertrand* excavation site 3 miles south of the visitor center. Admission to the refuge is $3.00 per vehicle. For more information call (712) 642–4121.

More of the history of the area can be viewed at the **Harrison County Museum and Welcome Center,** located 3 miles northeast of Missouri Valley on Highway 30. Included in the museum are ten buildings, including an 1853 log cabin, 1868 school, mill, harness shop, fur museum, broom factory, and chapel. The museum also serves as one of Iowa's official welcome centers and offers a large selection of brochures and other visitor information. The museum is open daily May through October, and the Welcome Center is open daily year-round. Call (712) 642–2114 for information.

Next head south to the Council Bluffs area. The city is named for the council meeting that took place near here in 1804 between the explorers Lewis and Clark and the chiefs of the Otoe and Missouri Indian tribes. Council Bluffs later became a major stopover point on the Mormon Trail, and it was here that Brigham Young was elected president of the Mormon Church in 1847. By the mid-1800s Council Bluffs had become a wild and lawless town, a place where "gambling and sin of almost every description flourished," to quote one observer of the day. The Ocean Wave Saloon was one of the most notorious sporting houses in the entire West until it burned to the ground during a violent thunderstorm (some held that it had been struck by lightning, while others believed it was the wrathful hand of God). Henry DeLong, a former regular customer of the establishment who had mended his ways, bought the property and gave it to the Methodist Church with the provision that it be used forever after as a church site. The Broadway Methodist Church now stands on the property, and it's most likely the only church in the country with a plaque on the front commemorating a saloon.

Council Bluffs' most famous and influential citizen was General Grenville M. Dodge, a man who has been called the greatest railroad builder of all time. Born in the East, Dodge first saw Council Bluffs while making a railroad survey and was so captivated that he made the city his home in 1853. In 1859 he met Abraham Lincoln and the two developed a strong friendship. After Lincoln became president he appointed Dodge as the chief engineer of the first transcontinental railroad. During the Civil War Dodge served with distinction in a number of positions and was responsible for creating the first military spy system. After the war he was elected to Congress without campaigning and later became an adviser to Presidents Grant, McKinley, Roosevelt, and Taft, as well as a business leader in Council Bluffs and the East.

Today you can visit the **General Dodge House** to learn more about the life and times of this remarkable man. The home was built in 1869 and was designed by the architect responsible for Terrace Hill in Des Moines (page 92). The Second Empire–style mansion stands on a high hillside overlooking the Missouri Valley and contains lavish furnishings; parquet floors; cherry, walnut, and butternut woodwork; and a number of "modern" conveniences quite unusual for the period. Today it has been restored to the opulence of the general's day and is open for tours.

The General Dodge House is located at 605 Third Street in Council Bluffs and is open from 10:00 A.M. to 5:00 P.M. Tuesday through Saturday and from 1:00 to 5:00 P.M. on Sunday. It is closed during the month of January, and the last tour begins each day at 4:00 P.M. Admission is $3.00 for adults and $1.50 for children. For more information call (712) 322–2406.

General Dodge's wife, Ruth Anne, is commemorated by the **Ruth Anne Dodge Memorial.** On the three nights preceding her death in 1916, Mrs. Dodge had a dream of being on a rocky shore and,

Tender Barbecue

How can you miss with a slogan like "You need no teeth to eat this meat"? Find out for yourself at **LaJuice's Bar-B-Q.** *This is the place to go while you're in the Council Bluffs area for rip-roaring barbecue and soul food. The menu has the more usual ribs and chicken and beef brisket and goes so far as to include pigs' ears and pigs' feet—remember, you're in Iowa!*

Proprietor Joyce Harper tells me that the sauce recipe has been handed down for generations "with my own deviations thrown in." Was that variations, I asked. "No," she replied emphatically, "deviations." *You have three temperatures of sauce to choose from: mild, which is okay for children; medium, which has a bite; and hot, which "makes your nose run but doesn't desensitize your taste buds." After all, the other half of LaJuice's motto is "Let us tantalize your taste buds." Food is takeout only (sides like potato salad and baked beans are also available), although there are plans to add some outdoor seating. Located at 728 Creektop Road, LaJuice's Bar-B-Q serves lunch and dinner Tuesday through Sunday. For more information call (712) 329–0093.*

through a mist, seeing a boat approach. In the prow was a beautiful young woman who Mrs. Dodge thought to be an angel. The woman carried a small bowl under one arm and extended the other arm to Mrs. Dodge in an invitation to drink of the water flowing from the vessel. Twice Mrs. Dodge refused the angel, but on the third night she accepted the invitation to drink—and died the next day.

Dodge's two daughters later commissioned Daniel Chester French, who also sculpted the *Lincoln Memorial* in Washington, to construct a statue of the angel in memory of their mother. Though the daughters were reportedly disappointed with the finished work, the monument is now considered to be one of French's finest works. Today you can see the graceful angel, cast in solid bronze, in Fairview Cemetery. As in Mrs. Dodge's dream, the heroic-sized statue holds a vessel of water and beckons with her hand.

The Ruth Anne Dodge Memorial, locally known as the Black Angel, is located in Fairview Cemetery at Lafayette and North Second Streets.

Another historic monument in Council Bluffs is the **Squirrel Cage Jail,** once considered the ultimate in prison facilities. The unique design was patented in 1881 by two Indiana men with the idea of providing "maximum security with minimum jailer attention." Also called a "lazy Susan" jail, the cell block consists of a three-story drum surrounded by a metal cage. Each of the three decks contains ten pie-shaped cells, with only one opening on each level of the drum. To enter a cell, the jailer would turn the central drum so that a cell doorway was lined up with the cage opening—like a squirrel cage. It may seem dehumanizing today, but in 1885 when it was opened, the jail was considered an improvement over the damp, unsanitary quarters prisoners had been kept in previously.

Though it remained in use up until the 1960s, the jail was declared a fire trap in 1969 because only three prisoners could be released at one time during an emergency. It was later in danger of being destroyed when the Pottawattamie County Historical Society launched a heroic effort to save it. The jail was named to the National Register of Historic Places in 1972 and is now owned and operated as a museum by the Historical Society.

On a tour of the Squirrel Cage Jail, you'll also see the jailer's quarters and office and a room filled with prison memorabilia. Today the site is one of only three "lazy Susan" jails still standing in this country and is unique in being the only three-story one.

The Squirrel Cage Jail is located at 226 Pearl Street in Council Bluffs. It is open Wednesday through Saturday from 10:00 A.M. to 4:00 P.M. and on Sunday from noon to 4:00 P.M. Admission is $3.00 for adults, $2.50 for seniors, and $1.25 for children. Call for reduced winter hours. For more information call (712) 323–2509.

Anyone with an interest in trains or rail history won't want to miss the **RailsWest Railroad Museum,** which is housed in the former Rock Island Depot that once served the city. Inside the 1898 structure are railroad memorabilia as well as a model railroad that depicts the railroad operations of the surrounding region. Don't miss the miniature railroad! The museum is located at Sixteenth Avenue and South Main Street and is open daily, except for Wednesday, Memorial Day through Labor Day. For more information call (712) 323–5182 or (712) 322–0612.

If you want to go to the movies while you're in Council Bluffs, just hop in your car and drive over to the **Council Bluffs Drive-In Theater** located at 1130 West South Omaha Bridge Road. This is one of the few remaining drive-in theaters in the country and shows new releases from April to October, beginning at dusk. Prices are $5.50 for adults and, just like in the old days, children under 12 get in for free. Concessions are also available.

If you have been following the Mormon Trail you may want to check out the Fairview Cemetery, where the high east end marks the site of Mormon pioneer graves. Buried here as well is Amelia Bloomer, the inventor of "the first trousers for women."

Is It a Bird, Is It a Plane?

*O*kay, you're standing around in Stanton. You've admired the church, the town, the view. Why are you suddenly, unaccountably overtaken by a powerful and relentless thirst? Not just any thirst, but a craving, an overwhelming desire, a passionate and undeniable urge for a cup of coffee. And not just for any coffee, but for "a cup of the richest kind."

You may, if you cast your eyes skyward, discover the cause, for looming on the skyline is the world's largest Swedish coffeepot! Stantonites claim it holds 125,000 cups, but it's really just a water tower in disguise. However, if you pay attention to the sign at the base of the water tower, you'll find that Stanton was the birthplace of Virginia Christine, who played Mrs. Olson of Folger's Coffee fame. Did she grow up in the shadow of the famous coffeepot and so go on to pursue her career, or was the coffeepot put there to commemorate her? I would prefer to believe the former. Please don't inform me if I happen to be wrong, and I just might buy you a cup of coffee.

A fine place to eat is *Pizza King* a combination steak and pizza restaurant at 1101 North Broadway. Although brothers Dan and Pete Poulos have offered a full menu ranging from sandwiches to fine steaks for thirty-five years, people always come back for their thin-crust pizza, which is known far and wide as the best in the area. Visitors include "regulars" within a 50-mile radius as well as frequent interstate travelers who jump off at the Highway 6 exit for just one more slice. Pizza King is open seven days a week from 4:00 P.M. to midnight; there is plenty of seating and prices are inexpensive to moderate.

A good place to stay if you're in the Council Bluffs area is the *Apple Orchard Inn,* a charming bed-and-breakfast that also serves gourmet meals, located in Missouri Valley, north on Highway 30. Three rooms are available, as well as a small cottage nestled in the orchard. Reservations are required for meals; call (712) 642–2418.

Council Bluffs is also home to the Bluffs Run Casino and two riverboat casinos, *Harveys* and *Ameristar.* For more information about these and other attractions in the city, call the Council Bluffs Convention and Visitors Bureau at (712) 325–1000.

From Council Bluffs you can also explore the *Wabash Trace Nature Trail,* which is quickly becoming one of southwest Iowa's premier attractions. The 63-mile trail stretches between Council Bluffs and the small town of Blanchard on the Iowa-Missouri border, following an old railroad bed through the Loess Hills and rolling farm country. The trail's gentle inclines are perfect for walking and biking and wind through many small towns where travelers can quench their thirsts and grab a bite to eat. The Council Bluffs trailhead is located on Highway 275, near the Iowa School for the Deaf and Lewis Central High School. The trail's user fee is $1.00 per day, $6.00 per year. For information call the Southwest Iowa Nature Trails office at (712) 322–2546.

Twenty-five miles east of Council Bluffs on Highway 6 you'll find the *Nishna Heritage Museum* in the town of Oakland. Housed originally in a 1905 dry goods and grocery store, the museum now comprises four lots. Don't miss the bathtub in the barber shop, the scooter-bike, the collection of bride's dresses and children's clothes, and especially the Buster Brown display!

About 25 miles east of Oakland is the small town of Lewis, home of the *Hitchcock House,* one of the remaining stations left in Iowa that were once stops on the Underground Railroad. Located on the route designated by the famous abolitionist John Brown, this brown stone house built in 1856 and inhabited by a sympathetic circuit preacher, his wife, and eight children, served as a shelter for escaping slaves en route to Canada before the onset of the Civil War. The house is open from April to September from 1:00 to 5:00 P.M. daily. Donations are appreciated. Call (712) 769–2323 for more information or to schedule a guided tour.

Northeast of Lewis on Highway 6 is the town of Atlantic. Here you can pay a visit to **Bittersweet Farm,** open from April 15 to December 15. Take a walk through their gardens of herbs and flowers and admire the towering maple trees. (There is also a collection of two-cylinder John Deere tractors and machinery.) You can purchase delightful herb products: vinegars, "dream pillows," sachets, and dish gardens. Bittersweet Farms (712–549-2357) is located at 1435 330th Street.

From Atlantic travel south to Villisca, which lies northeast of Essex on Highway 71. There you'll find a museum located at the site of one of the state's most notorious crimes. In 1912 an ax murderer killed eight people in a home in this small town, a crime that remains unsolved to this day. The murders have been the subject of a play and documentary and are still the subject of some speculation. The **Ax Murder House** where the killings took place has been restored to its 1912 appearance and is operated in conjunction with the **Olson-Linn Museum,** which contains dozens of antique cars, trucks, and tractors along with other historic artifacts. Begin your tour at the Olson-Linn Museum at 323 East Fourth Street, where you can view a half-hour video describing the murder case before you visit the Ax Murder House. The museums are open weekdays from 9:00 A.M. to 4:00 P.M., year-round, and on weekends from 1:00 to 4:00 P.M. from June 1 to October 1. For information call (712) 826–2756.

Northwest of Villisca on County Road M63, lies the community of Stanton, "the little white city," home of a predominantly Swedish population where all of the houses are painted white. Crowning the top of the hill around which the town is built is the beautiful gray-stoned Mamrelund Lutheran Church with its Gothic architecture and soaring steeple. You may also want to visit the Swedish Heritage and Cultural Center located downtown.

Southwest of Stanton at the junction of Highway 48 and County Road M41 lies the town of Essex. There the **Essex House** offers some surprises. One surprise is its owners. Carolyn and Alan Poulter are natives of England who moved to the United States in 1989 after hearing about an old hotel for sale in Essex from Carolyn's mother, who happens to be married to an Episcopal priest in nearby Shenandoah. The other surprises are the quality of the food and graciousness of the setting in a restaurant located in a town of only 1,000 people. The Essex House serves such entrees as peppered steak and marinated lamb steaks, and Alan's training as a chef is apparent in all the dishes.

The Essex House (800–309–3311) also offers two guest bedrooms to visitors. Located on Highway 48, the restaurant is open for lunch from noon to 2:00 P.M. and for dinner from 5:30 P.M. on Tuesday through Saturday. Reservations are recommended.

For your final stop in western Iowa, visit Clarinda, about 20 miles south of Villisca on Highway 71. Glenn Miller, the famous big band conductor, trombonist, and founder of the Glenn Miller Orchestra, was born here in 1904 and his birthplace, purchased by his daughter in 1989, has been restored by the *Glenn Miller Birthplace Society* and is open for tours. A great, though crowded, time to visit Clarinda is during the Glenn Miller Festival, usually held the second weekend in June. Highlights of the festival are informational talks and panels, question and answer periods, and performances by musical scholarship winners. It is capped off by the society's own big band, which uses Miller's original Café Rouge bandstands.

PLACES TO STAY IN PRAIRIE BORDERLAND

ARNOLDS PARK
Fillenwarth Beach,
87 Lakeshore Drive,
(712) 332–5646,
$50–$200

ORANGE CITY
Dutch Colony Inn,
706 Eighth Street SE,
(712) 737–3490

STORM LAKE
Sail Inn Motel,
1015 East Lakeshore Drive,
(712) 732–1160,
$35–$40

SIOUX CITY
Hilton Inn,
707 Fourth Street,
(800) 593–0555,
(712) 277–4101,
$99–$109

English Mansion Bed
and Breakfast,
1525 Douglas Street,
(712) 277–1386,
$90–$110

COUNCIL BLUFFS
Terra Jane Bed
and Breakfast,
24814 Greenview Road,
(712) 322–4200,
$89–$139

Best Western Metro Inn
& Suites,
3537 West Broadway,
(712) 328–3171,
$49–$99

ATLANTIC
Chestnut Charm Bed
and Breakfast,
1409 Chestnut Street,
(712) 243–5652,
$65–$250

SHENANDOAH
Tall Corn Motel,
Highway 59 &
Sheridan Avenue,
(712) 246–1550,
$35–$55

**PLACES TO EAT IN
PRAIRIE BORDERLAND**

ARNOLDS PARK
Smokin' Jakes,
117 Broadway,
Old Town,
(712) 332–5152

Yesterdays,
2 blocks west of
the stoplight,
(712) 332–2353

STORM LAKE
Ken-A-Bob Buffet,
606 Flindt Drive,
(712) 732–2648

SIOUX CITY
Luciano's Italian Bistro,
1019 Fourth Street,
(712) 258–5174

LAKE VIEW
Lakewood Ballroom,
Lakewood Drive,
(712) 657–3331

CARROLL
Tony's Restaurant,
Highways 71 and 30,
(712) 792–3792

WOODBINE
Bob's Cafe,
503 Walker Street,
(712) 647–2433

MODALE
Sour Mash,
Main Street,
(712) 645–9704

AUDUBON
Lil's Diner,
320 Broadway,
(712) 563–3171

ATLANTIC
Van's Chat & Chew,
509 West Seventh Street,
(712) 243–2312

CLARINDA
J Bruner's,
1100 East Washington
Street,
(712) 542–3364

Index

Entries for Restaurants and Lodgings appear in the special indexes on pages 180.

A

Adel, 96
Agency, 68
Air Power Museum, 69
Albert City, 152
Albert the Bull, 159
Albia, 71
Albia Restoration Days, 72
Allerton, 107
Amana Colonies, 29
Amana Colonies Golf Course, 33
Amana Colonies Nature Trail, 32
Amana Furniture Shop, 31
Amana Woolen Mill, 31
American Gothic House, 68
Ames, 118
Amish-Mennonite Community, 61
Anamosa, 55
Anderson Dance Pavilion, 153
Arnolds Park, 143
Arsenal Island, 45
Atherton House on the
    Boulevard, 96
Attica, 105
Aubrey's Vintage Collection, 96
Audobon, 159
Ax Murder House, 170

B

Backbone State Park, 23
Balltown, 6
Banowetz Antiques, 54
Basilica of St. Francis Xavier, 7
Battle of Pea Ridge Civil War
    Reenactment, 76
Bedstemor's House, 161

*Belle of Sioux City
    Riverboat Casino,* 155
Bellevue, 51
Bentonsport, 74
Bertrand Museum, 164
Bettendorf, 45
Bickelhaupt Arboretum, 51
Big Red Cedar, 140
Big Spirit Lake, 143
Big Treehouse, 116
Bily Clocks, 18
Bittersweet Farm, 171
Black Angel (Iowa City), 37
Black Angel (Council Bluffs), 167
Blakesburg, 69
Blanchard, 169
Blanden Memorial Art Museum, 126
Blank Park Zoo, 93
Bloomfield, 69
Bob Feller Hometown Exhibit, 97
Bock's Berry Farm, 38
Bonaparte, 74
Boone, 120
Boone and Scenic Valley
    Railroad, 120
Boone County, 120
Bridges of Madison County, The, 85
Britt, 131
Brooklyn, 90
Brunnier Gallery and Museum, 119
Buffalo Bill Cody Homestead, 48
Buffalo Bill Cody Museum, 48
Bulldog Beauty Contest, 96
Burlington, 80
Burlington Steamboat Days, 82
Burr Oak, 16
Butterfly Garden, 51

INDEX

C

C. B. & Q. Railroad Depot, 110
Carrie Lane Chapman Catt Childhood Home, 139
Carroll's Pumpkin Farm, 85
Casino Rock Island, 47
Cayler Prairie, 148
Cedar Bridge, 99
Cedar Falls, 23
Cedar Rapids, 56
Cedar Rapids Museum of Art, 58
Cedar Rock, 23
Cedar Valley Nature Trail, 58
Centerville, 72
Century Home, 150
Channel Cat Water Taxi, 47
Chariton, 106
Charles City, 139
Charles H. MacNider Museum, 135
Cherokee, 150
Chief Wapello Memorial Park, 68
Clarion, 131
Clayton, 9
Clear Lake, 113, 137
Clear Lake Fire Museum, 138
Clermont, 20
Clinton, 50
Clinton Area Showboat Theatre, 50
Colfax, 89
Columbus Junction, 65
Columbus Junction Swinging Bridge, 65
Community Country Store, 63
Community Orchard, 128
Coralville, 39
Cornell College, 59
Costello's Old Mill Gallery, 53
Council Bluffs, 165
Council Bluffs Drive-in Theater, 168
Country Relics Village, 129
Crystal Lake Cave, 6
Custom Surfaces Gallery, 42

Cutler-Donahoe Covered Bridge, 10
Czech Village, 56

D

Danish Bakery, 161
Danish Immigrant Museum, 160
Danish Windmill, 160
Davenport, 45
Davenport Museum of Art, 46
Davis County Historical Museum, 69
Decorah, 13
Denison, 157
Des Moines, 89
Des Moines Art Center, 93
Des Moines Botanical Center, 93
Des Moines Metro Opera, 103
DeSoto National Wildlife Refuge, 163
Devonian Fossil Gorge, 39
Diamond Jo Riverboat Casino, 5
Dickinson County Museum, 146
Dolliver Memorial State Park, 128
Donna Reed Festival for the Performing Arts, 158
Dorothy Decaut Nature Center, 155
Dow City, 158
Dows Mercantile Store & Fillmore Building, 130
Downey, 42
Dragon Boat Festival, 83
Drollinger's Amusements, 35
Dubuque, 1
Dubuque Arboretum and Botanical Gardens, 4
Dyersville, 6

E

Eagle Point Park and Nature Center, 50
Edel Blacksmith Shop, 116
Effigy Mounds National Monument, 12
Eldon, 68
Elk Horn, 159

Elkader, 9
Emmetsburg, 134
Ertl Toy Factory, 7
Essex, 171

F

Factory Stores of America
  Outlet Mall, 118
Fairfield, 67
Faith Mitchell Hat Collection, 22
Family Museum of Arts
  and Science, 46
Farm Park, 14
Farmhouse Museum, 119
Fenelon Place Elevator, 5
Festina, 19
Field of Dreams Baseball Diamond, 7
Fish Farm Mounds, 13
Five Flags Theater, 4
Flight 232 Memorial, 153
Flood Museum, 80
Floyd County Historical Museum, 140
Fort Atkinson, 19
Fort Atkinson Rendevous, 19
Fort Atkinson State Preserve, 19
Fort Dodge, 125
Fort Madison, 78
Fort Madison Farmington &
  Western Railroad, 79
Fort Museum, 126
4-H Schoolhouse Museum, 131
Francesca's House, 100
Frank Lloyd Wright
  Stockman House, 135
Frontier Days, 127
Future Birthplace of
  Captain James T. Kirk, 64

G

Gardner Cabin, 146
Gehlen House and Barn, 53
General Dodge House, 166

General Store Museum, 162
George M. Verity Riverboat
  Museum, 75
Gitchie Manitou State Preserve, 143
Glenn Miller Birthplace, 171
Grand Opera House, 4
Grant Wood Art Festival, 55
Grant Wood Scenic Byway, 53
Grant Wood Tourism Center
  and Gallery, 55
Gray, 159
Great Cardboard Boat Regatta, 107
Green's Sugar Bush, 20
Greenman Carriage Company, 141
Grinnell Historical Museum, 85
Grotto of the Redemption, 133
Grout Museum of History
  and Science, 25
Guttenberg, 7

H

Halloween Fun Night, 108
Harker House, 151
Harpers Ferry, 13
Harrison County, 163
Harrison County Museum and
  Welcome Center, 165
Haverhill, 116
Hayden Prairie, 17
Herbert Hoover Highway, 41
Herbert Hoover National
  Historic Site, 40
Heritage Farm and Coach Company, 25
Heritage Museum of
  Johnson County, 39
Heritage Museums, 66
Heritage Rose Garden, 159
Historic Fourth Street, 154
Historical and Coal Mining
  Museum, 73
Hitchcock House, 169
Hobo Museum, 133

INDEX

Homestead, 32
Hurstville Lime Kilns, 53

I

Ice House Museum, 24
Independence, 18
Indianola, 102
Inkpaduta Canoe Trail, 148
Iowa Arboretum, 123
Iowa Band Museum, 24
Iowa City, 34
Iowa Firefighters Memorial, 39
Iowa Great Lakes, 143
Iowa Hall, 36
Iowa House, 98
Iowa Polka Music Hall of Fame, 96
Iowa State Capitol, 91
Iowa State Historical Building, 92
Iowa State Men's Reformatory, 55
Iowa State University, 118
Iowa Trolley Park, 137
Iowa's Antique City, 162

J

Jasper County Historical Museum, 87
Jefferson, 124
John L. Lewis Museum of Mining
    and Labor, 105
John Wayne Birthplace, 100
Julefest, 162

K

Kalona, 61
Kalona Cheese House, 63
Kalona Fall Festival, 64
Kalona Historical Village, 64
Kalona Kountry Kreations, 63
Kalona Quilt and Textile Museum, 61
Kalona Quilt Show and Sale, 61
Karkosh Korners Display Gardens, 44
Kate Shelley High Bridge/Park and
    Railroad Museum, 121

Keith's Arab Heritage House, 152
Keokuk, 75
Keokuk Bald Eagle
    Appreciation Days, 77
Keokuk National Cemetery, 75
Keosauqua, 73
Keystone Bridge, 9
Kimballton, 159
Kinney Pioneer Museum, 136
Knoxville, 105

L

Lacey-Keosauqua State Park, 74
Lady Luck Riverboat Casino, 47
Lady of the Lake, 137
Lake Wapello State Park, 69
Lamoni, 108
Langworthy, 55
Lansing, 13
Laura Ingalls Wilder Museum, 16
Le Claire, 48
Leon, 107
Liberty Hall Historic Center, 108
Lily Lake, 32
Lincoln Highway, 124
Lincoln Highway Bridge, 115
Little Brown Church in the Vale, 26
Little Mermaid, 162
Living Heritage Tree Museum, 151
Living History Farms, 95
Lockmaster's House Heritage
    Museum, 8
Loess Hills, 155
Loess Hills Scenic Byway, 155
Lucas, 105
Lucas County Court House, 106
Luther, 123
Luther College, 14

M

MADRAC, 83
MacNider Museum, 135

Madison County, 98
Madison County Covered Bridges
    Festival, 99
Madison County Historical
    Complex, 101
Madison County Welcome
    Center, 99
Mahanay Bell Tower, 124
Maharishi International
    University, 67
Main Street Antiques, 41
Mamie Doud Eisenhower
    Birthplace, 122
Maquoketa, 53
Maquoketa Caves, 54
Maritime Museum, 146
Marquette, 11
Mars Hill, 69
Marshalltown, 115
Mason City, 135
Mason City Walking Tour, 135
Mathias Ham House, 3
Maytag Dairy Farms, 87
Maytag Historical Museum, 87
McCausland, 48
McGregor, 11
McHenry House, 157
McNay Research Center, 106
Mesquakie Bingo and Casino, 115
Mesquakie Indian Pow Wow, 113
Mid America Air Museum, 154
Midwest Old Threshers Reunion, 65
Midwest Sandhill Crane Count, 8
Millstream Brewing Company, 31
Miss Marquette, 11
Mississippi Belle II, 50
Mississippi River Museum, 1
Mississippi Valley Welcome
    Center, 49
Missouri Valley, 163
Moingona, 121
Mondamin, 163

Montauk, 20
Mosquito Park, 82
Motor Mill, 10
Mount Ayr, 108
Mount Pisgah Mormon National
    Monument, 109
Mount Pleasant, 65
Muscatine, 42
Muscatine Art Center, 43
Museum of Amana History, 31
Museum of Repertoire Americana, 66

N

Nashua, 27
Nathaniel Hamlin Park, 159
National Balloon Classic, 102
National Balloon Museum, 102
National Czech and Slovak Museum
    and Library, 56
National Farm Toy Museum, 6
National Hobo Convention, 131
National Museum of
    Veterinary Medicine, 126
National Rivers Hall of Fame, 1
National Sprint Car
    Championships, 105
National Sprint Car Hall of Fame and
    Museum, 105
Neal Smith Prairie Learning Center, 90
Nelson Pioneer Farm Museum, 70
Newton, 87
Nishna Heritage Museum, 169
Nordic Fest, 14
North Lee County Historical
    Museum, 80

O

Oakland, 169
Okoboji, 143
Old Bradford Pioneer Village, 27
Old Capitol, 35
Old Fort Madison, 79

INDEX

Old Mill, 150
Olson-Linn Museum, 171
On the Avenue, 77
Orange City, 149
Osborne Nature Center, 10
Oskaloosa, 70
Ottumwa, 69
Our Lady of Grace Grotto, 82

P

Palisades-Kepler State Park, 59
Pearl Button Museum, 43
Pella, 104
Pella Historical Village, 104
Perry, 97
Phelps House, 82
Pike's Peak State Park, 11
Pin Oak Marsh, 106
Pine Creek Grist Mill, 44
Piper's Grocery Store, 106
Pisgah, 163
Plum Grove, 38
Port of Burlington Welcome Center, 80
Porter House Museum, 15
Prairie Lights Books, 34
Prairie Pedlar, 156
President Riverboat Casino, 47
Pufferbilly Days, 121
Putnam Museum of Natural
    History and Science, 46

Q

Quad Cities, 45
Quasdorf Museum, 130–31
Quasqueton, 23
Queen II, 145

R

RAGBRAI (*Register's* Annual Great
    Bike Ride Across Iowa), 97
Railswest Railroad Museum, 168

Raj, The, 67
Rathbun Fish Hatchery, 72
Rathbun Lake, 72
Red Haw State Park, 106
Reiman Gardens, 118
Rensselaer Russell House Museum, 24
River Junction Trade Company, 11
Riverside, 66
Rochester Cemetery, 41
Rock Glenn-Rock Crest National
    Historic District, 135
Rock Island Arsenal Museum, 45
Rockford Fossil and Prairie Park, 141
Rose Festival, 117
Roseman Bridge, 99
Ruth Anne Dodge Memorial, 166

S

Salisbury House, 93
Sand Road Orchards, 38
Sanford Museum and
    Planetarium, 150
Santa Fe Swing Span Bridge, 80
Santa's Castle, 151
Science Station, 57
Scott County Park, 47
Seed Savers Heritage Farm, 16
Sergeant Floyd Monument, 152
Sergeant Floyd Welcome Center and
    Museum, 153
Simon E. Dow House, 158
Sioux City, 152
Sioux City Art Center, 155
Sioux City Public Museum, 154
Sisters Garden, 63
Snake Alley, 79
Sod House, 134
Spencer, 148
Spillville, 17
Spirit Lake Massacre Monument, 146
Spook Cave, 12

Springbrook General Store, 52
Squirrel Cage Jail, 167
St. Anthony of Padua Chapel, 19
St. Donatus, 53
Stanhope, 129
Stanton, 171
State Center, 117
State Hand Cornhusking
    Contest, 162
Stephens State Forest, 106
Stone City, 55
Storm Lake, 151
Story City, 117
Story City Carousel, 118
Strawberry Days, 22
Strawberry Point, 21
Stringtown Grocery, 63
Surf Ballroom, 113, 138

T

Tama, 115
Tama County Historical
    Museum, 115
Tanger Factory Outlet Center, 33
Telephone Museum, 125
Terrace Hill, 92
Tivoli Fest, 162
Toledo, 115
Toolesboro Indian Mounds, 81
Trainland U.S.A., 89
Trek Fest, 64
Tulip Festival, 149
Tulip Time, 104
Twilight, 49

U

Union Slough Wildlife Refuge, 133
University of Iowa, 33
University of Northern Iowa, 23
University of Okoboji, 146
Urbandale, 95

V

Valley Junction, 94
Van Buren County, 73
Van Horn's Antique
    Truck Museum, 136
Vander Veer Botanical Center, 46
Vesterheim, 14
Victorian Home and Carriage
    House Museum, 24
Victorian House Tour and
    Progressive Dinner, 3
Village of East Davenport, 47
Villisca, 170

W

Wabash Trace Nature Trail, 169
Waller, Robert James, 98
Walnut, 162
Walnut Country Opera House, 163
Walnut Creek National
    Wildlife Refuge, 89
Walnut Grove Pioneer Village, 47
Waterloo, 24
Watson's Grocery, 117
Waukon Junction, 13
Waverly, 26
Waverly Midwest Horse Sale, 26
Webster County, 125
West Bend, 133
West Branch, 40
West Des Moines, 94
Wexford Immaculate
    Conception Church, 13
Wildcat Den State Park, 44
Wilder Museum, 22
Wilderness Kingdom Zoo, 69
William M. Black, 1
Williamsburg, 33
Willowglen Nursery, 16
Wilton, 42
Winterset, 99

Woodbine, 158
World's Smallest Church, 19
Wyth House, 24
Winterset Art Center, 101

Z

Zellmer's Stage Door Dinner
Theater, 82
Zimmerman Lawn Ornaments, 55

Special Indexes

Restaurants
Big Muddy's, 82
Blue Highway Bakery Cafe, 109
Blue Willow Tea Room, 127
Bluestem Restaurant, 154
Bluff Lake Restaurant, 54
Bonaparte's Retreat, 75
Breitbach's Country Dining, 6
The Brewery, 37
Cafe de Klos, 58
Cellar, The, 78
Chart House, 44
Dayton House, 14
Emma's Tea Room, 34
Essex House, 171
Faithful Pilot, 49
Fitzpatrick's, 37
Hannah Marie Country Inn, 148
Hickory Park Restaurant, 119
Holiday Harry's, 51
Inn of the Six-toed Cat, 107
Iowa Machine Shed, 47
Ken's Cafe & Grill, 120
Kin Folks Eatin' Place, 105
La Corsette Maison Inn, 87
LaJuice's Bar-B-Q, 166
The Landmark, 3
Little Bohemia Tavern, 56
Liz Clark's, 78
Mandolin Inn, 3
Northside Cafe, 99
Northwestern Steakhouse, 136
Old Depot Restaurant, 97
Old World Inn, 19

Pizza King, 169
Raj, The, 67
Ryan House, 3
The Sanctuary, 37
The Shanti, 21
The Skean Block, 72
Stone's Restaurant, 115
Taste of Thailand, 94
Thymes Remembered Tea Room, 97
Vernon Inn, 58
White Springs Night Club, 12
Wilton Candy Kitchen, 42
Zuber's Dugout Restaurant, 32

Lodgings
Apple Orchard Inn, 169
Cklaytonian Bed and
Breakfast Inn, 9
Die Heimat Country Inn, 33
Dusk to Dawn Bed and
Breakfast, 33
FantaSuite Hotel, 43
Golden Haug Bed and
Breakfast, 39
Grand Anne Bed and
Breakfast, 78
Hancock House, 3
Hannah Marie Country Inn, 148
Hook's Point Country Inn, 128
Hotel Manning, 74
Hotel Pattee, 98
Inn of the Six-toed Cat, 107
Iowa House, 120
Kingsley Inn, 80

INDEX

La Corsette Maison Inn, 87
Mason House Inn, 74
Mont Rest, 52
Montgomery Mansion, 15
North Shore House, 138
Old Brewery, The, 8
Old World Inn, 19
Raj, The, 67

Redstone Inn, 3
Spring Side Inn, 52
Squiers Manor Bed and Breakfast, 54
Summerset Inn & Winery, 103
Traveling Companion, The, 162
Varner's Caboose, 45
Woodlands Bed and Breakfast, The, 48

About the Author

Lori Erickson is a freelance writer and native Iowan who grew up on a farm near Decorah. She holds degrees from Luther College and the University of Iowa, and her articles and essays have appeared in dozens of regional and national magazines and newspapers. She is the author of three collections of Iowa ghost stories published by Quixote Press and is a member of the Midwest Travel Writers Association.

Lori lives with her husband, Bob and sons, Owen and Carl, in Iowa City.

About the Editor

Tracy Stuhr is a recently hatched freelance writer and a native Iowan. She grew up in Cedar Rapids and received her B.A. from the University of Iowa. She was a banker for more than twenty years before returning to her first love, writing, two years ago. She is currently attending writing classes at the University of Iowa and is busily forging a new career.

Tracy makes her home in Iowa City, where she lives with her golden retriever, Saga, who has frequently been a companion during her travels around the state. As another native Iowan, Saga has her own rather definite opinions about the places mentioned in this book: In general, she prefers parks, whether small or large, and likes those with water best.